GODS OF WAR

GODS OF WAR

A Memoir of a German Soldier

Hans Werner Woltersdorf

Translated by Nancy Benvenga

PRESIDIO

Original German title, *Picknick Zwischen Biarritz and Shitomir*

First published 1990 in the United States by Presidio Press
31 Pamaron Way, Novato CA 94949

Distributed in Great Britain by
Greenhill Books
Park House, 1 Russell Gardens
London NW11 9NN

Library of Congress Cataloging-in-Publication Data

Woltersdorf, Hans Werner.
   [Picknick zwischen Biarritz und Shitomir. English]
   The gods of war : a memoir of a German soldier
Hans Werner Woltersdorf ; translated from the German by Nancy Benvenga.
     p.   cm.
   Translation of: Picknick zwischen Biarritz und Shitomir.
   ISBN 0-89141-402-9
   1. Woltersdorf, Hans Werner. 2. World War, 1939–1945—Personal
narratives, German. 3. Germany. Heer—Biography. 4. Soldiers-
Germany—Biography. I. Title.
D811.W6413 1990
940.54′82′092—dc20
                                            90–41386
                                               CIP

Printed in the United States of America

1

The caves at Lascaux were closed.

"What now?"

For five months, or to be exact, since New Year's morning 1961, which was when we planned our holiday, our itinerary through France to the Bay of Biscay, with a side trip through the Spanish Basque country, had been settled. Klaus had the sometimes irritating habit of organizing our trips with the pedantry one would expect of a general's staff: he worked out the main roads, side roads, resting places, and places to spend the night, right down to the hotels, and calculated the distances and the amount of time it would take to cover them. If he could, he would have gladly decided even what weather was required. Lore and Erika had to let him know in good time what places they wanted to see, after which no deviations were tolerated. Lore had assumed the role of cultural and historical travel guide and had prepared us during yesterday's evening meal: Lascaux had the best–preserved cave paintings of the Palaeolithic Age, discovered recently, only in 1940.

1940 . . .

In 1940 we had pushed forward to the Spanish border in a three–day forced march from Orléans and had passed only forty kilometers to the west of Terrascon. So, that was when the caves were discovered. Who discovered them, and why in 1940 of all times, when there must have been other problems to cope with?

"They're known as the Sistine Chapel of the Palaeolithic Age."

And now they were closed. Today of all days. In his itinerary and timetable Klaus hadn't allowed for this contingency. Placards and photos showed us what we would have seen if we had arrived there yesterday or not come until tomorrow.

"Doesn't something strike you as strange?" Klaus asked enigmatically.

Nothing struck us as strange.

"The hotel keeper in Terrascon knew that we wanted to visit the caves: he even explained how to get here and let us go on our way without telling us that the caves are closed today."

"So? Maybe he didn't know himself."

"Or maybe he thought, let them go, they'll find out soon enough, these Germans."

"You've been seeing ghosts ever since we came to France," said Erika. "Whether the French are friendly or indifferent, you're always interpreting it according to your prejudices."

"I have no prejudices. The French, on the other hand . . . and we're near Limoges and Tulle, close to Oradour. . . ."

Klaus had pleaded for a trip to Yugoslavia, but had been overruled by the rest of us, and what displeased him most was my intention to visit the little village in the Charente where, during the war, I spent five months forming and training a company of recruits to be used as replacements in the fighting on the Eastern front. Compared to what followed it was a splendid five months, a life of carefree abandon.

"So what do we do now? Drive on, or—"

"If it were up to me," Klaus said, and we all suspected what we would have to do if it were up to Klaus: stay here one more day, visit the caves, and then, with no detours or stops, drive directly to Hendaye. After all, I would only misuse the time that we had now gained to prolong the half hour that had been allotted to my village. He would even be willing to discard his itinerary in order to prevent that from happening.

"If it were up to you?"

"All right then, let's compromise. I propose that we take another little walking tour, a good hour. It's ideal weather for walking and an interesting area. We'll really be looking around at the hunting grounds of our Palaeolithic comrades!''

When the talk got round to walking or extensive sightseeing it gave the others a bad conscience for my sake, and they felt compelled to come up with useful suggestions for me since I couldn't keep up. Lore had the best idea: six kilometers away on the right–hand side of the road was a chapel, idyllic and very picturesque. They would allow an hour for their walking, while I could do her the favor of painting a picture of the chapel. We would meet there in an hour. Klaus looked at his watch: twelve minutes past nine.

I had taken up painting some time ago. Now I drove off to the chapel and sought the most advantageous position in which to park so that I could use the hood of the car as an easel.

I filled a bottle with water from a brook and unpacked my pad of paper, water colors and pencil. With pencil in my outstretched hand I took the bearings of the proportions and corners of my subject, as I had learned at school, and began sketching.

I let the blue–grey of the deeply sloping slate roof blend almost imperceptibly into the blue–grey of the wooded background. Actually, I had to manage with blue and orange as complementary colors. One–third clear sky, the distant ridge of hills quite faint, then a more energetic application of more orange for the bright meadows, a bit of black for the slate roof, and white dots for the reflected light. From time to time I leaned the pad of paper against the windshield so that I could step back and look at the picture. As soon as the brilliant orange of the masonry was added the picture would come to life! The wall in front of the chapel was far too high and would ruin the entire foreground, even if the opening for the rusty iron gate were made wider. I moved the huge, thick sycamore from the right–hand side to the left edge of the picture, because I needed its shadow to interrupt the otherwise continuous wall. And there was too much fresh greenery in the little churchyard, which didn't match the blue–orange combination, so I put predominantly bluish conifers there with some orange–colored dabs of flowers in between.

They had crept up quietly and were looking over my shoulder.

''But the sycamore is on the right!'' cried Erika. ''Why didn't you leave it there?''

"And the wall is much too low," Klaus put in.

"If you want the real thing, then take a photo," I said.

"A photo, of course!" Klaus always had his camera dangling around his neck, and in his short trousers he looked a caricature of the typical German tourist.

"A photo of the artist with his masterpiece, and the original behind. Ready, line up!" He knelt down, click, bent to the left, to the right, click, click, lay down on his stomach, click, crept up a small hill, click.

He was always in the best of moods after a walk and raved about everything I had missed, as if I had passed up the opportunity out of defiance and not because of my wooden leg. "When you roam through the countryside you see the loveliest subjects for painting, and the light, the weather! Isn't it splendid here? Maybe we ought to give ourselves another day here. . . ." And then he came out with what was most on his mind:

"And that village of yours, Montboyer or whatever it's called. I'd rather leave that to a later time, when it's all been forgotten."

"When what's been forgotten?"

"It's only sixteen years since the war ended, there must be many wounds still not healed."

"I never wounded anyone."

"Perhaps not, but does that make any difference, here near Limoges and Oradour? Yes, yes, I know, you weren't there, and partisan warfare is a horrible thing in which one injustice begets another on both sides. I'm glad that I never had anything to do with it."

"So am I."

"But you were in the Waffen–SS at the time, and even now the world thinks of that as the epitome of Nazism and injustice."

"I a Nazi? You should have told me off for that when you were still my cub squadron leader and were ashamed of me because I always managed to displease you whenever I reported for duty—"

"But that was quite different!"

"So? A person wasn't born a Nazi, he was trained as one, and you tried in vain, you insulted me and you tormented me at home because I wasn't good enough for your fancy service."

"You were only jealous of Stelzer and Blumenfeld."

"That was unreasonable too, to expect me to serve under old sticks like them. Blumenfeld who was stiff as a poker and that Stelzer who always got a heart flutter at the right time, whenever he had to strain himself.''

"Didn't Squadron Leader Schaettle always keep on friendly terms with you?''

"That was because he needed me as a showpiece in the Athletic Championships, the wheezing windbag! And yet I noticed how hard it was for him to have to declare me the winner over and over again. He would have preferred to cheat me of my laurels.''

"Are you back on your favorite theme again?'' Erika asked. "I could laugh myself to pieces whenever Big and Little Brother start arguing over who was the bigger Nazi.''

"At least I was never a member of a criminal organization,'' Klaus continued. "Joining the Waffen–SS was your crucial mistake.''

"You know very well that I went to Bremen to volunteer for the Marines.''

At that time, when the war had first broken out, I had wanted to join the Submarine Corps, and as I was only seventeen I was afraid that all the excitement might come to an end without me. But the Marines had just shut their bulkheads tight that day, while something like two thousand hopefuls stood in line to join the Waffen–SS. Hermann Bohlen, the big blond fellow who was the darling of all the girls, was among them and he called me over and dissuaded me from joining the floating coffins. The Waffen–SS, he said, was quite an elite crowd, just right for both of us. And so I joined him in line. Only one hundred fifty were taken; we were among them.

And then the slim corporal with the wily Tyrolese face stood before us.

"They've accepted you?'' he asked in amazement.

I nodded.

"The answer is *Jawohl!*''

"*Jawohl.*''

"*Jawohl*, Corporal! is the answer.''

"*Jawohl*, Corporal!'' He inspected me from top to bottom. That this slender little fellow was in the Waffen–SS amazed me.

"Have you any brothers or sisters?''

"Yes.''

"*Jawohl*, Corporal!"

"*Jawohl*, Corporal!"

"How many?"

"Three brothers and a sister."

"Are your parents still living?"

"*Jawohl.*"

"*Jawohl*, Corporal" is the answer, fellow! Are they all still alive?"

"*Jawohl*, Corporal."

"You'll never see them again," he said, and went off.

"Bastard!"

"Did you say something?"

"No, Corporal."

"You have to pull yourself together," said Hermann Bohlen. "These fellows are sharp."

"They won't get the best of me," I said, "especially a pipsqueak like him."

Klaus had the map on his knees, and while we enjoyed the scenery he studied the map intently; he was responsible for the schedule and the itinerary and was always having to prevail, especially against Lore, because she would keep trying to persuade him to make detours to the left or the right in order to make a quick visit to yet another worthy edifice, and she would moan and complain every time we philistines didn't acquiesce.

I had put a cross on the map at the spot where Montboyer must lie, which could be reached only by a succession of byroads. The closer we got to this cross, the more Klaus's misgivings and anxieties gnawed at him.

"Before we get there we should first come to an agreement about what we'll do if they run us out of town—or arrest you."

"Are you serious?" Erika asked.

"We can't be sure," said Klaus. "He seems to think that they'll lay out a red carpet for him, but I think they'll set the dogs on him."

I wouldn't let myself be provoked.

Erika turned to me. "Do you think so too?"

"Nonsense."

"He ought to have a better idea than you, Klaus."

"But you know him: an incorrigible optimist!"

"Better than a pessimist!" Lore came to my defense.

"All right then! If you won't listen to me, then on to the great adventure! I only hope the French *keine Sippenhaft praktizieren*. We've got about fifteen kilometers to go."

I reduced the speed. True, I could hide the fact that I was itching with excitement, but I couldn't deny it. And, if one has been permanently brainwashed into having a bad conscience, one begins to brood about it. Had we been involved with something that could be interpreted as despotism or injustice?

But what about Zinsheim, Lieutenant Zinsheim, the longest-serving Lieutenant in the Waffen–SS? He commanded the company to which I was assigned. Actually someone else was supposed to have been assigned to this company instead of me, but when he heard the name Zinsheim he asked for a transfer to another unit. Zinsheim, I learned, had already been a battalion commander and had been demoted for cowardice in facing the enemy. It is characteristic of this type of person to prove his courage by bullying his subordinates. Already the first time I met him I got a foretaste of this.

It was a cold, clear February night when I entered Montboyer. The sentry, a recruit who had been two weeks in the service, considered my arrival an important event, important enough to awaken the company commander, and this he did in a manner that closely resembled climbing through one's sweetheart's bedroom window. He bellowed over the road in the direction of Zinsheim's private quarters: "Lieutenant! Lieutenant! The Oberjunker is here!"

When that brought no response he threw tiny pebbles at the window. Then the light went on. Zinsheim opened the window and roared out, "What idiot is yelling like that?"

"Reporting to the Lieutenant that the Oberjunker has just arrived," the sentry said.

"Are you crazy, waking me up for a thing like that, you idiot? What's your name?"

He gave his name.

"Report to me first thing in the morning, you idiot!"

As a recruit I had a sergeant toward whom I had never heard a single insulting word said nor a curse uttered, although we had compiled a whole encyclopaedia of curses, nicknames, and swearwords which we used, not without justification, on the NCOs; we collected these words as other people collect stamps. Only once, when the violent–tempered Maerkinger had injured a comrade with a bayonet in an argument and then threatened him with his (unloaded) pistol, did a swearword escape the sergeant's lips. Quite rightly, too, and yet he immediately excused himself for it. I was impressed by this, and since that time I undertook never to use such swearwords against subordinates, unless, of course, I lost control, and then I would excuse myself immediately.

I did not get to bed until four o'clock that morning, and at eight I reported to Zinsheim, who lost no time in showing me just who ruled the roost.

"Our duty begins at six o'clock, take note of that once and for all!"

"I beg your pardon, Lieutenant, but how was I to know that? I was not informed of the routine, nor had quarters been prepared for me, although the regiment had reported that I was coming."

The atmosphere became tense, but since I was still his only officer, even if newly fledged and a reserve officer at that, he did not want to fall out with me completely, because training a newly formed company was degrading hackwork for someone who had commanded a battalion four years before. Ever since his demotion he hated the troops, the service, and the entire system. Therefore he needed me to do whatever he found unpleasant. When alcohol had loosened his tongue—such as happened on that first night in the battalion officers' mess—he poured forth scorn and derision on the other officers, insulted the doctor for being "unsoldierly," and insinuated to the commander, a doctor of zoology and botany, that without his good connections in the government he wouldn't even have survived officers' school. He insulted God, the world, and the entire lot of soldiers who never said anything but "Yes, Sir" and obeyed every damned order, no matter how idiotic it was. And since he met with neither agreement nor approval, but only with an awkward silence, he was on the point of imbibing still more courage with still more alcohol when the commander brought this, my first, so discordant evening at the officers' mess to an end.

But Zinsheim went on, full of courage and full of rage. And then it happened.

Needless to say I sat myself at the wheel of our first and only company vehicle, and that got his hackles up.

"Kindly move to the passenger seat!"

"But you're in no condition to drive—"

"How can you judge what condition I'm in, you snot–nose! I order you to move over to the passenger seat!"

"I'm also one of those who do not obey every bloody order, no matter how idiotic it is, Lieutenant," I said. Then he became violent and even reached for his pistol.

And then he took the VW, which was not even run in, and drove it at full throttle through the narrow streets to show how dashingly a real man can drive when he hardly has any blood left in his alcohol. We swerved towards the two nearly rectangular corners before and after the Tude bridge. He just managed to take the first corner with a loud screech of the tires, but at the left–hand corner that followed we landed in the ditch, and Zinsheim cursed the damned French who couldn't build decent roads, and complained about the pains in his back. I ran the remaining few kilometers into the village to fetch some people, who got the vehicle back on to the road. Zinsheim himself—because of his aching back—remained behind the wheel, put his foot down again, and roared into the village.

The sentry in front of the orderly room, who, on one hand, was concerned to recite his routine announcement to the company commander immediately, but on the other hand was at pains to keep out of the way of the swerving car, danced nervously to and fro. Nevertheless, Zinsheim got hold of him, this stupid sentry, this idiot, who, rubbing his knee which now hurt because of having been hit by the car, announced, "Nothing special to report!"

"No? I'll check that immediately!" said Zinsheim, as he left the car and noiselessly weaved his way through the village, looking for something special. When he reached the branch post office he stood still and listened. Then he shouted, "Sentry!"

Four sentries came rushing over. He ordered, "Halt!" and asked whether they heard anything.

"No."

"Someone is sending signals and you don't hear anything, you idiots?! Spies are sending signals right under your noses and you don't notice anything? Get on with it, arrest them!"

Suspecting that disaster was about to strike, I returned. Zinsheim shouted at me reproachfully that my soldiers had yet to notice how spies were radioing important information through the district and getting off scot–free.

Just then the soldiers came clattering back down the steps of the branch post office with two nightgowned figures between them, the post-master and his wife.

"Have you caught them? Red–handed? What were they doing? Where did you catch them?"

"They were lying in bed asleep, Lieutenant."

"You were asleep, you idiots!"

I reassured the couple from the post office and asked them to pardon the incident, but radio signals had been heard and it was thought that something was wrong. That was the telegraph, they explained, which recorded incoming telegrams day and night.

I tried to explain to Zinsheim how he had just made a fool of himself, upon which he shouted furiously at me and I shouted back until at last he shrieked orders that the two spies were to be locked up immediately, and I was responsible for the exact implementation of this order, and when he said "exact" then he meant exact. Then he swayed energetically away.

I brought the couple back into the post office and calmed them down. Next morning I explained to Zinsheim that I had had the effrontery not to carry out his senseless order, and left it to his discretion to institute court–martial proceedings against me because of this refusal to obey orders. He denied knowing anything about such an order or about the incident at all, and when I reminded him of his landing in the ditch he got the idea that it was I who had dared to drive the car despite being in a drunken state. But let's forget it, these things happen, and he would be the last person to ruin a young officer's career on account of a single faux pas, as had been done to him. Much worse than that were the back pains he got from the accident, and the pains in his shoulder joint. Rheumatism, excruciating rheumatism, unimaginable for anyone who did not have to suffer this scourge.

I was shocked and at the same time I felt pity, not because of the rheumatism (which I suspected was faked), but because here in front of me sat a man with a completely twisted character, neither a model nor a leader, a psychiatric case, unsuited even to lead a single squad into action. It could well have been people like Zinsheim who set fire to synagogues or killed defenseless people. There were people like Zin-sheim, but even we demoted them. We had to rid our troops of them.

I pretended to know something about rheumatism, and explained to him how such pains can throw the entire endocrine system, and thereby one's ability to think and act reasonably, off balance, and that because of this it was necessary to go to the hospital for thorough treatment. He did this too, and just in time, after word got out that our battalion was going to be transferred early to Russia as a replacement, in a hard winter campaign from which only a few men returned.

With a bar of chocolate for Madame and a packet of cigarettes for Monsieur I paid another apologetic visit to the branch post office.

2

Montboyer might well emerge from behind that hill over which the road gently undulated. First the church steeple would appear, and then the Boisse with its round tower would become visible on a hill on the right–hand side. I had had my quarters in one of the first houses on the left side of the street: a large room with an iron bed, a round table, and two chairs; otherwise, nothing but a good deal of space. For the round, cracked table I had bought from Madame Batiste a loud–colored cloth embroidered with artificial silk, which I later gave to Lore. She dubbed it the "liqueur cloth," thought it quite jolly, if kitschy, and used it to cover an ugly, makeshift piece of furniture.

Could that have been the woods where we practiced hand–to–hand and forest combat? Of course it was not the sort of woods we were familiar with from the Luneburg Heath but a neglected, bushy copse. A narrow path led through it, scarcely wide enough to move a 50mm antitank gun on it. This wooded lane must run into our road about four kilometers before Montboyer. I drove quite slowly.

"Do you want to stop here? Why? Do you have to?"

"From sheer excitement?"

A cross had stood where the two roads joined. That could have been it, a rusted iron cross with a picture of a saint painted on porcelain. Wilted flowers covered the base. I stopped, got out of the car, and pushed the flowers aside. It should still have been possible to see the place where the cement base had been repaired. At the time I had not had the opportunity to check whether my boys had replaced the cross properly in its base.

"What are you praying about?" asked Erika. "And on your knees, even!"

"Dear God, please hold the vicious dogs back when I come to Mont-boyer," joked Klaus.

One day the parish priest stood in the orderly room, beating tediously about the bush. He knew, of course, that we weren't church–goers, and yet God was there for everyone, even for us, and atheism was widespread in France too; in this respect we weren't exceptions, but still, one shouldn't go so far—

"What? How far?"

"To destroy the holy crosses."

"Who? Where? How?"

Here, on this spot, was one of them, and the other was on the road to the Boisse.

I had the company line up for roll call, and I went along, accompanied by the parish priest. It must have been funny, the way I paced up and down with Reverend Father inspecting the troops, but I could see from some of their faces that they didn't find it so comical at all.

"Those men who dismantled the holy crosses, forward three steps!"

Eight men of the antitank gun platoon and one artillery commander came forward three steps.

"What is the meaning of this?"

"You had ordered dummy tanks to be built, Untersturmfuehrer, for target practice with live ammunition—"

"Yes, well?"

"Something hard, iron, had to be in them so that the grenades would explode."

It was true, I had said that, and when they asked me what hard material they should use and where they should get it I had said, "Use your imagination."

I confessed this to the priest. Atheism was not to blame, then. I explained to him that most of these young soldiers came from the Catholic Balkan countries and from Poland and were most certainly no atheists. It wasn't easy for him, faced with these bedraggled sinners, to keep the offended look on his face.

"Who is a trained mason?"

Two men stepped forward.

"After work take these eight sinners and put the crosses back, and I mean in tip–top shape!"

"And where should we get the cement?"

"Use your—oh no, never mind! Get it from the sergeant!"

Now I finally had the chance to check whether the cross had been replaced in tip–top shape.

The parish priest had offered to procure cement, and since two trained masons were available we agreed on a penance that consisted of repairing a couple of minor details on the masonry of the presbytery and on the church as well. The good Lord and St. John would then see their way to forgiveness.

Reverend Father had yet another brilliant idea. A member of his flock had an armored ammunition trolley from the last war standing around the farmyard, which would be far more suitable for our target practice. We carted it away—as good as a real enemy tank for our combat practice with live ammunition, so that even the regimental commander himself took great pleasure in seeing us smash it up.

As a reward for this successful war performance, which we put on with the parish priest's assistance, the regimental band was posted to Montboyer to give an open–air concert. It took place on a Sunday morning in May. As Reverend Father's flock streamed out of the church after the organ had played the final chord, there, standing before them, was the forty–piece regimental band, instruments gleaming in the sun. Nothing of the sort had ever happened in Montboyer before.

You could have heard a pin drop as the band leader raised his baton and began the concert with "Old Comrades." The soldiers had dressed in their Sunday best and combed their hair, the church–goers mixed with the soldiers, and the irresistible oompah–pah of the instruments had quickly lured everyone, right down to the next–to–last citizen of Montboyer.

The last citizen of all, the village teacher, did not turn up. He avoided us like the plague.

It was a request concert. I had explained this to the mayor, and he and the town secretary went around and collected requests. Even Denise, the pretty, blonde, and shapely young teacher from the next village, was there. She had linked arms with Marianne, the dark girl from the Boisse, and made a point of looking past me as if I were air. She was *fâchée de moi:* we had quarrelled about something, and then she had sworn never to speak to me again. How did this quarrel actually start? We were always quarrelling, really, and Marianne had commented on these altercations with a saying that meant something like, "Teasing is a sign of affection." With the relatively few scraps of French I had at my command, a lot came out quite differently from the way it was meant. Actually I had wanted to explain to her that her tall, blonde, and blue–eyed beauty was more suited to my North German homeland than to the south of France, but instead what came out she took to mean "What a shame that you're French," whereupon she snapped back that she was proud of being French, which brought from me the rejoinder that at that time she really had no reason to be proud of France. And that did it.

Now she was standing to one side and was taking great pains to concentrate on the church steeple, so that she wouldn't be tempted to look in my direction, while Marianne insistently kept on and on at her and kept glancing over at me. At last Marianne tore herself loose and made her way over to me.

"Denise wants to hear 'The Blue Danube,' " she said, and I asked whether it was Denise's request or her own.

She laid a finger to her lips.

I knew that the Danube Waltz and *"Mon amour et ton amour"* were her favorite tunes.

I passed on the message that the Danube Waltz was my request too, and I also begged her pardon; it had been very silly of me to quarrel with her.

"Come to the Boisse this evening," Marianne said. "Denise will be there too and is staying the night with me."

The band played "The Blue Danube," the soldiers hummed, linked arms and swayed to it, and soon everyone joined in, including Denise, who smiled to me and nodded.

3

Twice now the steeple of Montboyer had come into view from the crest of a hill. There was also what must have been the signpost saying "Montboyer," although from a distance one couldn't be positive. We all saw it, but no one said a word. Embarrassed silence and anxious curiosity. The town appeared deserted, just as it had back then in the summer heat and during the midday break. A background of memories. To the left, level with the signpost and bordered by hedges and barbed wire, lay the meadow which sloped gently to the Tude, gently enough to serve as a sports field. The village youths played football there and we played handball. Only once did we condescend to play the vulgar game of football against the village youths. I assumed the role of referee, since the village teacher had declined it, and, of course, I was obliged to call every doubtful play in favor of the villagers. They won, and the event even made the local newspaper.

There, to the right under the big cherry tree, just behind the signpost, was the carpenter's workshop. A soldier from the First World War with a huge black moustache. Verdun. He was very reticent, and even the little he said was swallowed up by his moustache. *"Terrible, la guerre."* Sometimes I noticed him watching our exercises, hidden by bushes. One day I asked him if he could build a company chest.

"For lieutenants?"

I had no idea that there was a difference. He built the chest perfectly, and when I tried to instruct him on how to do it he simply waved me aside and wouldn't listen. What did I know about company chests!

He had two daughters, Monique and Jeanette. They lived diagonally to the left of the workshop and just next to my quarters. In the mornings, at midday, and in the evenings, whenever I went out on duty or returned from duty, I had to pass them. They sat in the window and sewed.

"Bonjour!"

"Bonjour, Monsieur!"

"Bonjour, Mesdames!"

"Bonjour, Monsieur Lieutenant!"

"Bonjour, Mademoiselle Jeanette, bonjour, Mademoiselle Monique!"

"Bonjour, Monsieur Lieutenant Werner!"

And so we got more closely acquainted. My cap was worn and greasy. Jeanette took it and turned it, and it was like new again. I collected it that evening at her friend Marianne's, at the Boisse, and after that we met there more and more often. Toni came along, and sometimes Zinsheim, whom they called Sissi, came too. Luckily he understood no French and the girls understood no German, so that when he insisted that I translate his sarcastically suggestive and nasty remarks I thought up something harmless to say.

The house appeared uninhabited, the workshop was deserted and dilapidated. The cherry tree was heavy with fruit and the blackbirds sat in it and feasted. *Les merles,* that's right, *les merles* was the word for blackbirds. Two women stood near the house and, full of curiosity, broke off their chat when they saw the car from Germany. Should I speak to them?

"Drive on," said Klaus, to prevent that.

The village was unchanged, and yet I had to correct my recollections. The little farm where the mortar platoon had been accommodated was not immediately next to Jeanette's house. I had completely forgotten the two or three small houses and sheds in between.

The farm was cultivated by an immigrant family from Poland. The farmer's wife spoke a bit of German and was an eager as well as a dreaded gossip who knew all and told all. But she would let nothing bother the young recruits in the mortar platoon; she mothered them, helped them with their laundry and their cleaning, occasionally even made extra soup for a treat, and settled arguments. Whenever I would turn up for inspection she would rush up to me, gabbling excitedly like a goose defending her brood, and assure me that everything was in order and she had already checked it all herself; then I could set my mind at ease. She had a seventeen–year–old son who spent the night in the barn along with the recruits, shared the field kitchen food with them, and was always present at drill and at field practice—even if it was at a distance of ten meters and minus steel helmet and weapons—though he always strove to imitate the others and to carry out the commands and the orders. He demonstrated for the village youths how well he had mastered the drill rules, the commands, and even the colorful, profane vocabulary of the instructor.

It was there, in front of the woodpile that dwindled with use over the winter, that the incident occurred. Once again I had appeared suddenly for an inspection. The farmer's wife came towards me, drying her hands on her apron, and assured me that everything was in order, "Herr Unter-sturmfuehrer." Her son stood erectly at attention in front of the woodpile, in order to demonstrate to me the level of his training, with a view to applying as a volunteer.

"Halt, you son of a bitch!" He hurled the command at me, clicked his heels together, and commanded, "To the right—forward march! One, two, three, four . . ." And then, with a deadly serious expression on his face, he sang, as if it were the National Anthem, the bawdiest of sailor's songs:

> *Ein Seemann, der im Hurenhaus erwacht,*
> *von Tripper–, Schankersorgen kaum genesen,*
> *gebumst hat er die liebe lange Nacht,*
> *in seinen Armen lag ein nacktes Wesen.*

The recruits, meanwhile, had swiftly retreated into the barn and were doubled up with laughter on the straw. They had rehearsed him for this performance.

"Why are you grinning like that?" asked Lore. "You must be thinking of something nasty!"

I turned right, into the unpaved road. On the left was where our kitchen had been put up; our parade and roll call ground was opposite, on the meadow owned by Monsieur Réau, the proprietor of the cognac distillery, whose house also accommodated our orderly room. Next to the kitchen lay Madame Batiste's little shop. We called her "the paintbox." Even her ears were powdered. With the aid of lipstick she managed to turn her thin, pinched mouth into full, scarlet, cherry lips, and her eyes looked as if she had just pulverized one hundred kilos of coal. But she fell over herself to be kind, and rumor had it that she was carrying on with the deputy platoon leader Schmieding, an elderly man of thirty-nine.

"Do you still remember that loud silk cloth, Lore?"

"The liqueur cloth?"

"That's right. I bought it in this little shop, from Madame Batiste."

"Aha."

And then Klaus moaned, "You can't simply drive on the meadow! It's bad enough that you even dare to show yourself here again, but now causing damage to an agricultural area as well! They'll set the dogs on us!"

Just let Monsieur Réau come and chase me away! Nearly every Sunday morning, when we were off duty, out of respect to the church–going populace we met secretly in Réau's parlour to celebrate the *"sainte messe des plus grands filous de Montboyer."* The mayor was there, as well as the town secretary and the garage owner, Sarasin, who had such a marvellous laugh. Réau would then sneak like a burglar to the wall cupboard, open the door to a forbidden secret, and bring out glasses and a carafe which he held up triumphantly like booty: Pineau Charantaise! Then he would put a finger to his lips, because it was forbidden to make Pineau during the war. *"Défendu!"* The devil knew why. At first we were allowed only to sip it, very solemnly, and had to marvel at how wonderful the forbidden fruit tasted. After three or four glasses the mood was wonderful. The town secretary tried to start off "The Marseillaise" as a chorale and then attempted *"Deutschland, Deutschland ueber alles,"* which was much better suited to a choral arrangement. Sarasin told the fifth or sixth installment of his story about how he had nearly recaptured Paris, and now he was at the point where he had finally arrived as a gun–layer at a field kitchen at Angoulême's loading depot. Two freight trains stood ready to depart for Paris, one of which carried nothing but supplies for the troops. An entire car full of cube sugar, for example, in order to sweeten the war. One car each full of anisette and Grand Marnier, since no Frenchman could reasonably be expected to fight and win without a digestive to wash down the fatty food. The food train was fifty cars long, which was why the story was so long as well; all of it ammunition for the field kitchen.

Even before the arrival of the real artillery a mood of unrest had spread through the early morning hours. It was maintained that the Germans were already there, in Angoulême, and a couple of shots actually were fired, the first and last shots of this war for Sarasin. And then two motorcycles with sidecars actually came driving along the railway platform. *"C'était la SS,"* which Sarasin translated as *"sans soucis,"* because they had come along quite carelessly, with no respect for the explosive super–power of field–kitchen ammunition. "We were supposed to leave everything standing there and go home, they said, the war had ended long ago—*'durant que vous avez dormis.'* So I went home, on foot, forty kilometers, with my rucksack full of field–kitchen ammunition, and then I did nothing for two weeks but eat and sleep."

"The one on the motorcycle could have been me," I said. "I was there at that time. Didn't you recognize me?"

"You were there? Oh, what did you do with the anisette? When I returned to Angoulême four weeks later there was none left! *Vous êtes un des plus grands filous de la SS!"*

"Now you've seen everything once more," said Klaus, "and so far we've been lucky, but rather than overstep the mark let's get out of here quickly now."

"Did I ever tell you about the swimming pool we made here? It's up there at the edge of the wood; you can't see it properly from here."

"A swimming pool?"

During the summer the water was very scarce here, and the little brook, the Tude, was almost completely dried up. But up there, at the edge of the wood, was a little spring that bubbled constantly and just as quickly seeped into the ground, unused. And so we and the local people dug out a basin, got hold of some cement and built a big pool. The decision to do this was arrived at after the fourth glass of Pineau during the *"sainte messe,"* which also inspired the mayor to plan his "Montboyer-le–bain" of the future, in which he would build palm–tree–lined avenues and a golf course and, naturally, a casino. From the colossal income that this would bring in he offered Sarasin a loan to build a luxury hotel next to his petrol station and bicycle workshop.

But the water that came dripping from the spring was meager, and our daily checks revealed that the level was rising scarcely more than a quarter centimeter per day. So we organized a liquid manure cart, rinsed it out to some extent, and carted in additional water from a long way away; and when we had finally got water up to our knees we officially opened the pool. In the mornings it was reserved for the civilians, in the afternoons for the soldiers, and in the evenings everyone could use it, while at night the insects, scorpions, lizards, adders, salamanders, and other animal life came. The problem was that the latter did not leave voluntarily. After a while the pool was used only for laundry, and the creatures finally died of the detergent.

"A boring, insignificant village like a thousand others," Klaus remarked, not suspecting how much the time–lapse photography of my mind had to tell me. Every house corner, every bit of undergrowth, every pathway conjured up, in fractions of a second, new associations from my faded memories, and before I could manage to put them in any chronological order they had already been replaced by others. I would have to come to just this place! How could I expect anyone else to do anything but find this a boring, insignificant village like a thousand others! The hedges that lined the road had spread out luxuriously, so that on both sides the branches scraped the paint on the car. The dogs barked furiously, just as they did way back then, when Toni and I went to the Boisse late in the evenings.

"They're letting the dogs loose, turn back!"

Even Lore and Erika were getting impatient now. "You surely don't want to go in here, do you? 'Hello, I'm the Lieutenant from way back, the Untersturmfuehrer, don't you remember me?' Do you think they'll be as glad to see you again as you are to be here?"

Marianne would certainly be glad, and would ask what had become of this person and that person. She was about twenty–three or twenty–four at that time, and we spent many happy and pleasant hours with the boys and girls from the village. That is something she wouldn't have been able simply to erase from her memory as if it had never happened, the mild summer nights, the soft moonlit songs, the little campfires with a midnight picnic and red wine, the linguistic misunderstandings with Toni, whose corrections of his translations led to new comic confusion. How we laughed, each of us in his or her own way, Monique loudly and shrilly, Marianne chuckling almost tonelessly, with tears pouring from her eyes. Three questions behind the door, and heaven forbid that Toni wouldn't admit that Monique was his favorite! Then she would dance only with the cat in her arms, and Toni brought the St. Bernard into the house to chase the cat away. Then, towards midnight, we charged back over the drill field to the village, doing somersaults, and the girls imitated our exercises, and one of us would have to escort Marianne back to the Boisse and be a long time in taking his leave of her. Perhaps she had long been married now, and her husband mustn't know anything about that time!

I drove slowly by the Boisse. The bushes had grown larger and an Alsatian had replaced the St. Bernard. However loudly they might protest, instead of driving back I turned into the wider road that still joined the main road near the carpenter's workshop. The two women were still standing there chattering. I stopped and rolled down the window.

"Excusez, mesdames . . ."

There was nothing they liked better than to excuse the fact that they had been spoken to.

"The carpenter with two daughters used to live in this house. Do you know where they are now?"

Oh yes, they knew, the one better than the other. The carpenter had died, although they couldn't agree on whether that was five, six, or seven years ago. But his wife was still alive, and Monique, who was married to someone from the railroad, had a fashion studio in Paris; Jeanette, however, was not married, and she lived with her mother and aunt in Chalais, six kilometers from here.

"Come out here, follow the main road all the way down, then go over the rail crossing, which is often closed because the trains from Paris to Bordeaux pass by there. And once over the crossing you don't go right towards Libourne, but straight ahead to the church, to the *marbre,* and right next to the *marbre* is the house where the mother and the aunt live, and Jeanette isn't married—"

"What did they say?"

"Actually they seemed quite friendly and enthusiastic; what did they say, then?"

"Jeanette lives with her aunt in Chalais." Twice they had emphasized that she wasn't married, as if they wanted to say that I could easily go and say hello.

"*Mariée* means married, doesn't it? That much I still remember from school."

"So, now you've done everything," Klaus decided, "even spoken with people. Monique is married, the other bird isn't; but let's go now, I'm hungry!"

I don't know why Klaus is able to repress the war and his army days so completely. I have never heard him talk about it. But it was, after all, our youth, and all the older folk I knew enthused about their youth, whether it was their training, their student days, or the First World War; they laughed about their pranks and the silly things they did, talked of their adventures, their thirst for action and their high spirits, full of nostalgia for this youth which is usually followed by the serious business of life.

And yet our youth, which was over as soon as it began, had a veil of awkward silence laid over it, as if we had spent it in prison, committed burglaries or arson, or stolen cars; and even those things would have been incomparably more harmless and understandable than to have taken part in Hitler's unjust war—and in the Waffen–SS, no less! But it was a fact of life, and I was a part of it; I did not leave my mark on this era, but it left its mark on me, and yet no dark spot existed that I had to be ashamed of, either now or at the time. And if it is true that a person's youth marks him for life, and if I am the way I am, then my youth is a part of that, and I want to keep it as it was.

And here, in Montboyer, was a poor imitation of that carefree time that a person has to live on for his entire life—only a few carefree months in which my memory packed in everything that other people could relate of their happy youth. I had nothing more to offer and would also have preferred Heidelberg, Marburg, or Goettingen; but it was here, and it wasn't so carefree either, because hanging over us like a menacing sword was the deadly serious business of the imminent march into the Russian inferno, which would demand of us the humanly impossible. And again and again there flashed into my mind the awareness that I

had to prepare the seventeen– and eighteen–year–old lads, scarcely younger than myself, to enter this inferno and survive in it.

They may well have cursed me every time I made them dig holes in
the hard ground in the burning heat in order to cram themselves into
the protective covering of the earth; every time they had to bring their
antitank guns, mortars, or infantry guns into position so that all the
movements became second nature to them; and when, stop watch in
hand, I demanded that it take not twenty but only ten seconds to be
ready to fire. They had to realize that "Take cover, charge, forward
march!" is no punishment drill or sadistic form of harassment but life
insurance. I once spoke to the Dutch soldiers in the fortress Grebbe
who had to defend it against our regiment's line of attack across a
one–kilometer field of advance. They found it weird and disconcerting
the way we disappeared as quickly as we had appeared before they
could take aim at us. Having expected that anyone advancing could be
picked off like ducks in a shooting gallery, they found themselves powerless to prevent the constantly approaching but ducking, bobbing, and
dodging steam roller; and so everyone survived, attackers as well as
defenders.

And how often did I have to go without sleep in Russia while we
continuously pushed forward against the enemy lines, or later, while
the Russians stormed our positions with ever new forces, day and night
without a respite, when we used Pervitin to keep awake and I had hardly
more than twenty–four hours' sleep in ten days. That is why I did night
drills that were talked about for a long time afterwards.

The normal daily routine was followed by the first night drill—without
sleep. It was miserable. Just as the men were thinking they would make
up the lost sleep the next day, I announced that they had only forty-
five minutes in which to wash and eat breakfast before resuming their
normal daily schedule. After this, they thought, they would sleep that
much better the following night. I will never forget their despairing
expressions when I announced that evening that they had to assemble
in one hour in full marching order with all weapons, light and heavy,
in order to repeat the night drill.

Already the drill went better.

At sunrise they stood there again, covered in dust, filthy, and wanting nothing more eagerly than to be able to hit the hay now. But it wasn't to be! Two hours later, weapon and gun roll call, because weapon care and constant readiness for action are essential! And since this roll call left a lot to be desired the normal duty rota was continued, without sleep.

When I asked them that evening who was dead tired, no one would admit it. "In that case I hope the night drill will finally go smoothly the third time round. Field marching order in one hour, like yesterday!"

Naturally the off–duty soldiers could take a cat nap while they were waiting.

"Sleep faster, comrades!" the sergeant advised. They had realized that one can make up many hours of sleep in a few moments.

"What is most important after an action?" I asked them at sunrise.

"Weapon and gun roll call!" they answered.

"Right, you have two hours. Then roll call in walking–out dress!"

Two hours later I inspected the weapons and guns and scratched the remaining dust out of the grooves with a match. They had a sense of foreboding.

"Who has been to Bordeaux?"

No one.

"Tomorrow morning at six o'clock we meet here again. Until then you can do what you want, sleep or go to Bordeaux. The train leaves in fifty minutes."

Howling with delight they took their weapons home, ran the two kilometers to the station, and reported for duty the next morning, fresh and happy. Nothing is more burdensome than having to suffer harassment and injustice, but nothing increases self–confidence more than having withstood hardships.

When, seven months later, the Russians had us surrounded in Zhitomir, I predicted that we wouldn't get much sleep over the next few days.

"We're used to that, Untersturmfuehrer," said Alfons. "You know: B—o—r—d—e—a—u—x!" He pronounced it the way it is written, to show how well he had learned French.

Alfons could neither read nor write, and there were others who hadn't learned more than to scrawl their names in capital letters. They came from Yugoslavia, Hungary, Rumania, or Poland—"adopted Germans." They had never learned to walk or stand properly, in the scouts or in any other youth organization, and came to us straight from the sugar beet field, the cowstall, or a herd of goats. Some had volunteered, others had not, but none of them had any idea of what was in store for them. In October 1939 twenty percent of my company of recruits might have consisted of college students, athletes, or at least well–trained scouts with a minimum of average intelligence, but in Montboyer I found a motley crew that made a mockery of any idea of "elite."

Alfons was my "orderly." Even at that time we had pompous titles for the simplest services. I could, in all good conscience, leave my private correspondence lying around in the presence of illiterate Alfons, an "orderly," just because it was a foreign word, was something fantastic for him, a distinction, an early career. He did not know what "elite" meant, and when I explained it to him he was very impressed that he, just he, who had not even learned to read or write, was one of them, and from then on he behaved like a member of the elite, walking erect, chest out, taking long, energetic steps with his short legs. Wherever a steel helmet could be seen in the column bobbing up and down with especial vigor, that was Alfons marching.

He was one of the first to earn the Iron Cross, Second Class. It was in Isiaslavl, a place north of Staro Konstantinov, through the middle of which the main front ran, alongside a brook. The Russians were on the other side, sometimes not more than twenty meters away from us. In a dugout on the edge of the brook the Russians were holed up in a machine–gun hideout, an excellent position from which they could, and did, fire at everything that moved as well as at every noise in the darkness of night. Unpleasant, extremely unpleasant, and there was no way of getting at this hideout.

Alfons had an idea.

Twice a day one of the few babushkas left in the village strolled calmly out of her house by the brook, with a yoke over her shoulders and two buckets on the chain. Exactly opposite the hideout she scooped water from the brook through an always freshly–broken hole in the ice, and then waddled back again.

The way Alfons persuaded the babushka to take off her clothes must have deserved an Academy Award. He only wanted her clothes, really, nothing other than her clothes, and only for five minutes. No, no under-wear, for God's sake, he had his own, and it wasn't much cleaner than hers. But he did need the scarf under which she tucked her hair. Under the blanket of the bed—and he still had to turn his back—she cast off one piece after another. While she watched, he practiced using the yoke and buckets, and also tried to imitate her waddle. *"Karasho? Da da?"* And since she had no comment—because she didn't know what he had in mind—she had to demonstrate it once more, and for this Alfons had to take the dress off again.

Then he was ready. Alfons put two hand grenades into the bucket and at dawn waddled down to the brook, broke the skin of ice, washed his hands, washed his face, and blinked through his outspread fingers over to the machine–gun hideout. They smoked Papirossis and waved with their little fingers. Alfons reached into the bucket, took out both hand grenades at the same time, and threw them as if they were fresh breakfast rolls.

There was a "bang" and Alfons filled both buckets with water and took them to the babushka.

"In the first place, my dear Alfons, civilians may not become involved in war activities; and secondly, the Hague Land Warfare Convention says that fighting may only be done in uniform. Didn't you know that?"

"No, Untersturmfuehrer."

And even though it was bitterly cold he kept the top part of his overcoat open wide enough that everyone could see the black, white, and red ribbon of his Iron Cross. Now he was really one of the elite.

4

The house just next to the *marbre,* she had said. What is a *marbre?*

I turned in the direction of Chalais and went quite slowly past Madame Andrea's pub. Was that she, on her knees, scrubbing the steps? Or was it her daughter, who had been sixteen then and on account of whom the soldiers visited this, the only watering hole in the village, whenever they had time? And because of this Madame Andrea, who served me my first crepes suzettes, had begged me to get her husband released from captivity, so that this one and only pub would grow up to our expectations. I looked into the matter and consequently ended up in an embarrassing situation. Her husband managed an estate near Berlin and didn't appear to have any great interest in a speedy homecoming. I put her off by saying that he couldn't get away before the next harvest.

One of Madame Andrea's regulars was Bobby, the town secretary's son and the mayor's brother–in–law. "Brother–in–law" wasn't quite correct, since the mayor was only having a love affair with his sister, but Bobby acted as if he had great influence with the mayor and the goings-on in the community because of this relationship. He was a loafer, a good–for–nothing, a lazybones and a schemer, and again and again he talked to me about my getting him a good job in Germany, because there was nothing happening in this boring dump. No one would have any use for such a lazybones in Germany, so I turned him down, whereupon he whispered to Madame Andrea that I had lied to her and had done nothing whatever about freeing her husband, because the Germans had absolutely no intention of freeing a prisoner of war or exchanging him for one who would immediately take over the management of the estate near Berlin . . . Berlin!

Lights-out, *couvre feu*, was at 11 P.M. for civilians as well as soldiers, but until then no one had bothered about it. But that evening, when Bobby drank one glass of red wine after another at Madame Andrea's and was persistently and suggestively provocative, I insisted on it and announced that at one minute past eleven the guards would come and arrest everyone who was still sitting around here. But Bobby just laughed scornfully and ordered another glass of wine shortly before eleven, while Andrea observed the scene tensely. At eleven o'clock I announced *"Couvre feu!"* and Bobby stretched his legs out still farther; but one minute later two guards appeared, took Bobby away, and locked him for the rest of the night in the provisional detention cell just next door in the Réau house, which also accommodated our orderly room.

By the next morning everyone knew about it, and everyone smirked, especially his father, whose German vocabulary amounted to *"Was ist los?"*

"Don't drive so far to the left!" Lore shouted. "You're dreaming."

"Of course he is, he's been dreaming the whole time," Erika put in.

The presbytery came after the Réau house and the cognac distillery. I spent my first nights here in the little hut just to the left behind the entrance. A bed and a chair, nothing more. The housekeeper was nick-named *"Madame à barbe."* Sparse hairs, a couple of centimeters long, grew on her chin and upper lip, and when she spoke she leaned forward and backward and tossed her right arm back and forth like a pump handle. It was whispered that she was the guarantor for the parish priest's having remained faithful to his vow of celibacy.

"If you keep dawdling like this we'll never get to Hendaye," muttered Klaus.

When the last houses had been left behind I accelerated. "Chalais 6 km," said the signpost. Before reaching the Tude bridge I had to slow down again. It was here that Zinsheim had driven into the ditch. When we came from Chalais, from the cinema or an evening at the front theater (although there was no front here), we made a halt here.

I saw them sitting there, the entire company, to the right and to the left on the bridge parapet and on the edges of the ditch. They sang, and when a young girl rode by on a bicycle they applauded to the rhythm of the pedals.

What became of them, the men of the Heavy Company, who were all of good will and who tried to make up with eagerness for what they lacked in practice, condition and skill; easy to inspire and easy to lead if they were led? I still went hot and cold when I thought of how after one single night only a third of them survived.

It was the night of Christmas Eve, 1943, in the Bulitschety Forest, between Kiev and Zhitomir. There had been front–line soldier packets and the Christmas post, which was already four or even eight weeks old. We had decorated the company command post, which was covered with thick tree trunks and lay not far from the antitank gun and mortar positions, for Christmas: covered crates with green tarpaulins, put up a little Christmas tree, and lit Hindenburg candles. The post had contained a letter from Lore. I wrote four letters that evening, one to Lore, one to Klaus, letters that never reached their destinations.

For about two weeks it had been relatively quiet in this zone, but now something seemed to be in the offing. Every quarter–hour Toni gave me messages from his scout, and the observer of the mortar train also confirmed that something was brewing up ahead. Russian artillery moved up, closer and closer. They immediately began to aim their sights. The easterly wind carried the clank of their tracks to us. More and more artillery moved up. Our mortars erupted intermittently. I passed the information to the battalion, the battalion passed it on to the regiment; but they didn't appear to take us seriously. After all, it was only some weeks ago that we were sent prematurely to Russia as a replacement battalion, without having finished our training, while the "*Das Reich*" Division, which had been involved in continuous fighting for ten months and was severely shattered by the struggle to recapture Zhitomir, was preparing to leave the main front to refresh themselves in the West, in the south of France, in the region of Montboyer. We were—and in no way unjustly—the replacements, with no experience at the front, and our alarmed reports were considered exaggerated.

A peculiar mood of festive expectancy had spread. The weather had changed, the hard frost had eased, and a strong wind brought mildness and the sounds of tank tracks. Tanks. Tanks are attack weapons. Was a most unchristian attack being planned for just now, at Christmas?[*]

It was 4 P.M. and already pitch black. Even the commander of the 1st Company, on our right wing, complained that the reports about the Russian preparations were not being taken seriously by the top brass. The Russians had worked their way up to fifty meters in front of their positions and, camouflaged in white overcoats, lay ready to pounce. The situation was tense to the breaking point. His men now absolutely needed to feel a sense of achievement. Toni was to try to open fire on the Russian position with his infantry guns.

I took a 50mm antitank gun from its position and led the 1st Company with it. In the light of the flares one could make out the black–and–white figures dotted in the snow as Russians. Toni's well–aimed fire forced them to take cover. When I could, I fixed them in the sights of my gun and fired grenades at them.

Now there was movement. Some of the Russians started crawling or jumping back. The first screams of the wounded could be heard. Our machine guns hammered on, and Toni intensified the firing.

A flare, fired too steeply, drifted back in the wind and illuminated the antitank gun. A tank grenade whizzed past our ears. Change of position! Hand grenades were flung back and forth. Cries, calls, commands. The whole Russian field was now on the move. The antitank gun continued to bark. They fled, out of sight of our flares.

In the sudden silence the groans, moans, and cries of the wounded could be heard. Would the Russians come for their comrades under the protective cover of darkness? Would they simply leave them to their fate? They must come for them—the moaning and crying had become intolerable.

Now, it seemed to me, after such a victory on our side we would have peace over Christmas. But then . . .

It started with a distant rumble, as from an earthquake. Then a scream, whiz, roar, and explosion. Sand oozed between the tree trunks and extinguished the candles. Trees splintered and disintegrated. The noise, the commotion came inexorably closer. Yard by yard the Russians advanced.

---

[*] Zhitomir was recaptured by the Soviets on 31 December.

The telephone lines were shot to pieces; the man in charge kept shouting, "Please report!" but the men had no time for that.

The Russian gun barrels had to be glowing now after such a barrage. Why had they not hit our dugout? Would it come, within a second, a minute? How long will they go on like this?

Eventually the barrage ceased and we stormed out of the dugout into a completely altered landscape. Broken-off tree crowns, naked tree trunks, fog mixed with smoke, a burning wood stove, shell–holes everywhere, tree trunks lying on their sides . . .

And sudden silence. Only in the distance shots and the rumble of cannon fire could be heard. We looked towards the main front line. Only fifty meters from our antitank gun position the outline of a T-34 tank was silhouetted against the dawn sky. Its gun was lowered. Close by, with its tracks skyward, was another one, pouring out smoke. But it was quiet up there. Nothing moved.

Then there was not much to think about, and not many orders to give. Stay together and don't shoot! We combed the woods, just as they did. Keep more to the right! But they were already there. More to the left, keep your distance going past the house! More and more Russians streamed into the bullet–riddled forester's lodge, as if they had already discovered great things there. Many of them were even running. Our front–line soldier packets! They were holding the little white cartons in their hands, digging biscuits and chocolates out of them, and lighting one of the six cigarettes that each packet contained. They were all smoking and chatting.

There were six of us, the company commander, a dispatch rider from each platoon, the radio operator, and myself. Don't shoot! Only when they've seen us and I give the sign, then hit the ground and open fire! But I could still see no suitable escape route. They were everywhere. We were now on a level with the forester's lodge. Some waved at us. Pay no attention! Ahead of us the woods seemed to grow thicker. Every-where branches were snapping, Russians were talking.

Now the first Russians had discovered our bunker and were disappearing into it. They would find opened front–line soldier packets—and my letters; one to Lore, one to Klaus, one to my mother. I was doing well, it said in them; we had won back Zhitomir and, for the moment, some quiet as well. Yesterday we had beaten off a timid attempt at an attack and would now surely be able to celebrate Christmas undisturbed.

We had reached the denser woods and no one appeared to be hard on our heels. Unbelievable, how long one can grope one's way through enemy–occupied woods with the deepest concentration and greatest effort, despite twenty-four hours without sleep. Was it occupied? Where were the voices and the snapping sounds coming from? Could it be our people? Wasn't there a tank standing there? Yes, it was a tank, a T-34. The crew members were sitting behind it, talking loudly and absorbed in the front–line soldier packets. Capture this T-34 and break through!

In one leap I was standing in front of them, my machine gun in firing position. They looked at me in amazed indignation, not believing that a German was standing there. Do I shoot or not? Did I try to shoot? Did my machine gun really fail to function, as I claimed later? One of them offered me a bar of chocolate. Get lost, man, get lost! Leave us the tank! They got up, threw their weapons away, stumbled backwards a few steps more to the fir thicket, turned round, put their hands down and ran like the devil.

Who among us knew his way around a T-34? Why was it standing here at all? In the middle of the woods? Breakdown or break, that was the question.

Excited voices from over there where they had fled, from the right. We veered off to the left. My machine gun had failed, thank God, otherwise all hell would have broken loose here! But they now knew that another troop of scattered Germans was lingering in their lines. They would be looking for us.

Was the sharp frost of the recent weeks over, or were we only warm from sheer excitement? The blanket of snow had grown very thin and was now hardly visible. We could not leave a trail in the snow, but the forest floor was no longer brittle as glass. We avoided treading on branches and did not speak a word. Meanwhile our thoughts flowed like a string of pearls, until they fastened on the fact that it was now Christmas morning—church bells—butter cake for breakfast—a book among the gifts, *The Army behind Barbed Wire* by Dwinger—being Russian prisoners of war, that was absolutely the last way out—we would sell ourselves dearly—we would not sell ourselves at all—we must come out of here again, we must!

Suddenly two Russians emerged from behind a pine tree; one of them carried a machine gun over his shoulder. They waved at us amicably with hands they kept in the air when they saw two rifle barrels aimed at them; then they raised their other hands too and let the machine gun fall. Fuchs, the freckled ethnic German from Poland, picked it up and relieved them of their weapons. They were to walk ahead of us and lead us out of the Russian lines. Fuchs translated that for them into Polish, and they said *"da, da"* and in their situation would have said *"da, da"* to anything in the hopes that the tables would soon be turned, for we were a long way from being out of the danger zone.

They walked ahead of us, sometimes bearing to the left, sometimes to the right, and when voices could be heard ahead of us to the right they headed away from them. Fuchs drove them to the left, where they followed only with reluctance. The woods grew thicker and were filled with young pine trees, the kind we would cut down for Christmas trees. They both took advantage of this by running away. Fuchs raised his gun to his shoulder; Wachter, the company commander, knocked it down: "Don't shoot!"

The two men fled in the direction of the voices, which could be heard, and we hastily veered off to the left. The feeling that the woods must soon come to an end did not deceive us. It grew lighter. We had a feeling of having run in a westerly direction, and from that way we thought we heard the sounds of engines. The German front? Our tanks? Fifty meters more and we would have reached the edge of the woods. We carefully crept along, then we crawled to the edge of the woods and strained to listen. The smell of burning. Voices that were not excitedly giving orders, but chatting casually. Laughing. Our people had nothing to laugh about; it must be Russians.

When we raised our heads we could see only sixty meters ahead of us. There to the right at the edge of the woods, that was where the burning smell was coming from; a little fire. They were brewing coffee or something to that effect and were squatting or standing around the fire. Front–line soldier packets! One of them was just throwing an empty packet into the flames. To our left, too, we could hear voices. In front of us was open terrain, farmland, and after that, a good kilometer away, a village. Our complete attention was drawn to the village. Who occupied it? Our troops, surely, but it didn't fit that the Russians had arranged a comfortable pause in the fighting and made little fires near the enemy.

We had no choice but to go over the open terrain. Should we stroll over it in a leisurely fashion, as if we were a group of Russians? The two men with the machine gun and the tank crew knew we were here; they would have informed on us long ago. We had to sprint as quickly as possible.

At home the bells would be ringing now, calling everyone to church; right now everyone would be trudging through the snow, wearing the new pullover, the new gloves or the shawl, breathing in the Christmas morning, peaceful, secure, full of hopes, and no one would have any idea of what a dangerous path lay before us. We removed our overcoats, our thick felt boots, and all superfluous equipment, and crouched, ready, in starting position. One more glance at the coffee–drinking, cigarette–smoking group, and then I hissed the starting signal.

Nothing happened. Ahead of me the men were puffing and panting and running as fast as they could, twenty, thirty meters. Then it got louder behind us: shouts and commands.

"Faster!" After fifty meters the first shot was fired. We darted from side to side and they shot at us as if it were a rabbit hunt. More and more weapons joined the hunt, and occasionally the ack–ack of a machine gun could be heard too. The group behind our left side had also noticed us and now joined the others.

"Separate! More distance! In jumps!" We spread out, threw ourselves down, sprang up again. Fifty meters ahead of us, if I weren't being completely deceived, was a ditch, a life–saving ditch! Wachter, up ahead, fell to the ground, and I could tell he hadn't done it on purpose. I lay down next to him.

"What's wrong, Wachter?"

"My right foot!"

I saw it: a bullet hole through the ankle, impossible to run any farther on it.

"Come on, Wachter! Only thirty meters more to the ditch, then you'll be safe. Run! Jump up, Wachter!"

He jumped up, buckled, jumped up again.

"Only a silly graze, Wachter, it just hurts, that's all. Run!"

He ran and he howled with pain. The first men had reached the ditch, raised their weapons to their shoulders and were aiming at the edge of the woods. "Covering fire!" I roared at them.

Damn! Even the village was occupied by the Russians. A troop of about ten Russians broke away from the village and came towards us. I dragged Wachter into the ditch. Only a few seconds to catch one's breath, to stop the huffing and puffing and consider the position. The ditch, obviously a drainage ditch, ran parallel to the edge of the woods and ended about two hundred meters to the right of us. Behind it we could see heaps, pyramid–shaped heaps. Peat.

Shots whistled away over us. "Take Wachter to the right, two of you stay with me!"

I started keeping tabs on the group that came from the village, while the other two watched the group at the edge of the woods. With well aimed independent fire we forced them under cover and followed Wachter, who was moaning more and more loudly. "Faster, Wachter, you're holding up the whole outfit! Don't think about your silly graze, run!"

The ditch was only a meter deep, and the ground was marshy; it squelched with every step. They dragged Wachter, who was all bent over, farther on. The group coming from the village moved closer to us. We opened fire on them, and after we had hit one of them they took cover. The group at the edge of the woods had also taken cover and they fired as soon as one of our heads could be seen.

"Farther, men, and faster! Wachter, don't just drag yourself. Run! A hundred meters more!"

And then? The mud was sticking to our shoes, knees and hands. Up ahead were the heaps of peat. The thaw had set in.

Why didn't they come? They only needed to cut off our path to the peat heaps, ten men would be enough; after all, we had only a little ammunition. We had left everything superfluous back at the edge of the woods. Why didn't they come?

They came. An armed personnel carrier had driven up to the edge of the woods—a German armored personnel carrier that had been captured.

"Faster, men, faster, run, run!"

A dozen Russians stood ready to climb into the armored tub. Was this the end? I imprinted the date of my death in my mind. Fallen on 25 December 1943, around 2 P.M. But we wouldn't make it that easy for them. My next–to–last magazine was in my machine gun. I aimed a couple of shots at the group that stood in readiness and drove them under cover. Every second of delay could help us, because seventy or perhaps only fifty meters up ahead our ditch led into a cross–ditch, which was wider, deeper and filled with brown water. The men got a move on; Wachter crawled on all fours and dragged his right leg after him.

The engine roared, the gears screeched, a machine gun from the armored personnel carrier gave the signal for the finale. The first of our men appeared to have reached the cross–ditch. The armored personnel carrier was being driven at full throttle, and it shot out onto the open terrain. At best I could reach the cross–ditch at the same time as it did, but Wachter crawled slowly, they hauled and dragged him along. I aimed my machine gun one more time—useless against the armor, but maybe . . . maybe it would stop.

It stopped, its engine roaring loudly. The tracks were spinning in the boggy sand. The armored car reversed and drove on again. Full throttle, only full throttle, but the tracks got stuck again and were spraying out fountains of dirt behind it.

Wachter had reached the cross–ditch. The brown water came up to our hips. The men dragged him through the four– to five–meter–wide ditch. The armored car could no longer even reverse. It had got stuck fast. The crew fired at us with all its weapons. Furiously. The men had reached the piles of peat and found cover there.

The Russians got out and were coming on foot. Now we had the advantage, because they had no cover. We fired on them with well aimed independent fire from two sides. They drew back. They drew back! I was the last to reach the water–filled cross–ditch.

"Everyone all right? No one wounded?"

No one wounded.

Wachter wanted to look at his wound, to take off the boot. "Cut it out, Wachter, we haven't got time now."

"I can't go any farther," Wachter whined. "Leave me here; I'll give you covering fire."

"Do you want to give up?"

"It's pointless. My ankle has been shot through, it's no graze, I know."

"Where did you get such nonsense! Don't be a sissy! What did you get this for?" I pulled at his Iron Cross First Class. "For bravery or for giving up like a coward? All right let's go, this way!" I pointed northwest. Someone broke off a small birch and wrapped the stump in his field cap, so that Wachter could use it under his armpit like a crutch. This worked for a couple of steps, then he broke down again.

"I have a fever."

"We're all hot, that's quite natural, so, forward!"

"You have a better chance of making it without me, let me stay."
"We'll all make it or none of us will, and now I don't want to hear
any more whining. Do you want no one to make it?"

A few shots still came after us, as if they wanted to wish us a good
homecoming; then they gave up. The bog was safe as houses, but after
a few hundred meters the ground was harder again. The men had been
dragging Wachter and now all their strength was spent. It was no more
use. Hahn was the strongest. I took him with me; up ahead, a little
over a mile away, there must be a road, and where there was a road
German or Russian vehicles would be coming. Maybe we could capture
one.

There was a road there, now clearly visible, but not a human being
as far as the eye could see, not even a crow. Everything seemed to
have fled from the heavy barrage. Where were friends, where were the
foe? Where were they, the rest of the company, the men from the Bannat,
from Transylvania, from Poland, the "adopted Germans" who had joined
with us, so full of confidence in our victory over the Russians?

There, on the wall of the Tude bridge, they had sat and sung and
laughed and clapped when a young girl came cycling. Then, during
the first weeks of their training, they had to hand in their letters home
unsealed; I was supposed to make random checks that they mentioned
no places or other items that were to be kept secret. No, they didn't do
that; but now and then there was someone who described our exercises
as though we were marching against the Russians. In these letters they
were heroes, victors, they landed bull's-eyes with their hand grenades
or knocked out tanks. They *had* knocked out tanks: the two up ahead
in the main front could only have been put out of action by our antitank
gun, which lay a short distance in front of their positions. I wondered
whether they would have the chance to write that to their girlfriends:
two tanks—or, as far as I'm concerned, two dozen, the fear and excitement
are the same. But now I had no idea what the situation was and did
not know where friend or foe were.

We lay in the ditch by the side of the road and waited, for more
than an hour now. Dusk had already begun to fall when a dark spot
could be seen on the road in the distance. It came from the village that
was already occupied by the Russians, a large village, as we could
now make out. The spot grew larger. Was that shooting we heard? It
was neither a tank nor a lorry, it was much too fast. It was a private

car, a German one, a Horch if I wasn't being deceived, and not full. Only the driver could be seen. A Russian or a German? A hundred meters more. We got ready to jump. Forty meters more. Now we jumped on to the road, holding our submachine guns in front of us. The driver stopped. His tensed–up face relaxed when he recognized us.

"For God's sake, don't do anything stupid," he cried, "jump in; they're coming now." He was a captain.

I got in behind him and said, "Please drive to the right over the field. There are three more of us there and one wounded."

"Back to the Russians? Are you crazy?"

"Drive to the right!"

"Hey!" I pressed the barrel of the submachine gun into his back.

"For God's sake, watch what you're doing!"

"If you turn off to the right I will watch."

"What the devil . . ."

He turned off to the right and hurried over the field. "Only about a kilometer more," I said.

"A kilometer, damn . . ."

He tore along so that I was afraid for the springs. Then they waved, Fuchs, Wachter and the others. Did they have tears in their eyes?

"We'd never have believed it, Untersturmfuehrer, really."

"The captain was so nice," I said.

"But now, on the double, dammit!" he said agitatedly. He helped Wachter onto the back seat and raced off again. Werner was his name, and he said he was the brother of Ilse Werner, whom everyone knew from the musical request concert. When we had reached the road again it came to light that he was attached to our neighbors on the right who were connected with the First Company, at the place where we had beaten back the little Russian attack; oh yes, he had known about this shoot–up, he remembered, but hadn't we noticed what a huge amount of artillery, infantry and tanks the Russians had brought up? The outcome of this attack was a foregone conclusion.

"We cleared out," he said. "Didn't you?"

"Cleared out? Without notifying us, your neighbors?"

"That was for the regiment to do."

Now everything became clear to me. While our sector was standing up to the attack, the Russians had marched through our neighbors unopposed and rolled up our position from the side and the back. The two knocked–out T-34s had attacked the antitank gun positions from the right flank.

In the following days more than sixty men returned in similarly bizarre fashions; the rest . . . those who had sat and sung and laughed, sitting on the wall of the Tude bridge . . .

The next day Wachter's foot was amputated. The doctor considered it out of the question that he could have taken a single step on his bullet–shattered ankle. "You can tell that one to your grandmother, but not to me," he said.

5

"Look at the sad expression on him!" said Erika.

"Is that so? Let's see! Is it because we're now leaving your beloved Montboyer?" Lore stroked my shoulder consolingly.

Klaus had the map on his knees and was giving directions. "All right, we're now about to go through Chalais, that's it just up ahead. Watch out, keep on the main road towards Libourne-Bordeaux. It's just after twelve o'clock, we ought to be thinking about our picnic now."

What is a *marbre?* The house right next to the *marbre,* they had said. The cattle market compounds must be just to the right of the entrance to Chalais. There they were. The marketplace, where the battalion orderly room and the cinema had been, must be just a bit farther on. Then left to the level crossing, and beyond that not right towards Libourne but straight ahead to the church.

"Where are you going? That was the signpost to Libourne!"

Jeanette's aunt's house had to be where the church spire towered above the roofs. Sometimes she spent several days in Chalais, at her aunt's, because she had customers in Chalais whom she could serve better from there. She was a seamstress.

The road forked right and left. Which way? I went left.

"What are you looking for here? Go back!"

Now I was by the church, which was surrounded by an unpaved square. Which of the many houses could it be? The square was devoid of people. It was noontime. No one there whom I could have asked. What could I ask, anyway; I didn't even know their family name. Had I ever known it at all? Slowly and searchingly I crossed over the church square.

"This is only for pedestrians! Do you want to get another ticket too? Turn around, stop your looking around, we're hungry!"

I looked at every house. Maybe, by chance, I would see her, sitting in a window and sewing. No one was sitting in a window and sewing, no one was there whom I could have asked.

Now Lore and Erika were grumbling too. Disappointed, I drove slowly back to the main road and turned off towards Libourne.

"Were you trying to find Jeanette?" asked Lore.

"Yes."

Outside the town, to the left, there was an avenue of poplars which led to a wine–growing estate. There must be a picnic place there. I turned in.

"Now what? Was there some bird living here too?"

"Picnic, you were so hungry."

"Good, let's have a picnic here!"

We got out. Erika spread out blankets and scattered pillows about; Lore got out wine, cheese and bread. Klaus stretched his legs.

"What's a *marbre,* Lore? Do you know what a *marbre* is?"

"Look it up in the dictionary!"

The dictionary, of course! *Marbre . . . marbre,* there it was: marble. In front of the church there was a monument—of marble? Could be. And right next to it, yes, next to it there was a house; that must have been it.

"Well, what does *marbre* mean?"

"It could mean a monument, the monument in front of the church, and the house next to it, that must be it."

"Do you want to go back there one more time?"

"But Lore! You're sending your husband to his old girlfriend?"

"That could have its advantages; otherwise he'll think that I'm the only one who's got older."

Klaus, the restless wanderer, was hanging around near the manor house and saw me drive away from a distance.

*   *   *

I could still remember this avenue of poplars. Back then, on that Sunday when the Company had a pass to Bordeaux, we rode by here on bicycles, Monique, Jeanette, Toni, and I, to the small river that flowed sluggishly by. Was it the Dordogne? The water was warm and muddy. Monique and Jeanette could not swim. Only a few French can. A little boat lay on the bank. When Toni rocked it violently the two girls clung anxiously to me. They had very white skin and avoided the sun. How childish and silly we were, like boisterous teenagers who had stolen a day off from school. We disappeared, diving, under the green water and, unseen, reached the little island that was overgrown by bushes.

"Où êtes–vous?"—"Where are you?" they called, looking around in desperation. Concealed by the bushes we made grunting animal noises. Monique buckled Toni's belt over her swimsuit and put his uniform jacket over it, went into the water up to her knees and threatened to dive under with the uniform jacket. Toni swam underwater, unseen, back to the bank, crept up behind her and threw her into the water before Jeanette could warn her. The uniform jacket was soaking wet. Monique snorted and screamed, Jeanette hit out at Toni, I came to help him, and then began the tussling, the chasing and the jumping into the water and back out again, until we collapsed on to the blanket, out of breath, and made peace. A splendid carefree day, which might have been even lovelier if the owner of the boat hadn't turned up to check that everything was all right.

On account of this there was a postlude. On this very Sunday morning the adjutant was overcome by the desire to take part in our *"sainte messe des plus grands filous"* and found the village empty, but for some sentries. I had not reported the change in the duty rota, the repeated night exercises or the passes to Bordeaux. "Has God completely deserted you then?!" I was to confess the matter to the commander himself and take the flak for it.

I tried to confess to the commander, but he was absolutely not in the mood to listen to me. The following Sunday he came to the *"sainte messe"* and brought along Vera Kaden, the well known *chanteuse,* who belonged to a troop entertainment ensemble which was just then making a guest appearance in Chalais. Other members of the ensemble were Maria von Schmedes, Stummelschlueter, the singer Emmerich, and Hansen, the Intendant of Hamburg Radio, a consummate balladeer.

After the *"messe"* the commander went walking with Vera Kaden towards the Boisse to show her the rare subtropical plants, since he was a doctor of botany. He did not want to know about what I had to confess to him, nor did he want me to accompany him. He sent me back into the village on a trivial errand and winked a couple of times through his glasses. Aha, understood! Before they had disappeared into the undergrowth Vera Kaden had linked her arm in his.

There was the monument. Was it marble? Certainly, for one definitely does not make saints out of plaster or cement. And the neighboring house was the one only the roof of which could be seen, because it lay in a little depression below the square and the road eastwards. A large, flowering rose bush concealed the view of the house. Awkwardly I paced down the path. There was no railing, only thorny roses. If Jeanette still remembered me as the cocky sportsman who somersaulted over the barbed wire, threw stones so far that they disappeared out of sight, swam underwater across the entire river and jumped over wide ditches, then now I was making my way very carefully, leaning on my walking–stick, down the path to the house.

A watering can, a little spade, flower pots—empty or planted with tiny seedlings—a bench, a hoe. The door to the house was painted blue and had small window panes. There was no bell or even a nameplate. I peeked cautiously through the glass. A living–room–cum–kitchen, and four people were seated at the dinner table. The most inconvenient time to come visiting. Should I once again . . . or—maybe I could just ask if they knew where Jeanette . . . Wasn't that she who straightened up and stared at the door as if she were seeing a vision?

She got up—and her eyes never left me, as if I were a ghost. I opened the door cautiously. Now the others had noticed; they turned around and stared at me. There was Jeanette's mother, and the other woman must be the aunt. They looked surprised from one to the other, to Jeanette, then to me again. What was happening? Who was that young man who had now likewise got up, knife and fork in his hand? Were they annoyed that I was daring to disturb their midday meal? No, they weren't annoyed. Something unexpected had happened. No one said a word, either *"bonjour"* or anything else, and I, too, had a lump in my throat. Jeanette came slowly over to me, took me by the hand and asked, *"C'est toi?"*

If it were I? Of course. *"C'est moi,"* I said, looking around in embarrassment. There were oil paintings lined up on a high ledge. Ukrainian farmhouses, too, had such a ledge on which the icons stood. Here there were oil paintings, some imitations of famous masters and others original landscapes and houses done in impasto. Some years ago I had begun to paint pictures, including oil paintings. A married couple, artists with whom I had become friends, had maintained that innate talent was required for painting, and I considered this nonsense. Everyone can paint, some people better than others. At school I had got average marks for drawing and painting and I wanted to prove that I, too, could paint, without being innately predisposed to it. And so I painted.

And here someone else was painting.

Since I could not think of anything better to say, I asked who had painted the pictures. I said *"painté"* and knew immediately that this was incorrect. *"Qui a painté ça?"*

"Ton fils," said Jeanette, still holding my hand.

How bad my French had become in the intervening years. *"Ton fils"* would mean "your son." Somehow we had misunderstood each other, and I formulated the question differently. *"Qui a fait les tableaux là?"*

And again she answered, *"Ton fils."*

And then he stood before me, the tall young man with blue eyes, the narrow head and the half–hearted attempt at whiskers and a moustache, half a head taller than I.

"Mon fils?"

No one made any further comments. They left me to my surprise and tensely awaited my reaction. Over the decades, however, I had learned to control myself, to think before speaking or acting. But at this moment I could not think, though thoughts raced inside me. A thousand things at once. Lore! Erika, Klaus! We had no children. Now, he, there, my son? He seemed to be asking, have you come at last? Where were you for so long? Cabbage was steaming on the table; there was a smell of garlic. Even the two old women stood near us in order to be in on the dramatic moment. Broken bread lay between the plates, a bottle of wine without a label. *Vin ordinaire.* I had disturbed their midday meal.

He did oil paintings, my son. Did I have innate artistic talent after all, which he had inherited? When . . . ? Where . . . ? Candlelight was reflected in the red–wine glasses. . . .

*   *   *

. . . back then, as it was now. It was on one of my last evenings in Montboyer. Jeanette's parents had gone away, to some family gathering or other, not far. Monique and Jeanette were alone in the house. They had closed the shutters and lit only the one candle. A mood of farewell was in the air. My God . . . was that when—?

"He's seventeen," said Jeanette, "he turned seventeen on April first."

Among the oil paintings there stood a photo of me in full uniform; I could not at all remember the existence of such a photo. It had always stood there, said Jeanette, ever since then, the whole time, no matter what . . .

"Il a tes yeux bleus, tu le vois?"

I saw. What must she have gone through because of this? I had a thousand questions on the tip of my tongue, but none of them came out. At last I tried to ask him his name, and he did not understand me because I was stuttering so and clearing my throat, so that I had to repeat the question a couple of times.

"Julien," he said.

"Julien?"

"Oui."

"I've interrupted your meal," I excused myself to the two ladies. They shook their heads and said, *"Non, monsieur, pas de tout!"*

The door was still open and outside the midday heat was building up in the hollow and causing beads of perspiration to break out on my forehead.

"Tu es blessé?" asked Jeanette.

"Oui."

"Qu'est-ce que tu as?"

"Perdu," I said, pointing to where my leg had been amputated.

"Mon Dieu," she said, pressing my arm harder. "But you're alive!"

I'm alive, yes. I usually answered such expressions of sympathy with some silly phrase, but since they were untranslatable I said, "Better a wooden leg than a wooden head." *Une tête de bois.* Maybe *"tête de bois"* had a completely different meaning in French?

"Unbelievable that you're still alive," she said, and then she told me that back then, in February or March 1944, when the *"Das Reich"* Division had been transferred to this area for a rest, she had shown the soldiers who had visited Montboyer again my picture and asked them where I was. *"Il est resté en Russie,"* they had said, he remained in Russia, and this she had interpreted as "fallen in Russia." And Monique had secretly written me a letter, although Jeanette had expressly forbidden her to do this, and the letter had come back several months later.

And so I was dead.

And now I had risen again, like a vision.

"Tu comprends comme je suis heureuse?"

We clambered up the road to the square where the monument was. Jeanette was still holding my arm. Julien flew on ahead to the car.

"C'est la tienne?"

"Oui."

He inspected it from all sides and finally opened the passenger door and sat inside.

"Qu'est-ce que tu penses?" asked Jeanette. What I was thinking? Too much to imagine. I tried to explain to her that I first had to assimilate this surprise. Naturally I had already made the decision, inwardly, to take Julien to Germany, but others would have a say in this, Lore, Julien and Jeanette. But I was still not clear-headed enough to bring this up, and so I simply asked her what she was thinking.

"Je suis heureuse que tu vives," she repeated.

Long live those who are declared dead. It wasn't the first time I had been declared dead. Hermann Bohlen, my classmate, had experienced the disaster of Bulitschety Forest from the rear positions and knew that I was up ahead, in the thick of it. By the time I rejoined my unit he had already gone away on leave, and had registered me on his list of the missing. Lore's sister occasionally listened to the BBC and heard there that the *"Das Reich"* Division had been wiped out at Zhitomir. She gently broke it to Lore, while Hermann Bohlen visited my mother and announced to her with a mournful expression that I was at least among the missing. My brother, too, was missing, or worse, at Stalingrad, so that she now had two really sad events to contemplate.

I tried to translate these complex thoughts to Jeanette, but I ended up in such difficulties with trying to find the right vocabulary that I gave up. Jeanette, however, had the impression that I wanted to tell her something very important and waited anxiously. And so I finally explained to her why and with whom I was here, and that we were intending to reach Hendaye by that evening. First I'll have to take care of all that, do you understand? And then I would return, but first I would send her a telegram.

She said that it was all right with her; I should do what I thought right. Merely knowing that I was still alive was happiness enough for her. And then suddenly she ran into the house, came back again immediately and pressed a photo of Julien into my hand.

"On his seventeenth birthday," she said.

Julien, meanwhile, had sat at the steering wheel, and when I opened the door on the driver's side he moved aside and said, "I—will—know—you."

His use of the words wasn't quite correct. "Do you know a bit of German?" I asked. He didn't understand me in German, so I asked him to say it in French.

He spoke much too quickly for me to be able to understand everything. He was about to get his driving license and had volunteered for the Marines, but first he had wanted to travel to Bremen to look for some member of my family, my parents or brothers or sisters.

Right! When someone asked me where I came from I used to say Bremen, the nearest large, well–known city. Julien would have looked in vain there for any relatives of mine.

"I'll come back," I said, but Julien didn't get out. He wanted to ride along a little way, to the edge of Chalais.

Jeanette's mother and aunt stood at the door. The food had gone cold in the meantime. They waved. *"Je reviendrai."*

Jeanette stood as if rooted to the spot and watched after us. I stopped at the last houses. Julien got out. *"Je reviendrai."* Through my rear–view mirror I saw him run away as if he had something very important to do.

I stayed there for a moment, to reflect in peace and quiet. But in a flash I realized that I had given them no address whatever, no visiting card. Did they even know my real name? They hadn't asked it, they didn't know who I was, what I did or where I lived. It never occurred to me whether they doubted that I would return, for my departure without leaving an address could have been taken as an escape. "Whatever you do is all right with me, the important thing is that you're alive," she had said.

I had exchanged hardly a word with the mother and aunt. I already knew that the father was no longer alive. He was very strict with his daughters, almost too strict. Once it was dark they were not allowed to leave the house anymore. The mother was the opposite and understood her daughters. She went walking with them in the evenings, delivered them to our rendezvous, walked on farther alone and collected them again ten or twenty minutes later.

Two kilometers more to the picnic area.

How would they take it? How would Lore react? However well you know someone you still don't know how they'll behave in such drastic circumstances.

Already I envisioned Julien in our house, in his own room, going to school or to college, mowing the lawn or romping in the swimming pool, but I saw him as much smaller than he really was. Seventeen years old and half a head taller than I!

I have never found it difficult to make quick decisions and carry them out with a detailed plan of action, but I still didn't know what I was going to say in the next few minutes. I laid the photo on top of the dashboard.

Lore and Erika were walking in the distance. The picnic site had already been cleared away. Klaus was standing by the road and seemed to be waiting impatiently for me.

"Where were you for so long? It's taken more than an hour. We finished the picnic a long time ago. There's nothing left to eat."

At home, in our family of seven, punctuality was the supreme law. Whoever did not appear on time for meals had to count on being punished with hunger for his tardiness.

"Come, get in!"

"I'll go these few meters on foot, I'll be spending a long enough time cramped into this crate!"

"Get in, I said!"

I handed him the photo.

"Who . . . what . . . ."

"That's my son."

"Whaaaat?"

"My son."

"How . . . where . . . since when . . . ? Are you crazy?"

Lore and Erika had spotted the car and were returning to the picnic site.

Klaus put the photo into the car atlas, snapped it shut and shoved it quickly into the glove compartment.

"Don't let anyone see that!"

"Why not?"

"You can't do that! You can't just say, this here is my son! What are you thinking of! Think what a shock it will be for Lore. You'll ruin the entire holiday for her—and for us, too. Why did you absolutely have to go back there again, my God!"

Then, in his way, he allowed his grey cells to work for me. "Did you promise them anything?" came out.

"Yes, that I would return."

"You want to go back there again? When?"

"In the next few days, I think."

"In the next few days? How do you see that happening? And then— what then?"

"Then I'll bring the boy to Germany."

"Have you said that you have a factory there?"

"No, they didn't even ask for my address, and I don't think they even know my full name."

"Thank God!"

Lore and Erika were coming closer.

"Thank God for what?"

"This has to be thought about thoroughly, quite thoroughly. But to start with, not a word about it, do you hear, or you'll ruin our entire holiday. Think of Lore! And do you think the boy will feel at home in Germany when he's grown up here as a Frenchman?"

"I don't know."

"Exactly; that has to be calmly considered—calmly, but not now. Later, after the holiday. Just don't show the photo and don't do anything impulsive or silly!"

Erika poked her head in through the window. "Well, is he telling you about his wartime experiences with the French girl? How many men did he shoot down then?"

Lore poked her head in through the other window and asked, "Well, did you meet her? Did you have lunch with her? It took you so long."

"I've not eaten anything, no."

"Where did she live, then?"

"In the house next to the monument in front of the church."

"What did she say, then? Did she recognize you right off? Was she still just as young as before? Tell us about it: you went in, said hello and then? What then?"

Erika asked, "Did they cut her hair off because of collaboration with the Germans—with the Waffen–SS, no less?"

"No, no," Klaus answered for me. "They didn't do anything to her. It was what you'd expect after twenty years. People are glad to see each other again, and then there isn't much more to say. Come, let's pack up, it's already very late."

"He hasn't eaten anything. Should I make you a roll with cheese?"

"No thanks, I'm not hungry."

"He's been living on air and love," said Erika.

Klaus hurried with the packing and drove us quickly on to the road to Bordeaux. "So, finally we have a clear run now," he said, "and once and for all an end to the damned war reminiscences!" He kept speaking of everything else possible to prevent me from coming out with the news of the discovery of my son.

"Isn't it splendid here!" he exclaimed. "And the weather! Are you aware that we're now in the most famous wine region in the world? Not far from here is a town that they've named after the renowned Cognac."

"It's the other way round," said Lore.

"The other way round? Fair enough, but *everhinque.*"

Everhinque! It was the Intendant, Hansen, who always had this crazy Latin hodgepodge on the tip of his tongue. He was the leader of the troop entertainment ensemble and had enjoyed the stay here so much that he added a few days extra and organized a special entertainment evening with the officers. They enjoyed the wine, the cognac and the forbidden Pineau, and Maria von Schmedes sang "I have red hair." As long as I had only heard her girlish voice on the radio she had embodied for me innocent maidenhood; but here, in the officers' mess, no one was able to surpass her dirty jokes and double entendres. Emmerich was very drunk when he sat down at the piano and sang the "Tsarevitch." He didn't sing it, he cried it, heart–rending his yearning for the angels, truly heart–rending, the way the tears rolled down his cheeks—and ours too. Then he sat there with a bottle of wine in his arms and bored around the edge of the label with the bottle opener.

"What are you doing, then, Emmerich?"

"Opening the bottle, can't you see that?"

"But not there?"

"Of course, it says so here: 'bore, do.' "

6

Julien was born on the first of April. 1944. Where was I then? In any case, a couple of thousand kilometers away from the Charente and completely clueless. Was I already in the Semlin sick bay? Or still in Odessa? Or had I not yet been wounded? When there are no Sundays you easily lose track of time. It was still bitterly cold, and we were rushed back and forth with the rest of the *"Das Reich"* Division. I was adjutant to Lex, the commander with the sure instinct for judging the situation correctly and always doing what was right. He was one of the few commanders whom I respected totally, who prepared all his actions from the point of view of obtaining a maximum effect with a minimum of losses.

Along its entire breadth the front was pushed farther and farther westwards, and we had the thankless task of protecting the removal of divisions that found themselves in difficult situations, usually occupying the enemy with an attack until the division had withdrawn.

Lex fell in the course of preparing such an attack. He satisfied himself as to the position and the ground and climbed up to Schlomka in the tank, as it crept very slowly up a hill, the binoculars to his eyes. "Stop, Schlomka, ten centimeters more—stop, a couple of centimeters more—stop! In no case, Schlomka, may you attack together with the infantry! Move out over there to the left, up to the clump of trees. Encircle the

Russians from behind, and move towards our attacking forces. Can you
see the clump of trees? Still a couple of centimeters higher—stop, stop!''

Then it happened. A tank gun shot into the binoculars had torn his
skull off.

''I couldn't see the clump of trees,'' Schlomka cried, ''and had to
drive a couple of centimeters higher still. That was too much, damn—
damn!''

Schlomka had never found out why he absolutely had to attack encir-
cling the Russians from the left, but he did it. And that was luck for
us. Since we needed every man for this attack I went along, and then I
saw how correctly Lex had calculated without realizing it. After we
threw the Russians out of the area, tanks attacked which looked like
our Panzers. But they were the first Stalin tanks, never seen before,
with armor plating that was impenetrable from the front. But they could
be knocked out from the rear, and Schlomka breathed down their necks,
shooting down one after another. Only one of them had already advanced
to the first houses. Unterkofler and I approached it casually, as if it
were one of our own Panzers. The crew had gotten out and were raising
their hands. Why they surrendered the first Stalin tank to us intact is a
puzzle to me to this day.

On this day the circle that stretched from east to west was closed at
Kamenez–Podolsk. We protected the retreats in the east. Most of our
vehicles and tanks had gotten bogged down in the mud at the onset of
the thaw. We marched at night and fought during the day. I covered
the road to the 101st Rifle Division on a horse, without saddle or bridle.
Dead tired. Before we reached our destination we were fired on from
the left. At dawn we saw the holes occupied by the Russians and provided
protective fire for the troop leader and his two men, who had sneaked
up to the positions from behind. They ran from hole to hole and fought
the Russians down with pistols, and when they ran out of ammunition
they used spades. An eerie sight in the early morning mist. A few
days earlier the troop leader had received the news that his family had
died in a bomb attack. He was not able to take his special leave.

Thus it was that we had begun the magic fire of the new day.

From ahead, from the left and right, shots could be heard. The men
whose removal we were supposed to be protecting were already coming
toward us, the Russians were pursuing them, a hopeless muddle of friend
and foe. My horse had long ago taken flight, and grenades were falling

right and left, ahead and behind. And then my left knee was hit. That part of my trousers was ripped to shreds and the blood flowed, but I could still run, until the dull blow against my right shoulder blade that followed shortly after. When I tried to say something to Unterkofler, Lex's successor, blood gurgled from my mouth, and he wouldn't have been able to answer, because his throat was shot through.

Even in memory I find it difficult to make any sense out of this muddled situation. All I know even now is that a load of soldiers and officers crowded around one of the last big freight airplanes that took off from the airport at Kamenez–Podolsk, which was already under bombardment. "Only the seriously wounded!" A captain of the Luftwaffe brandished his pistol and grabbed me by the collar. "And you? What do you want here?" I had to cough and I coughed a whole load of blood into his face.

A huge number of wounded were lying in the airplane like sardines in a tin. Unterkofler was somewhere, too. The six engines roared. I lay right under the petrol tank, from which petrol was constantly dripping. All the way to Odessa.

In Odessa we were given fresh underwear. Lice love fresh underwear. To lure them we wrapped fresh gauze bandages around our throats and thereby triggered off a Great Louse Migration. The fresh bandage announced its presence right down to our little toes; the lice got on the move and crawled slowly over our calves and our thighs, our stomachs and our backs, higher and higher, until they made their way to the throat bandages. Then we threw the bandages into the fire. Morawetz presorted his lice. Those that were still too small he put back on his chest. One can get used to domestic pets.

We lay for a few days in a hall of the airport at Odessa. The lice that hurled themselves onto our fresh underwear here came from all the countries of the world and brought typhus with them. The typhus broke out in the sick bay at Semlin, where Prince Eugene had once pitched his camp against the Turks. It was on Easter Sunday. I lay on the top floor and the air–raid warning was sounded. There was no time for them to take me down to the basement, so I saw it coming, the British bomber squadron: saw clusters of bombs falling from the sky; saw them coming closer and closer, shooting high into the air like one fountain of bricks, beams, and stones after another; and saw the last bomb burst on the ridge of the roof opposite. Then glass, stones, and window bars came showering down onto my bed. I was hot, scorching.

For several weeks I hovered at the upper limit of the fever thermometer in an exciting delirium. The basement room was tiled. Waging exciting battles night after night I beat off the partisans who had their eye on my decorations, which I had hidden in my night table. I lay in front of the door in the aisle, my submachine gun in firing position, and when they came the submachine gun failed; it always failed in the critical moment, but they put up their hands, ran away and abandoned the tank.

Then there was the lady from Panshova. She knew me from the time when we marched into Yugoslavia; however, I wasn't in Panshova at all but in a village in Swabia, before we captured Belgrade. She came with a large sack filled with food, sausages, ham, cheese, bread, and the light biscuits the Swabians always had ready to offer. No, I couldn't eat for the entire week; she must take it all away again, I told her, except for the ten lemons: these she must leave in the kitchen and say that they were only for me, only for me!

"And now, at last, I'd like my lemon juice," I told the nurse from Transylvania the next morning. I had acquired a squeaky falsetto voice.

"I'm sorry, but we haven't any lemon juice."

"Oh, yes, nurse, you have," I protested, "the lady from Panshova brought me ten lemons yesterday and left them in the kitchen. They're for me."

"A lady from Panshova? You had a visitor? Here in the isolation ward?"

I remembered everything about the incident and described yesterday's visit to her in minute detail, enumerated everything that was in the sack and demanded my lemon juice. She brought in the senior nurse for reinforcements. I related to her the incident with the lady from Panshova and repeated my protest that no one wanted to give me the lemon juice.

She stroked my head, which still reeked of camphor, and said, "You're imagining things, Lieutenant, the fever causes that."

"Imagining things?" I pondered intensely, to ascertain whether I was now awake or was imagining things. "Then the bit about the partisans isn't true either, or that my submachine gun . . . ."

She shook her head.

*   *   *

At this time, then, Julien was born, or may even have been two weeks old, and I was far away and never suspected. Even in my feverish dreams I did not return to the Charente: neither Jeanette nor the funny Sarasin appeared, but only war, war, war.

And now peace had returned. Incomprehensible. Back then it would never have occurred to me that seventeen years later, hale and hearty if no longer quite complete, I would come travelling through the Charente. And Lore was sitting behind me and had no idea of what was occupying my thoughts—and would be occupying her thoughts, too, if she had known about it.

I would tell her that evening.

Klaus could not shake off his anxiety. Before, he had been afraid that I would be sent packing in disgrace, or even arrested; now he was just as afraid that I would come out with the news about Julien at an inopportune moment and thereby ruin the entire holiday. Whenever a quiet moment threatened to break out in the car, when I might blurt out my bad tidings, he called out, "Isn't it splendid here? Just look!" And if there was nothing worth seeing, he would add, "The Atlantic lies over in that direction!"

Erika said, "You're overdoing your enthusiasm again. First you didn't want to go to France at all, and now every pylon is an Eiffel Tower to you."

Klaus's enthusiasm could not be stifled, and he seized every opportunity to prevent me from getting a word in. "Bordeaux ten kilometers! Did you see that? We've sometimes drunk Bordeaux, Erika, do you know that? And now we'll get to know Bordeaux."

The Garonne Bridge. Even now I still remembered, exactly, our advance from Orléans to the Spanish border in the course of a few days in 1940. The city began right after the bridge. As a motorcycle dispatch rider my task was to regulate the traffic on the thoroughfares in relay with my colleagues. I would stand at the junctions for a few moments, closing off the side streets, until I was relieved so that I, in turn, could relieve the next colleague.

Denise was in Bordeaux at that time, and she described to me her own experience of our entry into the city. When the first vehicles from our reconnaissance division had crossed the bridge the news spread like wildfire: the Germans are coming! Incomprehensible! No one had known exactly what was going on and where the front ran. Her uncle, with whom she lived, still had in his mind a picture of the rigid front of the First World War. And now the Germans were on the doorstep. She ran to hide in the cellar with her family, as if marauding mercenaries were about to plunder the city. But no shots were fired and there was nothing else to indicate that their fears were about to be realized. At length she timidly poked her head out of the cellar window to look out at the street. Many legs blocked her view and behind them one vehicle after another was roaring by. Then, out of curiosity, she, too, went up to the street. Soldiers were sitting on the grey vehicles as if on parade, and she dared to look the barbarians in the face. No, they did not have unruly beards. Under their helmets they looked like tortoises, young faces with blue eyes. Many even seemed friendly. One smiled and waved at her, and she quickly clasped her hands behind her back. But then the other people had waved back—and so, at last, did she.

"Were you there?"

"Yes."

"Where were you, on one of those vehicles too?"

"I was sitting on the motorcycle, controlling the traffic at the street crossings."

"If I had known that . . ."

"What?"

"I would have gone up to you and said, *'Bonjour, monsieur lieutenant Werner, ça va la guerre?'* "

"I wasn't a lieutenant yet at that time."

"No? A pity. Of course I wouldn't have spoken to a simple soldier."

Now policemen in blue were regulating the traffic and Klaus was searching for signposts. I had to drive over to the right and stop so that he could take time to see whether we had to turn off towards Arcachon or Mont de Marsan.

The road led directly south from Bordeaux through woods which, one often heard, were on fire. Here and there you could see areas of charred tree stumps. Back then we rested somewhere around here, on the march to the Spanish border, and because of the danger of fire we were ordered to build no fires and to be careful when smoking. Would I be able to find the place where we had paused in our march back then?

"Back then I bought myself a wine–red shirt in Mont de Marsan. It was amazing how we—"

"Don't bother me now with your old stories, I have to concentrate."

Don't bother me with your old stories! I would say the same thing to him the next time he trotted out his holiday slides and went off on totally irrelevant digressions. "That was where Erika left the hard-boiled eggs." "No, not the eggs, that's where I lost my glasses." "The glasses were two days after that, the slide's still coming." "You mean where the dog kept prowling around our picnic place? You were looking for your purse and finally found it in the trunk." "You're mixing everything up, Erika, that was in Yugoslavia." "Nonsense, we didn't even have the trunk with us then. . . ."

Yes, I would use these same words to interrupt the quarrelling that always accompanied the slide shows. "Don't bother us . . ." But now I was very quiet, considering everything that was going through my head.

I had a son.

If I were to say that now, the reaction would be very different from "Don't bother us with your old stories." It was on the tip of my tongue, and I was close to saying it when suddenly the Atlantic came into view.

"*Talata! Talata!*" Klaus cried enthusiastically. "Remember? Greek class with Mops Schaefer, Xenophon's *Anabasis:* 'And when they finally reached the coast after weeks–long marches they cried, *"Talata! Talata!"* ' "

Klaus greeted the Mediterranean with the same words the first time we went to Italy together and suddenly came upon the coast at Ventimiglia. Those are unavoidable associations, the same as those which now struck me when I saw the signpost for Biarritz. But I wouldn't bother them with my old stories.

Only at Dax I couldn't help saying, "My unit commander back then was called Ax, A—X." And Erika said, "That's an odd name, Ax, A—X, I've never heard that one before."

And now that I had their attention I continued, "In Dax someone played a nasty trick on me. We had camped here in the bullfighting arena . . ."

"Bullfighting arena?" asked Klaus. "Is there a bullfighting arena here?"

"Yes, we camped there and for the first time were able to go out, just as if it were peacetime—"

"Then there are bullfights here too?"

"Yes, of course. But before we went out there was uniform inspection. We had to have our uniforms in tip–top shape—"

"I thought they only had bullfights in Spain."

"In Spain the bulls are killed at the end, here they're not. And because it was so hot then I'd got myself a bottle of soft drink, drunk half of it—"

"If they're not killed, then what happens to them?"

"The bulls have a cockade between their horns. The sport consists of snatching the cockades from between the horns of the irritable bulls. Yes, and when I then returned from the pass to Dax I was very thirsty and was so glad to have my soft drink. I put the bottle to my mouth and—"

"So, we absolutely must see a bullfight. How far is it from Hendaye to Dax?"

"Look for yourself, you have the map! So, when I took a big gulp from the bottle it turned out to be—gasoline."

"Gasoline, isn't that dangerous?" asked Erika.

"Oh yes, I didn't smoke any cigarettes for three days, for fear I would explode."

"How did the gas get into your bottle? That's mean!"

"We need less than an hour to get from Hendaye to Dax," said Klaus. "I suggest we include a bullfight in Dax in our program."

"The men siphoned off gas from the vehicles to clean their things. They needed a bottle for this, and one of them took my soft–drink bottle."

"But that's stealing." Now Klaus switched on to my theme. "Stealing from a comrade. Didn't you have the death penalty for stealing from a comrade?"

"I never knew anything about the death penalty for stealing from a comrade—and in any case I never knew any case of stealing from a comrade."

"So then, what was this about your soft–drink bottle?"

"It was still there."

"And the drink?"

"Was only exchanged—for gas."

"Did you really swallow the gas?"

"Yes, I really swallowed it. I was parched."

"On the subject of thirst," Klaus interjected, "we could stop somewhere and get something to drink."

"That could have ended up badly, with the gasoline," said Erika, and Klaus commented, "But not for the Waffen–SS—tough as leather and hard as Krupp steel!"

In Hendaye the sun was just getting ready to sink into the sea. It was low tide. Klaus immediately took off his shoes and socks and ran in the mud flats, which I, too, had dearly loved to do on the North Sea coast. Out of fear that I might start talking nonsense in his absence he quickly returned, with the excuse that he had interrupted his jogging out of consideration for me.

The smell of garlic permeated the hotel. In the halls, in the dining room, even in the toilets it smelled of garlic. Of carbide. I asked the waitress whether there was anything available without garlic. After thinking for quite a while she discovered something without garlic: "Red wine."

Klaus constantly had to keep his wits about him to keep me from carrying out my plans. He organized the next few days in such a way that everything from our morning shaves to dinner was regulated, for tomorrow, for the day after tomorrow, and the day after that, with an excursion to Biarritz, a bullfight in Dax, and a trip into the Pyrenees. Naturally none of this was feasible without me and my car. He spread his map out over our empty dinner plates and tried to settle point after point with majority decisions in such a way that there was no possibility for me to plan a trip to Montboyer.

"Does everyone agree? The driver too—any objections?"

"Wait to see what the weather is like tomorrow," I said.

"High pressure over the Bay of Biscay. The weather is always beautiful here."

7

After the meal they wanted to take a little walk, "just around the corner," and I knew it would last several hours.

The hotel room was completely wallpapered, the doors, the door frames, the ceiling, and the cupboards. Ornamental patterns with large flowers. I lay on the bed and stared at the ceiling. The patterns became a map on which I returned to Montboyer with the rest of the division from the Zhitomir region at Christmas 1943. They were gathered there again, the mayor, Sarasin, Réau, the town secretary, and we sipped Pineau and talked of all that had happened in the meantime. Then I would have found out about Jeanette, and she herself, of course, would not have been in Montboyer but in Paris, with Monique, because Julien was born in Paris.

And then?

The film stopped here and dissolved into the reality of the Bulitschety Forest. For days we roamed around, searching, and kept ending up between the ubiquitous fronts, and we came to Studenizza, where a jumble of units from the army and the Waffen–SS, under constantly changing commands, were fending off constantly changing points of attack. In a bare room packed to the rafters with soldiers I found a corner in which I immediately sank into a deep sleep. It was already dark, perhaps even midnight, when I was hit violently. Hand grenades were exploding right near me, Russian heads in fur caps could be seen at the window, the glow of fires, soldiers shooting pistols at the Russians, while others had fixed their bayonets and were storming out. The entire town resounded like a fireworks display on New Year's Eve at home. Streaks of light whizzed past and over us. A four–barrelled antitank gun was firing down the street from all barrels, and at the end of the street soldiers were shouting, "Don't shoot, it's your own men!"

A bearded captain shouted to me, "The road to Zhitomir is free, retreat towards Zhitomir!"

I no longer know how I got to Zhitomir. There I met the battalion commander, who was obviously wandering aimlessly through the streets, while in the east end of the city violent battles were raging. Two hand grenades exploded right in front of us in a house entrance. "Damned partisans!" the commander cursed. The glow of fires was reflected in the glasses below his steel helmet. The rest of my company, without Wachter, were still with me. No one knew where the regiment command post was, and when we found it no one was there anymore.

At dawn we left Zhitomir on three motorcycles with side cars. The road leading west was completely blocked. Russian hedgechoppers dropped bombs and blocked the road even more. By the time the sun had risen the rumble of the battle from Zhitomir could be heard only distantly.

After barely an hour we reached a village named Godycha. It was New Year's Eve, calm and peaceful. The first houses we saw were empty. A little flock of sheep driven by two boys left the village in a westerly direction. At a little river the road curved to the right into the main part of the village. The first baggage train vehicles, with the emblems of our division, were standing here.

I saw it quite clearly on the hotel room ceiling, the 50mm antitank gun mounted to the provisionally–armored towing vehicle as a self–propelled gun. Then it occurred to me again that this antitank gun could not be brought into the Bulitschety Forest, because the barrel moved slightly to the right when fired and needed repairing. Now it stood there like a Christmas present. I stroked it as if it were a horse without which I would be hopelessly lost.

The sergeant couldn't believe his eyes when he saw us. He was old enough to be my father and took me into his arms like a son. "My dear Lieutenant, you're already on my 'missing' list, and Hahn too, and others, too, and . . . Now there are sixty of us again! And Wachter, where is Wachter?"

There was plenty to tell and plenty to eat and drink. The sergeant always had everything ready at the right time. It was New Year's Eve and I was home again. All the fatigue and all the strain were forgotten, and the days since Christmas were transformed by mulled wine and vodka into a series of comical tricks and boyish pranks, because, the sergeant announced, we would all now be returning to southwest France for a rest.

Once more I tried to reactivate the other film, the one where I returned to Montboyer and learned about Jeanette, but again reality prevailed. I saw the sergeant delete us from the list of the missing in a solemn act and noted next to Wachter's name, "Wounded, foot amputation." Although our Christmas Eve had been ruined we would spend New Year's Eve making up for what we had missed.

But the Russians always seemed to remember exactly when we were celebrating our holidays and when was the most suitable moment to spoil them. It was a few minutes before 1944, we had just filled our field mugs with vodka for a toast, ready to drink to our dead comrades and to our transfer to France, when the fireworks began that would drive out the old year and make way for the new.

It was as if they were part of the proceedings, the two or three deafening booms from the cannons of Russian T–34s, the rattling of submachine guns and the horrible shout of "Hurray."

Out!

The glow of fires illuminated the scene, a truck was burning along with one other vehicle, the ammunition truck! How did they get here at all? Amazing, the way one can switch from a happy toast to the New Year to concentrated defense in a few seconds. We hadn't wasted a single moment on considering the possibility of an attack by the Russians.

A tank engine roared, then the tank rattled on, firing and booming behind the houses, and rolled through the fences and hedges of the gardens only a few meters from us. The infantry dismounted. The sergeant emptied his submachine gun furiously at the tank. Shooting calms you down.

"Lieutenant!"

Karlemann, our number one gunner, was kneeling by the corner of the house and pointed with his outstretched arm to the street, to a T–34 that stood there, brightly illuminated by the burning ammunition truck, at the curve in the road at the edge of the village, some sixty meters away, with its barrel pointed exactly at our antitank gun. The antitank gun was standing in the shadows.

"Cover!"

It was just about to fire, and then our antitank gun, the beautiful antitank gun, would be blown to smithereens!

It didn't fire. Well, why didn't it fire?

"Have you loaded, Karlemann?"

"Yes, high–explosive shells."

"Take them out, load armor–piercing shells and shoot!"

What a suicide mission, I thought. Karlemann, the sharp, saucy Berliner, hadn't seen any serious action against tanks yet. There was deathly silence, only the burning truck was crackling. A large "M" in a white circle. "Munitions." The ammunition truck, only forty meters away, could explode at any moment. The gun loader had sneaked up to the antitank gun. Its barrel was aimed at the T–34. Carefully he unloaded the high–explosive shells and put in an armor–piercing shell. Only a soft click could be heard, then he crept down again.

"Fire, Karlemann!"

Karlemann knelt next to me. "Lieutenant . . . wouldn't you rather fire it yourself?"

I had brought it on myself. Nothing was good enough for me, nothing fast enough, nothing precise enough. Whoever knows better must also be able to do better. And fear, I had told them, was only a sign of insecurity, and insecurity comes when a person has not completely mastered his craft.

I crept behind the telescopic sight.

"You know, Lieutenant," whispered Karlemann, "hold it two or three meters to the left!"

The night–firing sight worked; the cross–hair lit up. Just a few turns of the aiming wheel, then I had the tank in my sights. I reminded myself of the two gunslingers in "High Noon." Who shoots first, me or the tank? At the hull? At the turret? Hold it two notches to the left, very calmly, very calmly. It's him or me.

Now, after ten seconds of eternity, the shot to end our suspense! The flare shot into the sky from the turret. Bull's-eye! Had the armor been penetrated, too?

"Reload!"

I had been left alone like the two gunslingers in "High Noon." Nothing moved, the tank stood there as if it had been abandoned by the crew. Only the flames of the two burning trucks crackled in the deathly silence. I looked for the armor–piercing shells and reloaded.

"Don't shoot," whispered the gun loader, "Karlemann is up there at the tank."

Karlemann had filled a grenade shell full of gasoline, sneaked up to the tank with it, doused the tank with gas and lighted it. Now the flames were raging.

Now Panzer engines were roaring in front of and behind us. The silhouette of a T–34 we hadn't noticed before, with mounted infantry, was moving in the vicinity of the burning tank, seeking cover behind a house.

"Get down, men, we'll get that one too!"

Then there was a dreadful explosion that drove us under cover. The ammunition truck? No, that was still crackling softly. It was the T–34. The turret lay near the tracks.

"Well done, Karlemann!"

Now he wanted to resume his gunner's position, but I didn't let him. The experience of success had encouraged him and all of them. Without bothering about the tank that must be somewhere behind us, we hit out at the tank that was behind the house. We heard its engine running. On speculation I shot the armor–piercing shell through the house; perhaps I got him. At least I had frightened him, for the engine roared and he hurried back to the runway at the highest possible speed. It was the road from Zhitomir to Staro Konstantinov. If the Russians were already marching there, we were cut off. . . .

Even the tank that had roared past us and was at our backs left the village hastily.

"Well, we've done it again!" said the sergeant. "The schnapps is getting cold. Cheers to the New Year that's already beginning!"

The glow of the fire was reflected in the glasses below his steel helmet.

The battalion commander had come all alone over the wooden bridge that connected the two sides of the village on the opposite sides of the river. With his unmistakable, awkward gait, he ambled past the burning trucks to observe the remains of the tank.

"He has even less fear than you," said Karlemann, who took it for granted that fear decreased in proportion to one's rank.

Then he came back and said appreciatively, "A wonderful shot. The whole turret gone with one blow. Zap!"

Then he spotted me. "Thank God you're here!"

And then he spoke softly and hoarsely. "To lose the whole battalion in a few days—you can hardly imagine what that's like. You're still too young."

I never saw him again. Not even in the following turbulent days. He was a good biologist and zoologist, the older officers said.

After the sergeant had briefed me on our geographical location it became obvious that we were cut off. The village lay at the fork of a river. The only access to the east was afforded by the bridge over the river. If we didn't succeed in building a new bridge by the mill west of the fork we would never get out of here.

I told the men that we would get hardly any sleep in the next few days, and then Alfons said, "But we've already practiced that, Lieutenant, remember: B—o—r—d—e—a—u—x!"

Towards 3 A.M. we dispersed over the wooden bridge into the part of the village on the other side of the river. The bank there sloped steeply down to the water's edge and was not suitable for bridge–building. The engineers had already reconnoitered and made all necessary preparations to build a bridge over the Teterev near the mill. Our escape route, then, took us over the wooden bridge into the south of the village, which we had just left, and then back over the Teterev near the mill. To be sure, there was marshy terrain here, and no road leading westward was marked. But this was our only chance to escape, if the engineers could get the bridge built.

Guards with walkie–talkies covered the southern edge of the village to the runway, from which we could hear the sounds of tracks and driving. The antitank gun guarded the wooden bridge and the roads leading there. All the trucks were brought into safety over the wooden bridge.

Dawn was already breaking when we could finally think of taking a catnap; but we had reckoned without the Russians. There they were again. The same "Hurraaay," the same rattling of submachine guns, and the same bangs from the barrels of rolling T–34s. They fired on the empty houses in the south of the village, and one of them dared to press forward to the river and head for the wooden bridge.

The antitank gun stood directly next to the house entrance. We were able to mount it, unseen.

Karlemann came one second too late. I was already seated at the telescopic sight. How annoyed he was! But he still wanted to be there, at least as gunner.

"High–explosive shells, Karlemann!"

"High–explosive shells, what for?"

"Don't ask silly questions, do as I say! And at the same time keep an armor–piercing shell handy!"

Because of the way its observation slits were arranged, the T–34 had a poor view. The mounted infantry was more dangerous initially. For a moment the tank stopped where the antitank gun had stood yesterday, swivelled its turret nervously back and forth, and then drove slowly on down to the bridge, less than a hundred meters away. Aim two lines short! Ratch—boom! Then they tumbled down and the tank driver hit the gas, rattled past the wooden bridge, and fled, seeking cover behind a house. The infantrymen who had tumbled off with a large basket dragged themselves to safety as best they could.

The tank took its position behind the house. We couldn't see it. What would he do? Was he searching for the antitank gun? Had he seen us? Was he keeping tabs on us?

The engine roared again and again. The tank tore ahead behind the house without having aimed its barrel in our direction; he drove up in front of the barrel of our gun as if on the military training ground, so that I was able to set my sights on him calmly. Ratch—boom! The shot found its mark, but the tank kept going. One more time: ratch—boom! Damn, he still hadn't had enough. Just then he ought to have reached the curve that would save him.

"Load! Aim at the track!" Ratch—boom! The god of war had mercy on me. I hit the track. The tank spun round and round and then lay motionless.

A pause. No rejoicing; instead, quiet. Karlemann came with a can of paint and painted two rings on the barrel. Now there were eight.

There was no reason to rejoice. On the runway closely packed columns were aiming westward, from which the distant rumbling of artillery reached us. Our chances of getting out of here were growing slimmer by the minute.

Some men had gone to the spot where the infantry had been shot down by the tank. They brought some booty along, a huge pannier filled with bread, butter, bacon and chocolate. But we never got round to enjoying it, because some men came by, waving excitedly and shouting, "Antitank gun ahead! Enemy tanks behind!"

Where was "behind"?

"They're coming from the northeast," they shouted, "a good dozen of them!" And that was where an engineer vehicle was standing, out in the open, with the cashbox on board. Fifteen thousand marks. Fifteen thousand marks! Something had to be done!

It was a big village. We still hadn't come to the end of it. A good dozen T-34s? And we, all alone? We hoped it was a hoax, an exaggeration, an error in counting!

No, there were eight, ten, eleven, twelve, a whole dozen. Along a wide front they rolled over the flat surface, still about fourteen hundred meters away. And in between was the engineer vehicle with the fifteen thousand marks. Two men ran with all their might back to the village.

From this distance we wouldn't even damage the bodywork, if we hit them at all. We had to wait until they were only 300 meters away. We could shoot at two, perhaps three of them before we ourselves would be shot at.

But once we had shot two of them down they would have gained enormous respect for our firepower; after all, they didn't know that we had only a simple antitank gun, which, moreover, was in need of repair. And so we would continue bluffing and act as if an insuperable line of antitank guns were standing here.

"Karlemann?"

He nodded and took his place. I announced positions and routes. We let them come up to a thousand meters, and then we opened fire. Two shots from one position, then quick change to a new position, two more shots, change of position, fire, change of position. When they had reached about six hundred meters they stopped, one or another of them fired, but they fired at thin air. Irresolutely, they considered what to do. Cover! Don't be seen! They had to believe that they were facing a strong and well hidden line of antitank guns from which they would get nothing but bloody heads.

The noise of battle flared up at our rear. It must be something at the bridge. Damnation! Were they still attacking? With tanks? Push off! Push off! We must get to the bridge!

They pushed off.

It was a wonderful moment, which made up for Christmas and New Year's Eve, but we had no time to enjoy it, because we had to get to the bridge.

"You can get your fifteen thousand marks back, but ten percent for us!"

The main action was already over by the time we got there. The last of the Russians could still be seen in the distance, running back towards the runway. The technical officer had mobilized mechanics, bakers, and cooks and they had thrown the Russians out again with zest. They had attacked without tanks. Thank God! They were back there and would take a good hour to get back to the runway. If they had known that scarcely a hundred camp followers and a damaged antitank gun were here! But they're no different from anyone else.

Now we finally had the opportunity to take a look at the tank that only a shot in the track had stopped. Had the first grenades not pierced it? Indeed, they had. The men looked into the tank, and they were near vomiting, so they didn't look further but instead went away, embarrassed. A headless torso, bloody flesh, and intestines were sticking to the walls. The camp followers said that the driver still had a rattling breath when they dragged him from the tank. He lay there, wearing a distinguished award for bravery. Already half dead, he tried to save the tank. I took his military papers and the award. Later, when it was all over, I would send them to his family and write to them that he had fought bravely to the last for his country . . . he had given his best . . . they could be proud of him . . . what does one write at such times?

Feeling nauseated, we drove to the southern edge of the village in order to seal off the runway.

It wasn't good to look into the tank we had shot, to look at the gruesome reality. One always sees oneself sticking to the walls in a thousand pieces like that, without a head, or being dragged from the tank with a death rattle in one's throat. The back of his head was gaping open and bloody brains were pouring out. He was foaming at the mouth and his breath was still rattling, the typical rattle after an injury to the back of the head. You're dead but your lungs are still puffing.

The mind wanders, but not that far away. Why didn't the tank shoot first that night? Then we would have been blown to bits, and the other man would have had to look at what he had done; then he would have felt the way we did. Were not we, the enemies on the battlefield, his real comrades, the companions in misfortune who in the arena of history had to play a dice game of fortune and misfortune, life and death, eye to eye, head to head? Faced with the shreds of flesh on the wall of the tank would we not long ago have reached a compromise concerning the future of our two nations?

There up ahead on the road the columns rolled westward. And then there was something else in us, the rudiments of an unfathomable hunting instinct, which drives one, against all logic and reason, to take great risks; which sees not danger and shreds of intestines but the enemy, success, victory, driven by a will to survive, even if it is through risking one's own life, for oneself, for the others, without grand words, without dramatic gestures, simply through doing. Those up ahead on the runway, for example, who were pressing ever onward towards the west in order to cut off our road, to annihilate us, they appealed to our will to survive, called forth the hunting instinct, and demanded that we did not simply look on passively and yield helplessly to our fate.

Karlemann was able to fire again, intermittently. Every fifth truck, two or three shots at most with high–explosive shells, then change position, like this morning against the twelve tanks. Meanwhile a bit of harassing fire with the machine gun. The idea was to make them believe there was an impregnable fortress here. Any desire they may have had to attack must be nipped in the bud.

The march westward began to flag. Burning trucks were blocking the road. Men ran around like excited ants. Then they positioned their mortars and artillery and found their range. The village was big, the farmhouses with their large gardens extended far into the surrounding fields.

There was movement behind us. The engineers had been slaving away without interruption. Now the bridge appeared passable. The first trucks rolled over it, testing it carefully, and then rumbled off westward, parallel to the runway, racing with the columns with which we had once created a traffic jam.

Dusk was already falling when the T-34s that we had driven off from the engineer vehicle that morning returned. The darkness swallowed up the happenings on the runway; the sounds of driving and tracks announced that the jams were cleared. Now our trucks, too, were flowing over the bridge. It was done!

We were hungry and thirsty and had earned a break. Only our ears were still alert to what was happening on the runway. The tank engines, which were still running, occupied our hearing's attention to the exclusion of all else.

They wouldn't dare to assault our fortress yet again. They had tried it at night and tried it by day, and had nothing to show for it but bloody heads. They would finally give us time to boil up some tea and eat from the captured booty. We parked the antitank gun in front of the house door, and while the boiling kettle sang we relived the day once more, suppressing the fear we had felt with a torrent of words. Everyone thought about, but no one mentioned, the shreds of flesh on the tank wall and the headless torso.

The engineers cleared away the mines they had planted on the road at midday. A dozen more vehicles, then all of them had got over. Once we, the last party, had crossed the bridge and blown it up, we would leave Russia and go to France.

Cheers! See you again in the Charente!

They simply wouldn't give up. For one brief instant we'd forgotten about them, and now they were here again, firing their cannons aimlessly in the darkness. Gradually, inexorably, they came closer, until, with incredulous horror, we watched them file past our antitank gun: all twelve tanks were there again!

I still get a chill down my spine when I think of this moment. A hopeless situation! Maybe we shouldn't have provoked them in the afternoon! Bravado, that's all it was, nothing but sheer bravado which could have jeopardized the bridge–building and the escape of our supply vehicle. I didn't want to think about it. This morning we had fooled them into thinking we had a strong defensive front, and now we were stuck with all twelve tanks again.

Everything proceeded like clockwork, without commands or orders. Even before the last tank had rattled past us, the engine of our one–ton tractor roared into action, shielded by their engine noise; everyone crouched in his place, and the gunner loaded a high–explosive shell. In the dark the tanks, with their poor visibility, were less of a danger to us than the mounted infantry. We fell into line right behind the last tank. Only their exhaust sparks gave us a clue as to their position, and we saw them, close together, turning right past the tank hulks from this morning, into the village, towards the old wooden bridge. They fired blindly into the village from their submachine guns. Our machine–gunner, who sat next to the driver behind the machine gun which hung on the armor plating, fired too, and aimed somewhat above the exhaust sparks at the invisible mounted infantry.

Our newly–built bridge! Had they already discovered it? Were any supply vehicles left behind? On the other side of the Teterev, only a short distance from the bridge, one of the gigantic piles of straw went up in flames and lit up the eerie scene. All the tanks had turned off to the right into the village and were fighting empty houses—but for one. We saw its silhouette in the glow of the fire. It was cutting us off from the bridge. The infantry was still mounted. Its barrel was aimed at the center of the village. Had they discovered the bridge?

"Fire!"

Screams, furious screams. The grenade landed below the turret. Infantry tumbled down. They may have thought that one of their colleagues had hit them while firing aimlessly in the night. Furiously he roared away after the others—and gave us a free path to the bridge.

"Are you finally here? Where were you for so long? We were just about to blow up the bridge."

In order to protect the bridge we positioned the antitank gun in the shadow of a heap of straw that was not burning yet.

The senseless shooting had stopped. Perhaps it had got around that one of their own tanks had been fired on. Here and there a rifle was fired.

A raiding party from the Flemish Langemark Volunteer Brigade approached from the west. It would have been impossible to explain to them why fighting was still taking place here, six kilometers into the Russian front. The supply train had long ago been written off as lost. They had the new bazookas with them. Two men positioned themselves at the bridge while the others penetrated the Russian–occupied village.

"Karlemann, bring me my fur coat from the antitank gun—and some chocolate."

I could have got these things myself, but by calling him back I saved

Karlemann's life. One single shot from a tank shattered the stillness. Karlemann turned round.

"Bull's–eye on the antitank gun, Lieutenant."

There was a farm some hundred meters to the west. We dragged ourselves towards it, tired, dreadfully tired. We had reached the point where we didn't care about anything. Except sleeping, sleeping, sleeping . . .

At daybreak we were awakened by artillery fire. We saw it flashing beyond the runway, and then the grenades rained down on Godycha. A quarter of an hour. Then they attacked. At the head, along a wide front, stood the twelve tanks, observing, shooting, and waiting until the infantry had moved up. Houses were going up in flames. They advanced in staggered waves. The artillery started bombarding the village on the other side of the Teterev. A reinforced regiment along a kilometer–wide front charged at our shadows of yesterday. They would all survive this attack, no one would end up as shreds on a wall. . . .

We dragged ourselves westward. Even we hadn't lost a single man during this time, only two vehicles. Somewhere and at some time we had to run into our own people.

We came too late. They were already rolling west out of Russia, towards France. Only one combat group, consisting of two reinforced battalions from the *"Das Reich"* Division, had remained behind for special action. They still needed an adjutant. I became Lex's adjutant.

"Il est resté en Russie," they said when Jeanette showed them my photo and asked where I was.

8

Lore had returned somewhat ahead of the others. She hadn't wanted to leave me alone for so long.

"Isn't that sweet of me?"

I took out the photo and handed it to her without a word. She regarded the unfamiliar face for a brief moment and looked at me as if she suspected that her entire world was about to collapse.

"Who—is—that?"

"My son."

She turned away from me, sat down at the other end of the bed, slowly turned her back to me, looked once more at the photo and pushed it back to me without looking round. Then I heard her sobbing.

No matter how well you think you know a person, you still never know in advance how they will behave in a situation like this.

It would have been pointless to say anything now, to explain or even to try to make excuses. All at once her world had changed, the future as well as the past, especially the past, in which she lived far more intensely and on which she fed much more than I did. I was thirteen and she was twelve years old when we met, at the vet's who looked after the livestock on her parents' farm and whose son was my classmate. We went to high school together and had dancing lessons together. To me she always remained the high–school girl, a rebellious individualist, always wanting what was special, tough, sporty.

For her I still had, even now, two legs. We had never broken off contact with each other. She always knew where I was and what I was doing, and what she didn't know, she suspected.

About this she knew and suspected nothing.

Neither had I.

It was taken quite for granted that we would get married, as obvious as the nose on one's face. She brought the engagement ring along when she visited me in hospital in Pirna in the summer of 1944. This was after the lung shrapnel, the shot through the knee, the typhus, and the thrombosis in my left leg. I was still only half the person I had been. It was time now that we got engaged, her father had said. Klaus had stopped in Pirna en route to Prague that very day, and so it was a real little family celebration. And three months later we got married. She had been deployed in Poland with a group of students for the building of the eastern defense ramparts, and the doctors had been trying to find new reasons to grant me leave, because I would still not be fit again for duty in the near future.

"If you're engaged, why don't you take leave to get married?"

Why not, then? And so we got married. I already had a son without knowing it.

What would have happened had I known? What would have happened had I not stayed so long in Godycha and remained with the combat group? What would I have written to her if I had already known then what I knew now? Then I would have taken part in the Battle of Normandy, and who knows what would have become of me!

Certainly she too must have been thinking the same thing, what would have happened if . . . Maybe she got the idea that I had, in fact, known or suspected. Why did I absolutely want to go to Montboyer? Why did I absolutely want to visit Jeanette? No, it was she herself who had finally talked me into it. Would I otherwise have gone back there again? Questions and doubts, doubts and questions.

When I woke from my reverie I could still hear her sobbing. It is good to cry if one can. I have never been able to.

The next morning the sun hid behind long shadows.

"Show me the picture again!"

She inspected it thoroughly.

"I don't like this attempt at a beard. That has to go. Then he would seem to be . . . quite a . . . nice . . . boy. What is he doing?"

"I don't know."

"You don't know? Didn't you find out, then?"

"No."

"How can you! Is he still in school? What has he been studying? What does his mother do? Is she married?"

"No."

"What does she do, then? Does she work?"

"Yes, of course."

"At what, then?"

"I don't know exactly. Back then she was a seamstress, she made clothes."

"You simply went away without finding out all this?"

"I said I'd come back."

"Then did you say where you are? Does she know you're married?"

"Yes."

"Do they have your address? Your business card?"

"No."

"No! And now they're sitting there waiting and waiting for you to return, waiting every day and knowing nothing about you, and you know nothing about them, and maybe they think you won't come back at all and have disappeared for good!"

"I don't think that they think that."

"They didn't even ask for your address?"

"No."

Now I had to tell what happened. She loved when someone told all the details, repeated every word, described every impression and every gesture.

Our breakfast together lasted two hours.

Naturally Klaus had put Erika in the picture, and they too had discussed the matter into the wee hours. Now the discussion continued. Klaus saw the situation from the legal point of view and was of the opinion that, because of the special circumstances, I really had no obligations and could even dispute everything; but then Lore and Erika sprang to the defense of Jeanette and Julien, especially Julien. I myself, on the other hand, came off poorly, not only because I had kept quiet about the situation but because they could no longer believe me about what had gone on earlier—at least not as far as this situation was concerned.

"I'd advise you not to visit any more old theaters of war," said Erika mockingly, "otherwise perhaps a daughter might turn up too."

"But you know what they did with girls in France," said Klaus. "What did they do to her?"

"I don't know."

"He doesn't know. He doesn't know anything at all," said Lore. "He didn't even know that . . . and that he then had a son."

"For once I'll believe him about that," Erika came to my aid. "How old were you then?"

"Twenty, twenty-one."

"And she?"

"A year or two older."

"How does she look?"

"I certainly don't want to know," Lore said.

"But I know," said Erika. "I've seen a whole series of photos from Montboyer in your album, and in one picture you're with Jeanette and between you there's a dog, a terrier."

"Toni's dog," I recalled.

"It was no chaperone, in any event!"

"Was that Jeanette?" Lore asked.

"Yes."

I drove to the post office and sent a telegram: *"Je reviendrai dimanche vers midi."*

Klaus had to revise all his daily schedules. We went for a day's swim, which meant that the others swam in the Atlantic, which was still much too cold, while I looked on as Lore let herself be tossed about by the high waves. I would gladly have shown her how you really should handle waves like that. How we had enjoyed diving into the North Sea waves that time near Cuxhaven! I had suddenly got the idea of scraping together a group of twenty–five young scouts one Whitsunday and cycling to Duhnen. They were wonderful days, with the most splendid weather, and then it all went up in smoke. Troop Leader Schaettle, who was both my German and my history teacher, gave me a serious dressing–down because I had made such a journey unauthorized and unannounced. Think what could have happened! Irresponsible, and unsuitable as a scout leader besides. The worst was that the others all thought it was fantastic, much nicer than the camp and the organized group trips. And what was still worse was that I had described the trip in the youth pages of our local newspaper just as it had been, arousing envy in all those who hadn't taken part.

Had she got my telegram? In any case I was burdened by the thought that they may have believed that they would never hear from me again.

I spent a sleepless night, woke up early, passed up breakfast, and drove off.

Sunny weather with a fresh Atlantic breeze. The waves dashed spray on to the steep shore. I had a 250–kilometer drive ahead of me. Taking into account the many towns I had to drive through, I would be there in just under four hours. I had packed my movie camera and intended to take a little detour to the shore at Biarritz to film the impressive waves as they played along the eroded cliffs.

Biarritz! Back then, in 1940, Baumbach and I were the first German soldiers to walk on the famous promenade at Biarritz. We were the company's motorcycle dispatch riders, Baumbach and I, and our officers had borrowed our motorcycles so that they could ride ahead to the Spanish border, where a welcoming reception for the German troop command was to take place. In exchange we got the company's Horch, and we used it to take a little trip to Biarritz.

We couldn't believe our eyes, to see that peaceful tourism was still going on here as if there was no war at all. We switched on the four–wheel drive and drove slalom–style past the sunbathers to the water. At first they looked on indignantly, then in amazement, then anxiously, and believed their eyes just as little as we did. German soldiers? Could it be? Should they flee in panic, or—? We gave them no reason for such a course of action.

"Let's go and have an elegant meal," Baumbach proposed, and he parked the car on the sandy beach, thirty meters from the restaurant, in the midst of people who had hesitantly gotten up from where they were lying, or come out of the water, and were observing at a respectful distance the drama that was now about to be played before their eyes, the drama of a war which was nothing compared to what would come later.

We took off our steel helmets, laid them on the seat, and left our weapons in the car. Wearing our thick motorcycle jackets we trudged through the sand towards the restaurant. It was nearly full.

Suddenly the room stood still. Some of the guests got up from their chairs, letting their napkins fall to the floor. What was about to happen?

We gave them friendly nods. *"Gardez vos places—ne dérangez–vous pas, bon appétit, bonjour."* For five years we had studied French in school, and we were delighted finally to be able to use it.

A waiter approached us, as plucky as a blackbird defending its nest: *"Messieurs???"*

We removed our heavy motorcycle jackets and handed them to him along with the belts on which our pistols hung. He took the jackets by the loops with two fingers extended, and took the belts in such a way as to assure us that he would not seize the pistols.

(I wondered whether that waiter were still there. Perhaps I might recognize him.)

"Est–ce qu'on peut se laver les mains?"

"Oui, messieurs, suivez-moi!"

We followed him to the toilet and washed our hands. The whispering and talking came to an abrupt halt when we returned to the dining room. The waiter led us to an empty table.

"La carte, s'il vous plaît!"

La carte, naturally. He hurried to fetch it, and when he placed it in front of us I told him, *"Lisez, s'il vous plaît!"*

Unusual; only the highest nobility had the menu read to them. After hesitating in surprise he began to read out the menu. I didn't understand a single word of his recitation. The only thing I remembered from my school vocabulary of what might appear on a menu was *ragout de mouton.* That, of course, was not on the menu, or at least for some obscure reason he hadn't read it out, and yet it must have been the best–known menu term in French vocabulary! I asked whether he had *ragout de mouton.*

To have the menu read to you and then order *ragout de mouton* must have been an inexplicable barbarian excess, to judge from the perplexed look on his face. And with the meal a Bordeaux, red and full-bodied.

I wanted to know whether we needed food coupons, but they hadn't taught us the word in high school. *Bons*—or *tickets? Timbres?* While a girl arranged plates, utensils, glasses and bread on the table a hand came from behind and laid food coupons on the table. Before I realized what had happened and could turn round to thank the person it was no longer possible to tell who the kind donor was.

The bathers outside stood on the beach in dense groups, engaged in intense discussions, and walked past the restaurant, peering in, dying of curiosity. They gave the Horch a wide berth, so that they wouldn't be suspected of having their eyes on the weapons in order to continue a war that was over before it had started here.

The waiter served the food. Baumbach tasted the wine and nodded as if he were a connoisseur. Children worked their way curiously over to our table. The mothers, of course, dragged them back, but they came again.

"Etes–vous allemands?"

"Oui, mon petit."

"Soldats allemands?"

"Oui, ma petite."

Their mothers dragged them back. We ate politely and left our table in much cleaner condition than the others were.

"Garçon, la note s'il vous plaît!"

They wanted to pay? Like real tourists, like all the others? First he put out his hands in refusal, but then he opened his purse when Baumbach offered him a large note. It was certainly quite expensive here. *"Gardez le reste,"* Baumbach said, without knowing if the note was even enough; but the waiter bowed deeply and hurried to fetch our jackets and the belts with the pistols, which he carried all the way to our car.

"Au revoir, mesdames, au revoir, messieurs!"

"Au revoir, messieurs, au revoir, messieurs!"

"Au revoir," the children called; they accompanied us to the car to explain to the bathers that we were German soldiers.

"Et les autres? Où sont les autres?"

"Ils ont justement touchés la frontière espagnole."

"The Germans have already reached the Spanish border!" spread like wildfire.

Our Horch burrowed its way through the loose sand.

"Bon séjour!"

"Merci, messieurs!"

*   *   *

I scanned the beach now with my camera and unconsciously lingered a moment at the place where the Horch had been parked; then I filmed the impressive waves and the people who clung to the cliffs and looked on.

Then it was time to push on. To my son.

The needle on the speedometer climbed to 150 kph.

"Bayonne."

Would I, by chance, be passing the boiler factory? I wondered whether the couple who owned the factory were still alive. They had a house not far from the orderly room which they only used on weekends. I didn't want to think about how I had disgraced myself back then.

Covered with dust and dirt I came from duty in the open field, past the company kitchen from which wafted the heavenly smell of lentil soup with ham, and there in the orderly room stood the maid in a white apron; she curtsied politely and handed me a card. Madame and Monsieur Boilermaker—weren't they called Buterac or something like that?—had the honor of inviting me to dinner. Right away. They were waiting.

While I was rinsing myself under the water pump in the brewery courtyard (there was no time to change my clothes) Monsieur Réau handed me a tasting glass filled with the newest cognac, and that before eating! I sprayed the dust from my army boots with a hose so that they sparkled like patent leather, but by the time I came within sight of Madame at the door of the house they had got just as dirty again, or dirtier. As village dignitaries they felt obliged to invite the other dignitaries. Me, for example.

She awaited me in a long, dark blue evening dress with an impressive chrysanthemum at her equally impressive bosom, and gave her greeting: *Très enchantée* and very pleased that I had accepted her invitation. Then she tucked her arm under my sweaty armpit and, with her huge bulk, determinedly steered me into the best parlor, where Monsieur Boilermaker was standing behind a battery of bottles. He asked me what I would like for an aperitif. I considered the huge array of bottles and hid my hands behind my back in order to dig the next–to–last bit of black out from under my fingernails.

Chartreuse? No, that was a digestive, perhaps a port? He and his wife preferred port before a meal. And before the toast he, too, held a little speech with *très enchanté* and so forth, and the port immediately blended with Réau's cognac sample to form a joyful duet.

Madame turned a couple of times on her own axis to draw to my attention the museum–like furnishings *à la* Louis Quatorze, Seize, Baroque, or Empire, but I stared at the six or seven different glasses at each plate and thought of the tin mug that went with my canteen, from which ersatz coffee tasted just as good as red wine, gin or vodka.

It was only a modest meal, she said: the war, you know, unfortunately not everything could be had that one would like to offer one's guests. Lentil soup. I wondered whether she had ever eaten lentil soup from a field kitchen. I didn't know what "lentils" were in French. Madame, indeed a bit put out that I hadn't sufficiently admired her ancient, impractical furniture, pushed a chair into the hollows of my knees, but I waited politely until Her Corpulence, Madame Boilermaker, had plopped down on to her Louis Seize. Then the angel of a maid came, curtsied and offered me a bowl of vegetables on a silver tray. Garlic! I was allergic to garlic and took just a little sample.

Oh, how modest he was, Monsieur Lieutenant Werner, but I assured them that I would take that much more of what followed. It was a prawn cocktail, superb and almost garlicless, if I wasn't being deceived. I took a bit more than half of this, while Monsieur stood behind me with a bottle and tried several times to get past my prawn–cocktail–shovelling arm, on my right or left, to pour me some wine. Which of the many glasses did he want to take? The big one for the white wine.

"Isn't it exquisite? From 1933. How old were you then?" *Quel âge,* she asked. I tried to estimate Madame's age and had the feeling that the table would heave up and down with every breath she took. In contrast to my hosts and fellow–eaters I was already nearly full from the prawn cocktail, and only then did things really begin happening: fillet of beef without sauce with two potatoes, then a pheasant or a duck—which it was I couldn't really tell under the thick mustard crust— closely followed by rabbit, and all the time yet another of the as yet unused glasses was filled with some high–proof yellow or green liquid. I stuffed down a puff pastry roll filled with ragout to keep everything from coming up again, but the curtsying maid still flitted to and fro. Thank God there was a war on—what would there have been to eat had it been peacetime!

Inspired by all the alcohol, my French flowed all the more fluently, if not more correctly. I told about how, in 1940, up there near Aire with only thirty-six men we had surprised and captured two French battalions, and how the commander cursed and shouted because he had surrendered to such a small horde. I wanted to throw up—and so did Monsieur, because he had been a commander at that time, although not exactly at Aire. I passed the cheese platter, without looking at it, to Madame, with such grace and flourish that a brie nearly fell into her lap. Whoops! Everything was spinning, and if it continued to spin my bed must come by at any moment! What else could I tell them in my fluent French, without treading on the tie or the chrysanthemum!

I got up jerkily so that the plates rattled, walked two laps of honor round the table and headed for a door. It led to the bedroom. The beds hadn't been made yet. Oh. Pardon. Neither had my bed, surely. The other door led outside, to fresh air. That damned Réau could have waited until after dinner with his cognac tasting!

Madame dragged me along while I frantically tried to think of what flattery I could use to accompany my departure, since that was customary. The enormous chrysanthemum impressed me most. And so: *"Vous avez là une très belle . . ."* Damn, what was "chrysanthemum" in French? *". . . une très belle rose sur votre . . ."* Bosom was *poitrine,* but that was hardly suitable. I pointed to the chrysanthemum a couple of times, or somewhere to that effect, until the appropriate word seemed to come to me: *"sur votre . . . soutien–gorge,"* yes, that was it: brassiere.

Coyly she looked down and thereby spotted my dirty boots. Barbarian! Philistine!

9

On the straight road to Bordeaux the speedometer needle again danced near its upper limits. Several signposts pointed the way to Arcachon, where the highest sand dunes in Europe are supposed to be. I didn't know the place personally, but Mr. Pollack, my representative and sole importer of my products into England, regularly spent his holidays there. On his way there he visited me to take holiday money from his commission account. He is Jewish and emigrated to England in 1938. Since he had not yet been naturalized when the war broke out he was put into an internment camp as an enemy German. He was confined there during the entire war, and when the war ended he was transported to an internment camp in Germany to be denazified. And so he hadn't many good things to say about the English.

He also knew Biarritz, and I told him about how I was the first German soldier to come there. Naturally he also knew that I was with the Waffen–SS; well then, I must have experienced all sorts of things, and when I came to London I had to visit his family and tell about the war in Russia, which fascinated them all. His sympathies, despite everything, were with the Germans, and he considered it a small revenge to be able to compete with the English through my products.

Bordeaux came into sight. Julien had intended to look for my family in Bremen. None of us lived in Bremen. My father had headed a book–

exporting business there for many years, but when the war broke out he was transferred to Berlin. Klaus lived in Hamburg, Kurt had a business in Hannover, Rainer had fallen in Stalingrad, and my sister lived in England. I stayed with her when I went to England on business.

How furious I was when I came home and learned that my sister had an English boyfriend. "Even you lost no time throwing yourself at the victors!" But Ken was a fine fellow. His father had told him to find a German girl to marry. At that time he was more German than many Germans, helped where he could, got gasoline and cigarettes, and even forged papers for me, because he thought it was more than shabby to persecute such elite troops, an unfair type of revenge for the many defeats that the Waffen–SS had inflicted on their opponents. He had been in Normandy and had experienced the Hitler Youth Division as well as the French! The British might have expected to be greeted as liberators by the French, but were much more likely to be sworn at. Until then everything had been intact and really peaceful, and now the victors wanted to bomb everything to bits, ruin and destroy everything— let them go back home! And when I asked him to drive me through London to Mr. Pollack, he let me off at the door and disappeared, because he couldn't understand how I could have assigned my lucrative agency for England to a Jew.

How would Julien have been able to find me—quite apart from the fact that he knew I was dead? He spoke no German, and even if he had found Klaus or Kurt, then what? Would they have accepted him at all as my son?

The road to Angoulême! It led over Chalais. What day was this, anyway? Sunday. On holiday, every day was Sunday. I tried to imagine how I would be received. But first I came to the avenue of poplars where we had picnicked, a picnic between Biarritz and Zhitomir, between heaven and hell, between today and yesterday. What would the present be without the past! Lifeless, empty, meaningless, a town, a village like a thousand others. And yet adventure and drama slumbered there.

There, next to the third poplar, was where I had stopped three days ago and shown Julien's photo to Klaus.

A photo of me had stood on the mantelpiece, among the oil paintings. When exactly had that photo been taken? Who had taken it? When and on what occasion had I given it to her? There were still so damned many gaps in my memory! If someone had asked me I would have sworn that such a photo of me certainly did not exist, nor had I given it to her. Only the photos of Toni, the photos from bathing in the Dordogne, and the photo with the terrier. Nothing else.

There was the gate, and to the right the road led to the *marbre*. The Mass had ended but many churchgoers were still standing in front of the church and the *marbre*. They broke off their conversations and looked with excitement and curiosity at the car that was now turning in to the church square. Curiously. Did they know? Julien detached himself from the group, rushed over, opened the car door and got in.

"Have you just come from Hendaye? When did you leave there? Then you must have driven very fast. How fast does the car go? *Voilà*, 180!"

I realized I was guilty of a shocking omission. "Is there a pastry shop in town? Is it open? Would your mother prefer chocolates or flowers?"

"We have flowers ourselves."

We parked in the market place and walked through the narrow shopping street. He greeted people on all sides. *"Ça va, Julien?" "Ça va, Marcel." "Holà, Claude!" "Holà, Julien!" "C'est ton père, Julien?" "Oui, Leon."*

We went into the pastry shop.

"The nicest box of chocolates you have," I said, and Julien pointed out what his grandmother and his great–aunt liked. Very kind of him to have thought of them too.

I stopped for gas. Julien got out, unscrewed the gas cap, and said, *"plein, s'il vous plaît,"* as if he filled up here every day.

All Chalais seemed to know that I was coming today. The young woman at the cash register, who was about Jeanette's age, regarded me furtively while the gas flowed into the tank. At length she got up her courage and asked, "Do you come from Karlsruhe?" She said "Karlsruhe" so that I had to ask her to repeat the question.

"Do you know Karl from Karlsruhe? Is he still alive? How is he?"

"I may know him, but there are many men named Karl. Do you know anything more about him?"

"He was tall, like you, and nice, very nice, and blond, like you."

"Many men were tall and blond—and nice too, of course."

"Bien sûr, oui, c'est vrai." When the owner of the gas station, probably

her husband, appeared, she suddenly became quite businesslike and counted out the money, chatted with Julien, and went round the car a couple of times.

"Many men fell," I said, "in fact most did."

"But maybe he's still alive," she whispered, "wounded perhaps, like you. If you're in Karlsruhe say hello to him."

"Vous êtes mariée?"

"Oui, quand même."

Jeanette was still surrounded by many churchgoers, and when they saw the car coming they stepped aside to make room for the coming drama. Julien put the biggest parcel into her hand and took the road down to the house in long strides to where Jeanette's mother was standing in a dark blue dress with a white collar.

"Je suis très heureuse, Monsieur, très heureuse. . . ."

Her voice was trembling. I recalled the customary greeting in France: a little kiss on the left cheek, another on the right and then another on the left, a nice custom really. In Germany we only offered our hand, and before that we only said *"Heil Hitler"* and had become so used to this that it stopped striking us as dreadfully silly. I tried to click my heels together and bow, as I had done back then, but she took me by the shoulders, kissed me on the left cheek, then on the right, and then again on the left.

And Jeanette did the same.

And the old aunt was occupied with the vegetables and the meat, held a huge knife in her hand and could offer me neither a hand nor an arm. From what I could understand from her torrent of words, she always did the cooking, just the cooking, and of course looked after the garden. The vegetables came from the garden. Jeanette had no time because she sewed, never did anything but sew, *toujours,* from morning to night. Not that she was complaining, no, that's just how it was. And since she had her hands full of bits of vegetables she at least held out her arm for me to take, and then decided to rinse off the bits of vegetables so that she could give me her hand; then she told me what there was to eat today. First a soup, of course.

Then we stood there and looked at one another.

"Sit down," Jeanette said, pushing an armchair my way, the only armchair there was. Now I was sitting while the others stood around me.

"Do you like cassis?" Julien asked. Of course I didn't know what cassis was, but I liked it and thought of Monsieur and Madame Boiler-maker from Bayonne. We drank cassis, and I asked what cassis was, and all four of them in turn explained to me how they made this drink themselves.

"Julien prefers grenadine," said Jeanette, and then we had the next subject of conversation until the aunt asked for the white tablecloth and the napkins to be found, for today the white tablecloth would be used, and also Julien had to fetch the glasses from the cupboard, the ones to the right on top.

There was garlic in the food. I wasn't hungry, which the aunt didn't understand at all; she kept refilling my plate, all the while regaling me with comments which I couldn't understand, because when she spoke she sounded as if she were yodelling, squeaking out one syllable in a falsetto and croaking the next syllable in a baritone. She must have been describing the ingredients and recipes in complete detail, and the less I understood the more I nodded to show my interest, which again induced her to give me yet another huge helping from one dish or another.

Julien had to tell about all the people he had met and what they had said, unfamiliar names, unfamiliar words. Since the war, I was completely out of practice in French; mentally I formulated words and questions I wanted to ask but didn't, because the family chatted and laughed and acted as if I weren't even there, although my presence was a very important event; because something or other would change, perhaps even today, but no one wanted to touch on this or to invite a discussion about it by asking premature questions.

Was I accustomed to drinking a cup of coffee with my meal? Yes, gladly.

Finally the mother began to talk about the war. She asked about the young *menusier* from Rumania who sometimes helped her husband in the workshop during his free time. I'd had no idea about this, nor did I know who the *menusier* from Rumania could have been, although I thought I had been informed about everything that was happening in the village. I surely was not speaking an untruth when I said that unfortunately he had fallen, on that Christmas Eve of 1943. She deplored the dreadful war and the many young people who had died in it. He was *très gentil,* the *menusier* from Rumania, *très gentil.*

"And Toni?" Jeanette asked. "Is Toni still alive?" Her mother listened, full of interest.

"Maybe," I said. "He survived those terrible days at the end of

1943 and was supposed to go to officers' school. He may still be alive.''

Le bel Toni! He came from Villach in Austria, had crinkly light blond hair and a dimple in his chin. He was Monique's heart–throb. She spoke no German and he spoke no French, and so their misunderstandings were a constant source of amusement. You could hear them laughing more than talking. Once Toni hadn't turned up at the Boisse at the appointed time and Monique wanted to get even. She picked a huge, thorny thistle, wrapped it up as if it were a bouquet of flowers, and wrote a sarcastic greeting to go with it; that is, she tried to formulate a sarcastic greeting, but what came out after hours spent translating literally from a dictionary was, ''I send you this from my embryo.'' We couldn't figure out just how and where she had got hold of ''embryo,'' but for weeks it was a buzz–word that gave rise to an endless variety of combinations and triggered off roars of laughter, whereupon Monique would pummel Toni furiously until he took her comfortingly into his arms.

Mind you, it would have been embarrassing to recall the ''embryo'' incident just now.

''And what is Monique doing?''

''She's in Paris,'' all four of them said in chorus. She had a small fashion salon there with many good clients, and her husband, Jacques, was an engineer with the railway, so that they got all their rail trips for free.

Still no one had asked me how it had gone for me, how it was going for me, and what I was doing now, nor was a single word said about how it had gone for Jeanette after the war.

I suggested that we take a ride to Montboyer, with a slight detour past the railway station. Jeanette had accompanied me there in the early morning hours when I went away on leave and never returned, because the battalion was then transferred to the Pyrenees and from there to the mouth of the Rhône.

Julien was enthusiastic. We could drive past Jacqueline's and get Robert at the same time. Jacqueline was his girlfriend of the moment. But the mother and the aunt understood that I wanted the opportunity to speak with Jeanette alone, and they dissuaded him from his plans.

No, Jeanette was not to help in the kitchen now. Just go, just go!

''Are you married?'' was the first thing she asked when we had got into the car.

"Yes."

"Do you have children?"

"No."

"Are you alone in . . . in Hendaye?"

I had told her all this three days ago, but then her mind must well have been elsewhere.

"Klaus and his wife are along."

"Who is Klaus?"

The road she was directing me to take was unfamiliar to me: a narrow road, just wide enough for one car, past the small farms, blooming meadows, and hedges. Yellow, white, and multicolored butterflies flew from flower to flower, a dog trotted ahead of us. Serenity and peace on a Sunday in May.

"Klaus is my brother."

"What did she say, your wife, about Julien?"

The cows looked up at us with bored curiosity. I stopped at a place where the road widened. The crickets were chirping excitedly.

"She asked what happened to you—after the war—because of Julien."

Bees and wasps assaulted the closed windows of the car, the crickets fiddled in shrill dissonances, a dog barked furiously. Her eyes filled, and before she said anything she buried her head in my shoulder. I guessed more than I understood of her story, which was continually punctuated by sobs. The furiously barking dog was now wagging his tail, inviting us to play. Cows approached the fence, bringing their calves along, chewing and chewing. She dried her eyes and sat up straight again.

"And you? What happened to your leg?"

I drove on, slowly. The fresh greenery of the hedges rustled against the bodywork; fragrant air wafted in through the open roof. Neither the mood nor the surroundings lent themselves to reliving the war just now.

The level crossing gate was closed.

"Il faut claquesonner," Jeanette said, sounding the horn. A woman came out of the little house, opened the gate, gave a friendly nod and closed the gate again. Then the road led up the wooded hill from which Montboyer is visible. Were they still there, the ditches and positions which we had dug for the antitank gun and mortar positions?

Jeanette touched my leg, cautiously, as if she might hurt me. "Is it the left one?"

"Yes."

*   *   *

Back then there had first been only a thrombosis in the thigh after the knee wound and the typhus. That was nothing to fool around with, the doctors had said. "The next time you strain yourself it can loosen and end up in front of your heart; that's the end of you." But it was my decision as to whether or not I wanted to undergo the complicated operation. I didn't want to, and the thrombosis didn't loosen. I'd had enough of hospitals.

A few days after the attempt on Hitler's life I arrived at the replacement unit in Rastenburg, East Prussia, right near the famous Wolf's Lair. The commander was overjoyed. "You're just the man I wanted," he greeted me. "Here I have instructions from the Wolf's Lair, signed by Bormann."

As a result of the attempt on Hitler's life they obviously didn't have complete confidence in some of the sentries any longer. We had to relieve them. For this purpose a decorated officer, experienced at the front, was required.

"Wasn't such a person to be found here?"

I went off to the Wolf's Lair with a troop of six–week recruits. If Russian paratroopers landed I was to beat a way out of here for the government heads with the aid of captured Russian T–34s standing at the ready. The atmosphere was hectic and absolutely crackling with tension. I remained standing, when I heard an all too familiar voice coming through the ventilation shaft of a bunker. Goebbels.

". . . and in the future you are to give no more radio talks unless the text is personally approved by me. Your attacks against the German nobility have brought the Officers' Corps and the generals—the noble backbone of the German Army—into unpardonable discredit, you have divided the German people, and encouraged them to insubordination against a ruling class whose loyalty is to be questioned less now than at any time. . . ."

Although he was very angry he remained so much in control of himself while speaking that every sentence of this dressing–down could have been passed for printing. The sinner was Robert Ley. I had heard his radio speech after July 20th, in which he termed the assassins "blue–blooded swine," and the fact that he had again been drinking too much was unmistakable.

No, the atmosphere was oppressive, and right after the events of the first night I was determined to get out of there again as soon as possible. Some of my recruits had taken up posts within the camp, and after midnight it happened. Around this time Hitler used to carry on relaxing conversations with artists, scientists, or other such persons who had nothing to do with war and politics. His two secretaries were usually present. On their way home they passed by one of my double sentries and awakened unseemly desires in them: "Hey there, dolls, are you on the beat so late?"

The next morning an appropriate complaint lay on Martin Bormann's desk, and I had to pay the penalty. "Here there is only one answer to the slightest breach of security: court martial! Once more and you've had it!"

That did it! The duty doctor, from whom I wanted nothing more than a new zinc liniment bandage to keep my leg from swelling too much, was indignant that I had been assigned here at all. After some telephone calls he gave me my marching orders and said, "Tomorrow you will go to a health resort for at least four weeks. In Sellin on the island of Ruegen. Does that appeal to you?"

Sellin did appeal to me, much better than the comrades in the SS spa hospital did, who were not comrades but uniformed civilians from various SS head offices in Berlin, who had long ago formed their own state within a state. They were neither wounded nor ill; they merely had good connections in the network and granted mutual approval for health–spa visits as holidays at the state's expense. Besides myself there was only one other officer from the front with whom I formed a clique against the clique.

There was someone else who felt attracted to us two front soldiers. He had lost a leg in the Polish campaign and, in the meantime, had acclimatized himself quite civilly to the personnel head office. He heard of my literary ambitions and had seen from the files that I was qualified to lead a war–correspondent unit.

"Then you'd be just the person we're looking for."

"Why, what for?"

In Pforzheim a new department was to be built which would collect and edit the training material for future National Socialist commanding officers. It was news to me that we, too, were now to have a kind of Commissariat.

"You have extensive experience at the front, appropriate educational background and ambitions; you're exactly the right man. You'd have a salary of seven hundred marks, double what you're getting now."

I had no idea what salary I was getting, and anyway, that would have been the last thing that would have attracted me; but I had wanted to be a journalist, and maybe this was . . . but then came the damper:

"And then you'll never have to go back to the front!"

That is what annoyed me so much about these civil servants. They wore our uniforms, decorated themselves with our ranks, and considered themselves far too valuable to be wasted at the front, too good to be expected to end up as shreds of flesh on the bulkhead of a tank or even to have to see this. It was they who, with their signatures and a few strokes of the pen, sealed our fate, the fate of soldiers, of families, of entire peoples. And here they cured the wounds that they thereby inflicted on others.

One day there came the last straw.

The hospital sergeant had a silver plate in his head as a result of having been shot in the head. His motoric speech center was damaged, and so he stuttered. And because the service at the midday meal wasn't fast enough for some Hauptsturmfuehrer or other, the Hauptsturmfuehrer summoned the hospital sergeant. "I'm really going to give him hell," he announced to his colleagues, and then he showed them how to go about it. Now the sergeant stood there, clicked his heels and answered the most offensive insults with nothing more than, "Yes, H–h–hauptsturmfuehrer!" And the Hauptsturmfuehrer kept making fun of the man's stuttering and got a great kick out of criticizing him for his total incompetence.

That was the last straw for me.

I took the sergeant by the arm and escorted him from the barrage of insults.

"And who are you to meddle in this!?" the Hauptsturmfuehrer shouted at me.

"I would prefer to speak to you about this in private, Hauptsturmfuehrer, if you don't mind."

He followed me into an adjoining room. Once inside I seized him by the tie and strangled him until he was red as a beet. "If I ever see such a thing again, you bastard of a Hauptsturmfuehrer, I'll see to it that you have a real reason for spending four weeks in hospital!"

Then I let him breathe again and left the room, and the bastard never even complained, but acted instead as if nothing had happened.

Then there was the gynecologist with the slender hands, over six feet tall, much too tall to be able to survive on normal food rations in Berlin. That was his illness—and his supplementary cure for it was three different meal–ticket affairs with war widows. I was always hearing him calling for harder, more drastic action against these weaklings and cowards.

The senior consultant set a good example. When he was in the building at all he had no time, because he devoted it to his yacht which lay in the harbour at Binz, and which, naturally—nearly everyone could confirm this—he made available to the SS Command Center anytime they wanted, for the purpose of the relaxation of the chosen few.

"I could arrange for your cure to be prolonged for two more weeks," he offered me as if it were a great favor.

"No thank you, I'd like to rejoin my unit as quickly as possible." He thought I was mad. Was I? Perhaps I would have been spared much, but I have been completely cured of looking back in hindsight or wishing that I had made different decisions, for the sole reason that life is much better when we don't entertain such thoughts. In the situation as it was, on the other hand, to have decided in favor of one of the more comfortable and less risky alternatives would always have been dull for me later.

My unit was my home, my family, which I had to protect, especially from those who were always ordering harder and more drastic measures against such weaklings.

SS-Untersturmführer
Woltersdorf, 1943

Author and Jeanette. Montboyer, May 1943.

Author and Lore, engaged. 1944.

Julien and Hans; father and son. 1962.

5 cm antitank gun in Russia. Improvised mount on tow truck. February 1944.

SS-Hauptsturmführer Lex is awarded the Knights Cross. December 1943.

Assault Unit at Isjaslawl.
Accompanied by Filmreport
Grigpleit. February 1944.

Foxhole at Mal Bratalow, west of Zhitomir. Hauptsturmführer Lex inspects.

10

The little village lay peacefully at our feet and the church perched protectively like a mother hen over the houses. I had stopped in a curve in the open sand road and was trying to recall the inhabitants of the individual houses and their roles in the usual village gossip. They had their nicknames, just as they'd given nicknames to quite a few of our soldiers. They called the sergeant "Father Christmas," and the armorer was "Squint–eye," although he didn't squint at all but just cocked his head to one side when he was concentrating on someone.

"And your leg?" Jeanette wanted to know. "How did that happen, when did you lose it?"

Ah, yes, the leg! The thrombosis wasn't to blame for that. After the short leave the doctor in the hospital in Berlin still didn't want to release me for duty. He looked for further reasons for leave.

"Do you have a girlfriend? Are you engaged?"

"Yes."

"Then there we have it: you'll get married! That's good for three more weeks."

I travelled to Poland, to the "Warthegau," as that region was known at the time. Lore was there in a deployment of female students. I went to call for her.

"Get married? So suddenly? My parents will be flabbergasted!"

101

No, it was best if I didn't tell Jeanette about this honeymoon leave; maybe just the part about Robert. An international brigade of Yugoslavs, Poles, and French were working on Lore's farm. Robert was a French POW who was in command and assumed the role of manager. He ran the farm as if it were his own. True, there was a prisoners' camp, with a barracks and a gate and real barbed wire around it, but exactly who had the key to it could never really be ascertained. The oldest and lamest in this unit was the prison warder, the watchman, whose chief task consisted of making up the duty roster of which farmers had to provide the breakfast, lunch, and dinner. Robert greeted me like an old pal and noted regretfully that my swollen elephant leg made me unsuited to field work. If necessary I could help in the stable or the kitchen.

On the second evening Robert said goodby, a weapon over his shoulder. The old fool of a warden had again forgotten where the key was, and so Robert was forced to make a detour around the camp to where he had a rendezvous with his girlfriend. In the bakery. It was lovely and warm there and smelled of fresh bread. He showed me the key to the camp gate and, with his finger, pulled his right eyelid down. Wooden eye on guard!

Jeanette laughed delightedly. When two people are really fond of each other it doesn't matter whether they are French or German, free or in prison.

How I envied Robert, who was able to stay on the farm, near Lore, and do very useful work, while I, who was unfit for field work, was fit enough to lead my company again. Full of timid hopes I limped off to the Battle of the Bulge and, together with those who had come back alive again, dragged myself through snow and cold and the recently-bombed city of Koblenz to the other side of the Rhine.

We had hardly enough time to collect everyone and take stock when freight trains started rolling in to transport us to our next adventure. Despite all the strain the blood clot had still not loosened and blocked my heart, yet my leg kept getting heavier, confirming for me Einstein's formula, $E = mc^2$, whereby energy is transformed into mass.

Our transport out was strictly secret. Even the highest ranks did not know where we were going. Only one person knew: I. A few hours before loading, a young girl was waiting in my quarters with a small case in her hand: "Oh, please take me along!"

"Along? Where?"

"To Prague. My fiancé is studying there. We want to get married."

Nothing against getting married, but why to Prague? "Are we going to Prague?"

She only wanted to go along as far as Vienna. From there she would somehow get to Prague.

To Vienna, then; it was not difficult to figure out that from there it would be Hungary, where intense fighting had broken out at Lake Balaton.

The continuous change from the American and English way of fighting to that of the Russians was certainly not very healthy, but for the hierarchy the events were taking place only on a globe, in a few centimeters and with little flags, that we had to fill out with body, soul, and life. We actually landed in the *puszta*[*] and were rechristened on the way. Our regiment was no longer called *"Der Fuehrer"* but Otto or Heinrich. *Der Fuehrer* was probably ashamed of our shabby remains. The units had their commanders' first names, and because we were to fight in the south we called ourselves "Combat Group North" to deceive our opponents. But even otherwise no one would have recognized our former unit. One of my chief guards was a one–armed lieutenant for whom the army no longer had any use, and the other chief guard was a sergeant with three years' experience of the paper war. And anyone else who returned from the Battle of the Bulge in one piece could thank the fact that there had not been enough gasoline to take them all the way to the front. But fresh replacements were due to come.

They came—though one could hardly have called them "fresh." Most of them could have been my father. They showed me their hernias, their gout, and the photos of their grown children, and I showed them my elephant leg and the lieutenant's missing arm, which comforted them. Some radical hero had combed the remotest places to find this bunch— an elite that was designed to inspire fear in us rather than in the Russians. When I surveyed the battered ranks of my battered company I was still unwilling to admit that we had lost the war, but the subliminal feeling

[*] Grassy plains of Hungary.

rose up in me that we couldn't possibly win it. At this point I did not want to think about what alternatives there could have been, and at any rate there was no time to think about it, because we had only two or at most three weeks in which to whip this crew into an elite brigade for the Eastern front.

Naturally I had long been aware that the dreaded Waffen–SS was really not so fear–inspiring; it was hardly as if a collection of elite individuals had gathered here by chance. Quite otherwise: the Waffen–SS was still living on the laurels earned by its very first volunteers. Those who wore its uniform now had to be aware of their commitment to heroism. Of course each of us was scared, but we did not talk about it or allow it to show. Consequently each man believed that he was the only one to have this unworthy feeling, and so the only thing to do was to put up a show of bravado; and everyone in turn was affected and influenced by his comrades' show of bravado. Fear and courage alike could be spread from the top to the bottom, from the bottom to the top ranks; thus I resolved to spread the image of courage and bravery as quickly as a plague in order to weld this crew of men together in heroic comradeship.

Hard training also had a useful side effect, in that the men regarded their respective commanders as the common enemy, and nothing unites people more than shared rage against someone or something.

We were ten days into training and had hardly begun when the general situation required us to continue our training on the battlefield. But first the sendoff! It was a merry farewell, with splendidly improvised entertainment. The lad with the long, curly hair who always seemed to have two left hands with mortars, got up and crooned the "Song of the Volga Boatmen" in such a way that tears of Lake Balaton wine rolled down our cheeks. The sergeant whistled a two–part yodel, and an orchestra of bottles, a washboard, combs, and empty cartridge cases conjured up a version of the "Triumphal March" from *Aida*. We drank the wine from washbasins that were passed round, a Hungarian told Jewish jokes so authentically that he was awarded the Star of David, and a juggler juggled five hand grenades and whirled them in front of, next to, behind, above, and below himself so that we got quite dizzy. The old corporal from the U–boat bunker sat on the thigh of my swollen leg and said to me in caressing tones, "You crafty devil, you're really a nice fellow and can always do everything better, but that trick with the h–h–handgre-nades, that you c–c–can't do, want to b–b–bet?''

I took two hand grenades, secretly unscrewed the fuse of one and let the porcelain knob hang out of the stem; then I clumsily juggled it in the air and unfortunately caught only the release button. The now–ignited hand grenade rolled under the men.

Someone spotted the rolling danger and screamed with all his might, ''Take cover!'' and the entire crowd tried to dive out of the way within the seven–second incubation period. That was enough sobering–up to bring us back to the serious business at hand.

A Rumanian army corps was to blame for the emergency. It had cleared out of its position at Raab and the Russians had thrust themselves into it, thereby causing the greatest possible confusion in the general situation. We were going to fill the gap before the Russians did.

In the uncertain light of dawn I led a charge and, as the noise of ammunition from friend and foe alike rendered communication impossi-ble, I had to show my men how to do it. Jump up, forward march, move eastward. When I jumped up and ran fifteen meters they ran only ten, and when I remained under cover for ten seconds they remained for fifteen, and when I beckoned them forward they waved back in a friendly gesture.

In front of us there sloped a depression in the midst of which a stream flowed. We jumped in, easily visible from all sides. I was in front and crossed the brook, the cold water pleasantly cooling my swollen leg. We're not going to make it, I thought as I staggered over uncultivated fields, unaware of the fact that a Stalin tank was parked on our flank. From the tank came machine–gun fire that whipped up lots of little dirt fountains all around me. He had me in his sights and would not be at peace until he had clipped off the single spearhead of the troop. I kept praying that if my leg was hit it would be the left one, which was not of much use to me anyway. My prayer was heard. At the next leap forward, march, march; then something smashed against my left foot and knocked me down.

The airman first–class who was hopping right behind me announced at the top of his voice, as if it were a cry of victory, ''The chief has been hit!''

The news of my heroic death spread like wildfire and seemed to unite the men, although the danger of losing the counterattack relieved them of the obligation to observe a moment of silence in my memory. And so I stood up again and hobbled a few steps eastward, to show them the way, only to topple over again just as quickly, which elicited a correction from the airman first–class: "The chief is only wounded! Medics!"

It seemed as if I were leading a company of medics, because one medic after another came to drag me back to the rear. In the process a real stampede ensued that would have challenged any gunner to pull in the reins. Shouting curses and abuses I ordered them to press forward, and then I was no longer the head but a lonely tail.

Our young, not yet fully qualified battalion doctor cut my boot off with his own hands, inspected the hole above the ankle, stuck a plaster over it, and thought I should come back to his surgery at the next opportunity. But at my next visit he suggested changing doctors because he could not explain why my lower leg was taut and ready to burst and exceedingly painful. There I lay, in the back of a truck, with a fever, and next to me lay the dead antitank gunner, and someone was standing next to the vehicle, looking at me sadly with his big brown eyes. It was one of my typhus roommates from Semlin; he had completely recovered since then and wanted at all costs to be in on the final victory.

"Keep a bed free for me, comrade!" he said; then he turned eastward towards the dawn.

The man who was tapping on my bad leg and smelling the hole above the ankle looked like a real doctor, since he wore a white coat with many dark red blood spots.

"Have you been hit there?" he asked.

"From five hundred meters away with a machine gun," I said.

"Then there must be an exit wound there!"

"Maybe it's still in there."

"No, nothing's there."

"It hurts badly below the knee. Maybe it's lodged there."

"Nonsense, how would it get there?"

The X–ray revealed the nonsense below the knee. It must have been a ricochet that spun upwards from the ankle through the calf to the knee, oddly enough without damaging anything important or vital, which was as baffling as it was serious.

At once a chloroform mask was clapped to my face and at the count of twenty-four I was out.

The burning, oppressive pain was blown away; the leg was light as a feather. Where the knee had been there was a thick wad of bandages. The nurse pressed my head to her soft bosom and said, "It was gangrene."

"Gangrene, like hell! For that the whole leg had to come off?"

"Otherwise you would have died," she said, "and your wife and children would never have seen you again. . . ."

"I have no children. . . ."

11

"*Mais, tu avais un enfant,*" Jeanette said, stroking my arm as if she had to continue the nurse's comforting. "He was already a year old then, nearly a year old."

"Was he much of a problem?"

"*Ah non, il était très gentil, Julien.*"

"And—the people?"

"*Les gosses disaient Boche, mais ce m'était égal. J'ais souhaitée un fils, un garçon—comme toi.*"

All hell must have broken loose here back then, when one Frenchman was terrorizing the other, but I didn't even want to ask about it and so I let the car roll slowly downhill.

There lay the farm that belonged to the mayor, with whom we exchanged cigarettes and other goods from the army stores for eggs and meat. The 17– and 18–year–old lads weren't supposed to smoke or to drink any liquor, but to have good food to eat.

"Do you remember?" There, on her way from Chalais, she had stood with her bicycle in the shadow of the acacia, in order to meet me as if by chance, since the last time we met we had forgotten to arrange our next rendezvous. The armorer had had his workshop just opposite.

The car made its way up the road to the Boisse as if of its own accord. "Shouldn't we say hello to Marianne?"

"She would certainly be glad to see you again, but she's married and her husband is very jealous. Whenever we talk about those times it fuels his jealousy. Maybe another time."

Another time! She took it for granted that I hadn't come here for the last time. So did I: she merely made me conscious of the fact. We meandered slowly through alleys and fields and now and then she asked me, *"Tu te rappelles?"*

Oh, yes! Everywhere memories flew through my head. Were they the same memories as hers?

"Everyone's life has its nicest time," she pondered. "It was never again so lovely as then." And when I didn't answer she asked, *"Et pour toi?"*

"Aussi," I said, and I meant it. Compared to what went before and what came after, my period here was an oasis. Here I was free from the pressure of watchful, ordering, critical, and commanding superiors. I was an awkward subordinate and suffered more than I would admit from the demands of obedience. I could count on the fingers of one hand the few persons whom I acknowledged as authorities and to whom I was prepared to submit. And if I didn't acknowledge them as such I let it be known, which often infuriated my instructors and superiors. "I'll wipe that cynical grin off your face!" With special duties or punishment drills. I had no time for the subservient muscle–men who acted authoritarian because they weren't authoritative.

Back then there was someone here who reminded me of myself; Scharf was his name, from Halle, an intelligent lad with character. I could tell what was going on inside his head when he stood before his instructors, clicked his heels together and said, *"Jawohl,* Corporal!"* He was not so stupid as to give a cynical smirk the way I did, which added to the provocation, but he couldn't hide what was going on inside himself from me when he said *"Jawohl"* with a straight face; his instructors felt intuitively that he didn't accept them, and they tried to force his acceptance through exaggerated commands or clumsy camaraderie.

No, when I saw this going on I never interfered. He had to learn to accept such attitudes. Like most people, he would always have someone over him, be dependent on someone, and there would always be those who would rely on a pose, or some injustice, intrigue, or demonstration of power to attempt to compensate for what they lacked. Nowhere would he find the understanding or justice that he would expect or demand, not as a soldier and not in civilian life. To learn this through experience, to defend oneself against it without rebelling against it, to endure the depths of injustice and degradation without giving up and without losing one's self–control, those are the necessary conditions for really being in control of one's life.

I made him a chief gunner; he was better than the older men, and for his eighteenth birthday I took the initiative to have him promoted to corporal, a move to which most of my officer colleagues in the battalion objected.

While we were being transported to Russia in the autumn, Scharf got appendicitis, just when we happened to be near Halle. He wasn't pretending, as the others thought, and yet I still couldn't help suspecting that his psyche had a role in this: the anticipation of his test under the critical eyes of those who considered him immature, a test which he absolutely wanted to undergo in order to justify his early promotion. I never saw him again.

But I heard about him. Persch, the commander of the Second Battalion, told me about a very young corporal, just discharged from sick bay, who had torn up his convalescent leave permit so he could get to the front. Persch had entrusted him with a daredevil raid. By night he led his raiding party through a minefield that went through the Russian lines, noiselessly took care of the Russian sentries, blew up an ammunition dump, and created a state of hopeless chaos so that he and his men could make their way back through the Russian lines. Going out he went first, coming back he came last; he brought all his men back in one piece, but then, just as he thought he'd made it, he stepped on a mine.

It was Scharf. "A splendid boy," said Persch, "so young and inexperienced, and the way he led his first mission, no one else could have done it any better. A real pity."

This damned war!

There was very little that got me down the way Persch's tale did.

I, too, had once torn up my convalescent leave permit, so that I could come to Russia. It was 1941. We had returned from the Balkan campaign and I was lying in a hospital near Linz when the war with Russia broke out. Two weeks earlier the division had already been transferred to action stations in the east. When I insisted on leaving the hospital I got three weeks' convalescent leave.

Three weeks!

The war had lasted eighteen days in Poland. Norway could hardly be called more than a surprise coup. The war in France had taken a bit longer. In Yugoslavia a captain had taken Belgrade with seven men and so brought that campaign to a premature end. The war in Russia was already eight days old and there was no news about how the fronts were developing. Three weeks' convalescent leave! By then, I reckoned, my comrades could already have marched on Moscow—without me.

And so in Linz I got out of the train that was carrying soldiers on leave and I tore up my convalescent leave permit, because in Linz our division had a vehicle pool among which there must have been something that had not yet left for Russia.

I reported there.

"Do you have a driving license?" the orderly–room sergeant asked me. I eagerly answered, "Yes!"

"Then come with me!"

We wound our way through masses of trucks in varying stages of road–worthiness, and somewhere motorcycles could be seen; my driving license was valid only for motorcycles. At last he stopped in front of an old war horse.

"A Panhard," the sergeant explained, "five tons, right–hand steering, French. To be delivered at the Light Communications Unit. It's somewhat overloaded with five tons of cable, so drive carefully and collect your marching papers from the orderly room."

That was the end of the matter for him, while my courage diminished each time I walked round the monster. My previous experience with trucks amounted to sitting in the back of a one–and–a–half–tonner, and I didn't even know what it looked like inside the driver's cab.

In the orderly room I asked whether they didn't have a partner for me, all alone . . .

Yes, a latecomer had just arrived who could be my partner.

"Can you drive a truck?"

"No."

"Neither can I."

But one can learn.

So there we were, sitting high up in the driver's cab, looking at the ground way down below. The steering wheel, which rose up vertically from the floor of the cab, reminded me of a sluice in the Mittellandkanal, which was also opened with a wheel like that, while we speculated on the significance of the other levers, pedals, and buttons, and remembered that such a vehicle would certainly not have a kick–starter but a starting button. We pressed every possible button—ouch, that one was the cigarette lighter and my index finger was the cigarette. Otherwise there was hardly anything there that could have been a starter. While we crawled around on all fours in the driver's cab to look for it the engine suddenly sprang to life of its own accord and chugged along. Fabulous! The miracle was brought about by a button located in the floor next to the steering column. One of us had stepped on it by accident.

And how did you turn the thing off again?

In the meantime we found no other solution than to put it in fourth gear, suddenly disengage the clutch and pull the handbrake at the same time. True, it did a frog–hop that caused the five tons of cable to shudder, but it stood still.

The sergeant waited impatiently for us finally to clear out, and before he could notice that both of us had only motorcycle licenses I expertly let the engine give a couple of roars, put it in first gear, and cautiously crawled out of the exit. The road just happened to be empty, so that, thank God, I didn't have to stop on the hill and then start again. Meanwhile I kept it in first gear and roared along the road at four kph, keeping pace with the pedestrians and waving to the horse–drawn carriages to overtake us.

Outside the city I risked second gear. Now the speed was even causing wind to hum against the window, and it was only the cyclists we had to let overtake us now. Then third gear, then fourth, and soon I was feeling so sure of myself that I risked eating a sandwich and smoking a cigarette while driving.

Just before we reached Vienna my partner began his driving lessons. On the Mariahelferstrasse he tried in vain to change down from third to second gear; as a result the problem of how we were going to make a sharp left turn at the next traffic light became bigger, the closer we got to the light. It was the evening rush hour and traffic was heavy. We didn't realize that the light was red until the trolley had slammed on its emergency brakes and screeched loudly to a halt a few meters in front of us, its bell clanging angrily. In the end the driver was prepared to give us the right of way, since we wanted urgently to get to Russia before our comrades had marched on Moscow, but our engine had died. And when the starter ground into operation the truck was still in third gear, so that we kept frog–hopping closer and closer to the trolley. Couldn't it just move a bit to the side! Meanwhile the light was obstinately changing from red to yellow to green and again to red, while people were honking behind us, clanging in front of us, and cursing to the right and left of us, until we had achieved direct physical contact with the trolley.

How did we ever get out of that mess? I don't remember. In any case we did get out of it, since in the late evening hours we landed, exhausted, at a farmhouse and pleaded for quarters for the night.

The people were just as unfriendly as the quarters, which were in the stable, and breakfast wasn't offered either, since the next day was Sunday and everyone on the farm was going to church.

Our Viennese dilemma could be attributed to the fact that we didn't know how to shift into reverse. And so instead of having breakfast we practiced with the gearstick until we established that you had to give it a good push downwards and then to the right. Now we got the truck to go backwards!

Our orders took us over Ostrau, towards Radom and Pulavy to Minsk. For the time being there was still a blackout on all news about the front, so our fantasies about where we would find our units ranged from Minsk to the Urals. We had long ago become perfect truck drivers and made faster and faster progress, driven as we were by the urge to overcome the news blackout through personal reconnaissance.

We couldn't miss the roads of our division's advance, because to the left and right there were Russian vehicles and weapons, mountains of rifles and machine guns, horse–drawn and motorized supply vehicles, light and heavy artillery, tanks, munitions vehicles, bakery trucks, dead horses, and endless columns of prisoners. For ten, twenty, fifty kilometers, nothing but vehicles, cannon, weapons and ammunition, the equipment of entire armies, all left behind by the Russian invasion army.

My co-driver kept mumbling to himself, "Christ! Think if they had attacked first! Think if all this had rolled westwards! Damn! Is there no end to this? Hell . . ."

Beyond Minsk we first met up with men from our division. We asked for news of the Light Communications Unit.

"Well," said the sergeant, examining the vehicle from all sides. "You are a lovely sight. Have you come from up ahead?"

"No, from behind. Why?"

Our lovely old Panhard had hardly any color left. The sideboards had been badly scratched and splintered by the many trees along the roads, the narrow bridges, fence–posts, and the like; the bumpers, fenders, and doors were as battered as if we had been driving a reconnaissance mission right at the front from the first day.

By sheer accident I discovered supply vehicles with the tactical symbol of the Antitank Division. And my motorcycle was there, fully loaded, waiting for me.

"Cheers, buddy! I have to go up ahead now. You can do the rest alone, and most of the dents and scratches are your fault anyway. . . ."

Three hours later I was in the midst of the spearhead to the east. My comrades still hadn't reached Moscow, and who knows whether we would have made it if I hadn't been wounded again shortly before my convalescent leave had officially ended.

"Tu te rappelles?" Jeanette asked, bringing me back to the present.

"Oui, je me rappelle."

We had been prowling around here one Sunday afternoon, Monique, Toni, Jeanette, and I. In fact it was the only time we had a rendezvous in broad daylight and in the immediate vicinity of the village. Toni had his little terrier along, which sounded the alarm just in time whenever a stranger approached. The boys from the village must not see us here; they were jealous. We sat over there among the bushes and took photos. After the war we were all going to meet here again and have a picnic, and Monique listed the peacetime delicacies that she would prepare. And the dog would get the leftovers. If we were married, the men could bring their wives and the women could bring their husbands; and, of course, the children too. And so we estimated roughly the number of people for whom Monique would have to prepare the picnic.

"Down there is where you played sports," Jeanette said, pointing to the soccer field. "I watched you sometimes. You always jumped the farthest and the highest, and you were always the fastest."

"Oui, je me rappelle."

"And now . . . you can't do any of that anymore. Was it bad?"

*   *   *

Considering the many possibilities and probabilities, fate had been kind to me. Of all those who had been crowded together with me like sardines in the cattle car and transported off towards Vienna, with whom would I have wanted to change places? There were moans, groans, and whimpers in that car; the smell of pus, urine, stomach and lung wounds, and it was cold. We lay on straw, each of us covered only by a woollen blanket. The train waited for hours on sidings.

After many days a doctor finally came crawling breathlessly into our car. He had long ago given up reacting to the many wishes, pleas, and complaints, indeed listening to them at all, and he concentrated on his task of distinguishing the nearly dead from the still alive, making room for new wounded, and changing dressings only when it was necessary. In my case it was necessary.

"I'm afraid we have no chloroform," he said. "Grit your teeth!"

Then he tore the whole septic kit and caboodle from my stump in one go. While dozing off in the last few days I had imagined a leg amputation in the Middle Ages to be something like that. I heard the angels singing in heaven, but they didn't take me along into their sweet anesthesia. Thousands of ants were biting on the keyboard of my exposed nerve endings, my big toe became cramped, someone kept giving me a good kick in the shin, my calf was slowly being cut open from bottom to top with a blunt knife, while a circular saw laboriously grated through the sole of my foot.

On the one hand I was fully occupied defending myself against these tortures; but on the other hand I carried out some highly interesting physiological studies as to how and why the nerve endings suddenly exposed by an amputation magically produce a whole series of painful experiences that are not occurring in reality. I concentrated on the fact that there was neither a knee nor a calf, neither a big toe nor a sole of the foot, that no one was kicking me in the shin, that no ants were biting on the nerves, and that no circular saw was buzzing. There were just several nerve endings lying exposed, to which absolutely nothing was happening. Now the doctor was washing away the entire mess with a yellowish antiseptic; I saw it but I was feeling something quite different: someone, it seemed, was stretching my tendons like a bowstring, holding a burning candle under my heel, tugging at my toenails, and trying to rotate my foot 180 degrees. If fantasy is a proof of the special intelligence of *Homo sapiens*, here it was being caused by tiny electrophysiological impulses of about sixty microvolts, which ran along my nerve tissues into my brain.

Consciousness of pain arises only in the cortical region of the frontal lobes, but that is not where it hurts; instead, from there we project the contents of our consciousness to the peripheral areas of the body, where we think we are feeling the pain. The fact, the reality, is no more than these sixty microvolts. They can be measured but not felt; instead we are compelled to translate them into learned, heard–of, read–about experiences of medieval torture chambers with glowing tongs, gnawing rats, and thumbscrews; we must spin and weave entire webs of experiences around them, in order to feel, with gruesome pleasure, what is not happening at all. What a malicious idea of nature!

At night I woke up because my left foot was freezing, and when I had carefully spread out the blanket to cover the nonexistent foot, I felt the soothing warmth. Of course, my conscious had quickly come to terms with the fact that the leg was no longer there, but in my subconscious, in which I had learned as an infant to experience the phenomenal world of pain and to localize it, I still have two legs. To that extent, anyway, what is not there is far from not there.

12

Once again we were sitting in the place where we sat back then and took the photo with the dog between us. "In any case, it was no chaperone," Erika had said. The bushes had grown higher and cut off our view of the village. It was Sunday again, just like that other time, and it could almost have been exactly eighteen years ago to the day. The carefree joyfulness of a bygone age could not be conjured up at will. We felt this, and perhaps Jeanette felt it especially. Perhaps she saw me quite differently, overshadowed by an epoch which others were now writing about, commenting on, and making movies about, an epoch whose main focus was on the persecution of innocent people, on concentration camps, torture, and genocide, war guilt and invasions of innocent, peaceful countries, an epoch inseparably bound up with the SS, the epitome of all that was gruesome and evil, bound up with Oradour and Tulle and that symbol that I, too, had worn back then.

"And—how did the war end for you? Were you taken prisoner? By the Russians, the Americans or the English? After all you were SS, 'sans soucis' as Monsieur Sarasin said."

My POW troubles were to begin soon enough. However, our cattle car odyssey first ended in a little place in Czechoslovakia, north of Linz.

In German it was called Beneschau and it was still far away from the rattling of machine guns, from tanks and grenades, in the agreeable, peaceful spring sunshine. I was assigned one of the twenty beds, which had fresh linen, in the provisionally furnished schoolroom, and was given coffee in real cups and lunch with shiny spoons and sometimes with knives and forks, too. Six of the twenty officers belonged to the Waffen–SS.

On Hitler's birthday, April 20th, a National Socialist commanding officer visited us, a man from the institution that would give me seven hundred marks per month and free accommodation in Pforzheim in return for my help in editing their training material. With a pithy Teutonic saying adapted for the purpose—''Leg lost, nothing lost—courage lost, everything lost''—he presented me with the gold badge for my sixth or seventh injury and cited examples from history in which things that were believed lost had still led to victory through loyalty, courage, and bravery.

He did this all quite clumsily, and it was obvious that he hadn't himself thought up the verses which he dutifully recited. Not that we scornfully or bitterly booed the man, no, we clutched at every straw and hoped for a change or miracle. In retrospect one might assume that in these last leisure hours of this miserable, endless war it ought to have occurred to us to reflect about sense and nonsense, guilt and innocence, and all the collective problems with which those times were burdened. But what later came to light was still in the future, back then. No word about persecution of the Jews, mass exterminations or genocide; the name Auschwitz or Maidanek would have meant nothing more to us than the name of any other unknown village. Nothing was there that could have burdened our collective consciences, and the SS had not yet become the alibi of a nation from which one distanced oneself or at which one pointed one's finger in order to ease one's own conscience.

Nor could I say that certain taboos existed about which we shamefully or guiltily kept silent, or that we would have sprung automatically to our feet at the mention of the name of Hitler or one of his ministers; no, it was taken for granted that Bormann and Himmler weren't liked, that Goering was an eccentric boaster, Goebbels a sly Jesuit, and Hess a big idealist. We had respect for Guderian, Rommel, and Doenitz, but not for Keitel, and still less for the dilettantes of July 20th, who were prepared to sacrifice others, but not themselves, for their patriotic ideals. We felt powerless before the immeasurable material superiority of the Americans, without which the Russians and British would have capitulated long since, and we did not understand why Hitler had declared war on them, for whatever reasons.

"Enjoy the war, for the peace will be dreadful," was our motto, and it was nourished daily by refugees from the east, by soldiers and officers who had driven the Russians from German–occupied areas and discovered the traces of indescribable atrocities and violence. It was that which stuck like a lump in our throats and united us in common rage at having to lie here powerless and passive. Everything that would have been worthy of discussion as criticism of our own affairs paled into insignificance next to this dreadful happening. Was the wish father to the thought or was there justification for expecting that the Americans, who had entered the war for human rights and human values, would now join with us against the greater danger from the East? Wouldn't Churchill, anti–Bolshevism incarnate, now finally have to realize who his real enemy was?

And so we took things easy until the bitter end on May 8th. The bad tidings, and the things we were able to read between the lines, inspired a macabre sense of humor in us. We got gooseflesh listening to the gruesome stories that refugees in soulless bodies told, not only about the Russians, but now about the Poles and Czechs as well.

Then the Americans came. Right in front of our hospital they built a cordon, a demarcation line, to receive the troops and civilians who were streaming back. Now they would finally realize what their allies in the East were up to!

But that's not how it happened.

It was much worse!

Those who were able stood at the window, watched, and told those of us who were lying down what was going on. A motorcycle with sidecar, carrying an officer and two men from the Waffen–SS, had arrived. They surrendered their weapons and the vehicle. The two men were allowed to continue on foot, but the officer was led away by the Americans. They accompanied him part of the way, just fifty meters on. Then a salvo from submachine guns was heard. The three Americans returned, alone.

"Did you see that? They shot the lieutenant! Did you see that? They're shooting all the Waffen–SS officers!"

That had to be a mistake! Why? Why?!

Our comrades from the Wehrmacht didn't stand around thinking for long. They went down to the hospital's administrative quarters, destroyed all files that showed that we belonged to the Waffen–SS, started new medical sheets for us with Wehrmacht ranks, got us Wehrmacht uniforms, and assigned us to new Wehrmacht units. I was with the "Linz Regiment," a unit thrown together from men who were on leave or scattered.

And thus began a new odyssey for me, the continuation of the war, between the fronts and without weapons, as quarry pursued with a hatred that was incomprehensible to me. We talked about reasons, causes, and mistakes that could explain it, but we could only assume that the mere symbol of our uniforms, which were also worn by the Gestapo, the Security Service, and the concentration camp guards, was the reason we were being persecuted. How could people make such superficial judgments! Or was it simply nothing more than primitive revenge, getting back at an elite group that had long ago ceased to be elite?

I never figured it out.

We had to evacuate the hospital in the shortest possible time. We lay on stretchers or stood on crutches in front of the building. We commandeered a postal–service bus and painted red crosses on it. A blind man sat at one door and a double amputee at the other.

Fifteen kilometers along the road and so far so good, when a frantically–waving French captain stopped our bus. "Heil Hitler, comrades," he said, and we thought he was pulling our leg. No, he wanted us to take him along, because the next day the area would be occupied by the Russians, and he didn't want to fall into their hands. We took him along. Shortly thereafter we were led to a large field where tens of thousands of civilians and soldiers were already living. The terrain was surrounded by barbed wire, and every ten meters there stood an American guard.

"We have to get out of here, comrades, otherwise we'll be handed over to the Russians," said the French captain.

"They can't do that," said the major with the amputated lower leg. "That's against the conventions of war. We've surrendered to the Yanks, not the Russians."

But the Frenchman didn't believe in these conventions of war and arranged for our bus to drive on. After about ten kilometers we were directed to a farmhouse. We were already in Austria. Here at least were nurses and an improvised hospital.

The wildest rumors were circulating: We would be handed over to the Russians here—no, to the Czechs—a dreadful massacre of Germans was to take place in Prague and spread to other cities—parts of the SS *"Das Reich"* Division had pressed on back to Prague to end the massacre and free the Germans—Here the Waffen–SS would be singled out and handed over to the Russians—no, not handed over, but shot, but just the officers—They wouldn't be shot, but incorporated into the U.S. Army to help them fight the Russians—

All false. The people here, ex–soldiers not yet allocated to prison camps, who were capable of mining or farming would be sorted out and immediately released to work places.

Others promoted themselves to the rank of milker or groom. Stamps and stamp pads materialized, as did empty military passbooks, Wehrmacht driving licenses, and typewriters. Again and again Americans invaded the place and gathered up groups of people who had to strip to the waist and raise their left arm. Then we saw some of them being shoved on to trucks with rifle butts.

"What are they looking for?"

"Waffen–SS, they have their blood group tattooed on their upper left arms."

Did I have one of those? I couldn't remember when or how it was done, since we were vaccinated and injected so often, but I had blood group O, and it really was tattooed under my upper left arm.

We grabbed one of the medics so that he could tell us how, and with what, such a thing could be eradicated, but he didn't know. Someone had a medical encyclopedia which said that it was not possible to remove tattoos without leaving a scar.

Nevertheless, one medical orderly had the right solution: donkey's milk! If you injected with that, the tattoo would fade. A kingdom for a donkey—but there were none. Smoking nitrous acid could also be used, with care, to corrode a tattoo. Some people got an ugly eczema from this, which made them look even more suspicious. Corn plaster could be used to loosen and remove the skin layers bit by bit. A kingdom for corn plaster! I got some of it allocated to me. I owed a kingdom, but even the corn plaster didn't help.

Someone had a radio, and the main subject of all reports, conversations, interviews and discussions was: concentration camps. Pictures were painted of gruesome mountains of corpses, emaciated, starved, exhausted bodies; mass graves, corpses in cattle cars, people behind barbed wire; women beseechingly stretching out their arms towards their children, maltreated with rifle butts and crammed into freight cars like cattle. And it was all accompanied by texts that sweepingly condemned the SS as inventors of, responsible for, and executors of every conceivable bestiality. Names were mentioned: Buchenwald, Bergen–Belsen, Dachau and Mauthausen, right near us. Until then Dachau was the only place I had heard of. One or two hundred prisoners from Dachau had been staying at the Cadet School for the Waffen–SS in Bad Toelz. Their duties were to keep the premises and equipment in order, and to prepare the material required for carrying out our work.

Next to me there lay a strangely obstinate colleague, whose uniform showed all too clearly that the collar patch and the eagle emblem on the arm had just recently been removed. He had a curious square flesh wound, the size of the palm of a hand, on his upper leg.

"How did that happen?" I asked him.

The story he told me about a grenade splinter did not at all fit the strange wound.

"Where were you then?"

Then he put a finger to his lips and whispered, "With the *'Das Reich'* Division."

Oh, how interesting! I asked him for names and dates, wanted to know whether this person or that one were still alive, where they had been sent after I was wounded. His uniform showed that he had an officer's rank, but all he knew about this division was its name. I drove him into a corner, until he finally revealed that he had been with a concentration camp unit in the East. The camp was supposed to be surrendered to the Russians, along with the people who could no longer be transported off to the West, but shortly before that an uprising broke out among the prisoners and all the guards were killed, lynched or stoned. He escaped as if by a miracle.

"And what's this that they keep talking about on the radio?"

"It wasn't like that, believe me: it wasn't like that! I'm maybe the only survivor who can witness to how it really was, but who would believe me!"

"Is it all a lie?"

"Yes and no," he said. "I can only say what I know about our camp. The final weeks were horrible. No more rations came, no more medical supplies. The people got ill, they lost weight, and it kept getting more and more difficult to keep order. Even our own people lost their nerve in this extreme situation. But do you think we would have held out until the end to hand the camp over in an orderly fashion if we had been these murderers?''

I no longer knew what to believe. Perhaps there were people who, constantly associating with prisoners—for whatever reasons they may have been locked up—lost the measure of and feeling for what is human; people who regarded the shooting of defenseless people as the ultimate in keeping order; people who considered this a proper form of discipline. In any case, what an ideal opportunity for the victors to present their own war as a crusade for humanity and justice, and to conceal their own atrocities, especially those of the Russians, behind a gruesome concentration camp happening!

And this guy here with the self–inflicted flesh wound was even trying to sneak into the *"Das Reich"* Division and to besmirch us as well. Why were they given the same uniform! The raids for tattoos were repeated daily, but the alarm system functioned. Those without tattoos drew attention to themselves, while we hid under the straw over which they were lying crosswise.

We were moved from Linz to a school on the north bank of the Danube. At least when we were on the farm we were able to find something or other from which to extract a few calories, whereas here my war without weapons became a war without rations as well, and it was no less bitter. There was simply nothing at all to eat; but then, too, there were no raids.

My neighbor in my straw mattress was a real lieutenant, tattooless. His name was Rase. He was a forest warden from East Prussia and was now homeless. We enthused about our school days and the morning break when we unpacked and took huge bites out of our thick slices of bread. Rase still had all his limbs and was constantly out and about, organizing something. He brought leaves, grasses, and herbs and, thanks to his training, he knew what could be done with them. He washed them, chopped them into little bits, salted them and boiled the mixture over a Hindenburg candle to make a soup that we began to spoon down before it cooled enough to eat. We calculated the number of calories we had inhaled, along with the heat generated by the cooking, converted them into work output, and then calculated how long we would be able to live on them if we did without the work. Meat! Rase sized up my good leg and drew to my attention what a waste it was that I had not brought along the sawn–off leg as a reserve supply of iron, even if gangrene would not have tasted particularly good; though there would certainly have been a usable joint of some kilos left above the knee. . . .

That there would ever be a time when we would get sick and tired of lots of fat and the daily bit of ham was unthinkable, and it would have been just as absurd to predict that our society would one day fritter away millions in order to do away with the harmful, unaesthetic and pathological effects of overeating. And so the only bit of hope remaining for me and Rase was that when the follow–up amputation was done on my leg, some extra kilos of flesh could be cut off and saved for consumption.

I went stalking along the corridor to suggest this to the senior physician, and he was coming towards me from the other end. But before we met, the door of what had been the second-grade classroom opened, a man with a somewhat familiar face emerged, saw me, clicked his heels, raised his arm in a German salute, and called loudly and snappily, "Heil Hitler, Obersturmfuehrer!"

"Have you completely taken leave of your senses?!" I hissed at him. During his training period he would never have dreamed that one day I would have answered such an impeccable salute in this way. Besides— and for this reason the American swoops on tattoos were superfluous— former prisoners from the Mauthausen concentration camp were being accommodated in a side wing so that they could be nursed back to health with white bread, butter, real coffee, and corned beef, and they were understandably allergic to SS ranks.

"Obersturmfuehrer?" the chief physician asked quietly. I said nothing, and he gestured for me to follow him and headed for a door which he closed behind me.

"Do you still have . . . ?"

I nodded.

I exposed my upper left arm. He injected me with something to freeze the tattooed area, then cut out the tattoo very carefully, layer by layer, mumbling that hopefully the subcutaneous layer would not be damaged.

If I were now very careful and would see to it that it did not fester, then perhaps hardly anything would be visible.

Now I felt a bit better, but not very much; for everyone who was released from here as cured had to be processed through the release camp at Wegscheid, which had been an annex of Mauthausen. And there they inspected upper left arms with a magnifying glass. And those who were not completely flawless got to be sparring partners for some professional boxers before being transported with all the trimmings to Mauthausen, in order there to begin the twenty–year exile promised by Montgomery.

That they actually carted off to Mauthausen on piggyback a young man who only had one arm left of all his limbs—and precisely the arm with the tattoo—was too much even for a former Mauthausen prisoner who worked here as a barber and cut my hair free of charge (even Rase didn't think any edible soup could be made from my hair). Barbers are sensitive people, especially this one, who himself had a son liable for military service and who did not know whether the son had ended up with the Volkssturm, the Wehrmacht, or even the Waffen–SS. And anyhow, the Yanks! They should talk! Granted, Mauthausen was no paradise, but what they got there in "meager" daily rations a wounded person here was expected to survive on for two weeks. Many of his fellow prisoners had secretly passed something on to the poor souls and cripples. . . .

"But all the beatings and torture," I asked, "what about that?"

"Oh, my!" he said. "They were something. Look!" He showed me his deformed shin. "Kicked to bits."

"By SS people?"

"They wouldn't get their own hands dirty. They had the kapos for that."

"What are kapos?"

"Camp big shots, prisoners themselves, traitors to their own kind."

"Why were you in Mauthausen?"

"For undermining the military potential. And yet by then there was no military potential left to undermine."

"How does one do that—as a barber?"

"You're constantly talking with your customers. They want to be entertained, after all. If a baker comes you talk about bread and cakes;

if a doctor comes you admire the medical arts; if a Nazi comes you talk about the genius of Hitler; if a reactionary comes, a Sossie,* Nazi, or Commie, then Hitler isn't such a genius. And then there came a young lad, just seventeen, I had to cut a few inches off his lovely head of hair. What a shame! He was going to become a soldier. You're crazy, I whispered to him; I was thinking of my own son. The war is lost. Why still keep on shooting? Then I gave him a couple of tips, vinegar with pepper and a lovely case of jaundice and so on. But one of the customers must have been a fanatic, someone from the SS maybe, he blew the whistle on me.''

"Then you couldn't have been in Mauthausen long.''

"I was waiting for my trial there. Undermining the military potential is punishable by death. God! How I prayed that the Yanks would come first!''

"Were there many dead?''

"Two kapos were killed.''

"And the SS?''

"The top brass took to their heels in good time, of course, and the little guys were friendly as hell at the end. What the Yanks did with them, I don't know.''

Rase now had a problem. He was about to be discharged as cured, but he no longer had a home to which he could be discharged. We solved the problem with a reciprocal deal: I wrote a letter of introduction to Lore, Rase would play postman and gave Lore's farm as his home address. Rase was enthusiastic, and I now had to describe to him exactly how his new home in Lower Saxony looked, the house with the big winter garden, the stables and barns, the location of the fields, pastures and woods; he wanted to retimber, to shoot wild pigs and pheasants, to cultivate tobacco and carve himself a pipe, and I could hardly sleep nights, since hares, pheasants, and wild pigs were coming closer and closer to me, fatter and fatter and prepared with sauce and potatoes, and when I was at last able to help myself to them I woke up.

Before Rase moved to the release camp with my letter to Lore in his pocket he wanted to show me once more where he used to pick the

* Social Democrat.

greens for our soups. I tried to jump down three steps at a time on my crutches, but hadn't taken into account that the steps had been freshly polished, so that the rubber stoppers skidded like blades on an ice rink. In a reflex movement I put out my left leg to catch myself, with the result that the end of my stump went smashing against the edge of a step. The impact vibrated up my spinal column right to my skull and took the air out of me.

The wound bled and bled for days without showing any sign of ever stopping. There was no question of giving me anything to eat in order to strengthen me. Rase said goodbye, looking extremely apprehensive, and promised to shoot me a wild pig as soon as possible. Until then I had to try to hold out. Then he was gone, and with him my daily soup.

Not even the senior physician could move one of the concentration camp prisoners, who were living like lords, to part with a few crumbs for me. The barber was not there anymore.

My rescuing angel came in the brawny figure of the former European heavyweight champion boxer, whose name I remembered at once: Andreas Diener. I was hooked up to his circulatory system until Andreas Diener was KO and I was, to some extent, OK again. He was supposed to have gotten an egg for that, and he must certainly have gotten it at some time or other.

When the senior physician saw me lying there, exuding so much vitality, he wanted to attempt the follow–up amputation immediately, that is, to remove another small piece from my thigh. But he needed the flesh to cover the bone, so there would be nothing left over for me. That was how our bargain turned out; under the circumstances I wasn't enthusiastic about the way the negotiations were going, but he whispered to me that the Russians would occupy the part of the city north of the Danube in the next few days, and then our nonexistent daily food rations would be cut in half, while I, on the other hand, having just undergone an operation, would have a chance of being transferred to a hospital in the American zone. And so we shook on it.

And yet the bargain was reached under unfair terms, because he hadn't told me that there was absolutely no more chloroform to be had, but only local anesthetic that was injected into the spinal column with thick hypodermic syringes. But this method had the advantage that I could watch the operation and check that no cheating was going on with my flesh. If I were lucky I would faint and thus substitute natural methods for the chloroform, which in any case wasn't very healthy.

But I didn't faint; instead I followed every minute of the proceedings. The area below the pelvis grew heavier and heavier, and more and more numb. After the doctor had cut the flesh like an orange, lifted it up and exposed the bone, he took a quite ordinary saw, the kind my father had once used to saw the garden shed behind our house into shape, and sawed away around my bone. In addition I had a dazzling view of the neighboring table, where they had cut someone's throat open and dug out the larynx, air tubes, vocal chords, and other innards, and were snipping around at them and stuffing them all back in again, as into a straw mattress. Thank goodness my stomach was so empty that I couldn't even feel nauseated, and in any case my appetite had long been a thing of the past.

"It's not much use anymore," he in the red–spattered overall was saying as he rolled himself a cigarette out of newspaper and bits from cigarette stubs, "but we still have to sew him up." Then they heaved the patient, who until then had been sitting on a chair, onto a classroom desk, where he was sewn together again. In the next patient they were searching the intestines for a grenade fragment which disappeared round the next corner whenever they tried to grab it.

"Always keep your head down, please," said the senior physician. "If you raise it the anesthetic goes to your head, and, so far as I remember, no one has survived that."

With my dulled senses I could feel him finely and neatly separating the nerve ends from one another, so that I would not have to suffer too much from phantom pains later on. Then he snipped off some more bits of fat and—simply tossed them into the bucket; I didn't protest, since my appetite was gone anyway. "Now hold these two laps of skin together," he asked me; he fetched needle and thread and, with expert sailor's knots, sewed the whole thing together. The stump now looked like a turtle's mouth protected by a metal grid.

13

"Stop, that's terrible!" Jeanette cried. She held her hands over both ears and got up to run a few steps. "And this Mr. Rase, did he get to Lore?"

"Yes."

"What did she say?"

"Thank God, she said, it could have been worse, I could have been blinded or my face disfigured from burns."

"Terrible, this war! And—did Mr. Rase shoot a wild pig and bring you anything to eat?"

"Of course not. The Germans weren't even allowed to possess a hunting weapon."

"And when did they finally give you something to eat?"

A few days after the operation the news filtered through that the Russians would occupy the part of Linz on the north bank of the Danube. The Americans closed the bridge to prevent a mass flight, and we were thinking quite seriously of secretly swimming the Danube at night. But there the former concentration camp prisoners came to our rescue, since most of them didn't want to end up in Russian hands either. They organized horse–drawn carriages and trucks and took us along with them over the Danube bridge. Here the Americans hadn't thought of looking for tattoos.

I landed in a hospital run by nuns and felt as if I were in paradise when I got a real bed with fresh linen and a lunch consisting of sweet apple rice. It was unbelievable: breakfast, lunch and dinner, solicitous nurses, and a visit from a doctor every other day. Sometimes Americans came too, but they weren't looking for tattoos but for wristwatches, medals, and decorations to trade cigarettes for. Anyone who still had anything to trade kept it for himself anyway, but we made a sport out of driving the prices higher and higher until our mouths were watering, and then sending them away without having struck a deal.

Some weeks later I transferred to what was once a palatial villa: part hospital, part boarding school, but above all a place where artificial limbs were made. It looked like a charnel house inside: great heaps of used and discarded artificial arms and legs from both World Wars, which an orthopaedic physician and some do–it–yourselfers were trying to re-model into suitable items.

I was a guest in Room 14, and my roommate was a lieutenant from Vienna named Manfred whose lower leg had been amputated. For the moment he was far from enthusiastic about having to share his room with a stolid Prussian, especially since he and his civilian accomplice, a carpet dealer and bookmaker called Tuvarisch, were involved in dealings that were obviously not completely aboveboard. He dealt with converts to the Catholic Church and to Austria's new Communist Party, among other things, and accepted alcohol in the form of valerian or liniment as payment.

However, I had my own problems and was in no way offended when the two mystery–mongers left me alone more often than not. In my luggage I still had an empty military passbook which had grown old and needed to have new life put into it. And, of course, with stamps. I had got hold of some plaster from the artificial limb workshop and made a cast of a pedestal the size of a stamp. With a pin, I carved in the plaster the eagle emblem with a swastika. I cast the model in wax using a liquified Hindenburg candle. The first solemn stamp samples were shattering. Not even the most superficial Yank could have mistaken this cross between a vulture and an anteater for the German eagle.

Then I heard footsteps approaching and the door was opened. Of course I was prepared to shove all my equipment under the pillow in the wink of an eye, but the draught caused the piece of paper with my stamp experiments to land right at Manfred's feet. He regarded the picture puzzle with amusement.

"Waffen–SS?"

I tried to explain how, when hastily vacating the hospital in Czechoslovakia, all my papers . . . but he immediately seized my left arm and looked.

"Oh, my!" he said, "if the guys in Wegscheid discover that, it won't matter how perfect your military passbook is."

Tuvarisch might be able to help, but his limited possibilities were soon exhausted in view of the fact that I was a German, and a stolid Prussian at that. In any case, Manfred no longer had any reservations about revealing to me his past and his future, which required him to board a ship to his brother in Argentina as soon as possible. His brother's huge villa would have room for me as well, and five times as much beef per capita was eaten in Argentina as in German Austria.

Tuvarisch suggested I become a Communist, but that went against my grain, since I had written a high school paper on dialectical materialism and discovered too many flaws in it. It all ended with Manfred sailing alone to the fleshpots of Argentina, and five years later he sent me a photo of himself, a well–proportioned playboy lounging in a deck chair in front of his brother's posh villa. But after Peron was toppled he ended up in Germany again and now heads the Latin American export division in my factory.

"And how did you yourself get out again?" Jeanette asked.

There was a chubby little nurse there named Ursula. I called her Bear Cub, and she always addressed me as "Herr Lieutenant," as if she could thus force everything to be as it had been. She had been tense and on edge for a few days, and once I was able to get her to open up about her problems the tears ran down her cheeks.

Her father, she said, had been transferred to Linz five years ago and worked there as a senior civil servant in the employment exchange. There home was in Stettin. Now, because they were Germans, they had been given a short time within which to leave Austria. But where were they to go? Back to Stettin to the Russians or the Poles? No way, never!

In the next room there lay a lieutenant who had already been in Russian hands, but since his leg had been amputated he had had the good fortune to be shifted onto the Americans. He had told her stories about the Russians and Poles, stories of mass atrocities, torture, and senseless murders. Whenever he started in with those stories Bear Cub would run out of the room. And now she herself was going to be handed over to the Russians! She would rather kill herself.

Naturally she hadn't expected any help from me, but when she mentioned that they were allowed to take their furniture and household goods along in a boxcar I got a brilliant idea of how we could help each other. She brought her father in and we held a council of war. Provided that my parents' home in Verden was still standing, and that it was possible to live closely in what had been our rooms as children, it could at least serve as an address we could go to. To be on the safe side, naturally, they would hide me among the furniture in their boxcar and take me along.

This was a cause for celebration, as this plan had to work. As long as plans are still plans they are always successful. Bear Cub baked a Madeira cake and Mr. Senior Civil Servant sacrificed his last bottle of liqueur. Verden, yes, that was so similar to Stettin, a person could feel at home there. I had to describe the house, sketch its layout and the rooms in which they were already planning their furniture, even if it would be just one of the rooms and some use of the kitchen, and seldom did I find such an interested audience when I told about my high school days. They could help my mother and Bear Cub, as a nurse, could look after me along the way and . . . and . . . and . . .

But there was still one snag.

They looked at me in dismay. Was the whole beautiful plan going to go up in smoke?

I showed them the scar under my upper arm.

Then Bear Cub threw her arms around my neck, for now we would be sworn conspirators and would help one another without having to be indebted to one another. They would give some good thought to my hiding place. Under a heap of beds, and on top of them her mother, ill, very ill, typhus, cholera, something contagious, and Bear Cub would sit up there as nurse and warn everyone not to come too close.

Mr. Senior Civil Servant was a correct official who had a horror of dishonest methods. After all, he nit-pickingly discovered, I too was a

German who had to be deported, and if this were correctly dealt with my departure from the country could even be done quite officially, with the appropriate documents.

Tuvarisch got me the address; then I took my crutches under my arms and made my first sortie alone into the town. My first destination was only the nearest tram stop, where a small demonstration by potential passengers was already in progress. The tram, which was already nearly full, approached and was stormed, so that those disembarking were nearly prevented from doing so. It seemed hopeless for me to try to get on.

Then a resolute female ticket collector, who was just as dirty as the tram, braced herself against the stream of people and shrieked above the crowd in a tone of voice which was impossible to ignore, "Let the cripple get on first!"

She said "creeple" instead of "cripple," and there was no doubt that she meant me. It went right through me, but the crowd actually did make room for me and let me run the gauntlet through the path they had cleared. Behind me they milled together again and the ticket collector escorted me to the VIP box for "creeples" and pregnant women. There I sat, the former sportsman, decathlete, and aspirant to the 1940 Olympics in kayak pairs, never again to stand on a victor's pedestal, but instead to be relegated to the extra places for cripples and pregnant women. Lousy war!

Suitably enraged, I stalked into the American department in charge of hospitals. The friendly soldier with the close–fitting trousers and the sports shirt offered me a chair, and the girl in uniform translated that I could wait there a moment.

The "moment" lasted somewhat longer than that, and I began wondering whether the soldier may have seen action at Baraque Fraiture[*] or Bastogne. In that case I would have loved to know what his experience had been—the plain truth, without polemics, without bias. I would have loved to know whether he had been full of confidence or full of fear; what his attitude towards us was; how he felt about fighting this war in a foreign land for a foreign cause. I would have gladly explained my view of it all to him, and it wouldn't have been very flattering to him and his comrades, for it wasn't they, but their virtually inexhaustible

---

[*] A crossing near Malmédy in Belgium.

supply of bombs, grenades, weapons, and equipment, that filled us with respect. They were afraid of the nights and stopped their attacks if they heard the rat–a–tat from one of our machine guns. Then they battered us with a huge shower of grenades.

Maybe he would say that it would have been pretty stupid to run heroically into bursts of fire from machine guns. A reasonable amount of fear preserves you from death or leg amputations like this. If our politicians send us to war without enough grenades and weapons, then we don't play along. We're not idiots—like you!

Would there have been any point in discussing it with him at all? His country isn't surrounded by a dozen hostile neighbors; it isn't in danger and hasn't been attacked. He fought far from home in a crusade, for an ideal that was different from our understanding of a nation, a people, and a tradition. Besides, he came from an America that hadn't developed organically, but was a country of immigrants from the four corners of the earth, without tradition, without history. There had never been kings and princes in his country. The British, Irish, and Germans would never have subjected themselves to a Frenchman, nor the French to an Italian sovereign. In his great country democracy was the only means of coexistence in a mixture of peoples. This idea of trying to impose democratic freedom upon European nations had already come to nothing after the First World War.

Would he be able to see this and understand us? What motivation did he have for coming into the war? What for? Against what? For the Poles? For France or the British Empire? Or simply against Germany? What did he know about our European problems?

The girl woke me and took me to the major. Robert E. Carr was his name, the plate on his door said. A headquarter chief's nameplate on the door! A new fad! Was the name more important than the function? They were operating under the name of "Public Welfare." The people here were actually behaving not like vengeful victors, but like people from a charitable organization.

I explained to the major that I, as a German, had to leave Austria with my relatives. By chance I had ended up in a hospital here where my relatives lived, and so it would indeed be expedient for us to leave together.

He could see the point of that, and then came what I had expected: I should in that case go to the release camp in Wegscheid and get myself proper discharge papers.

But no, I explained, because if I were to be discharged from the Wehrmacht I would, as a civilian, no longer be able to claim free hospital treatment, and would have to pay for everything, even my artificial limbs and so forth, out of my own pocket. But I had no money, where was I to get it!?

The part about the money convinced him, and he understood that I wanted no more and no less than to be transferred from the hospital in Linz to a hospital in Hannover. My relatives had assured me of transport and even of the care of my cousin, a nurse. The major sent for a welfare lieutenant, who typed out the text I wanted as I dictated it to him. The major signed it and the lieutenant stamped it at the bottom with a thick red stamp.

It was one of the loveliest documents I ever held in my hands, especially since it officially confirmed my rank as a lieutenant in the Wehrmacht.

I stalked back to the hospital on my crutches so that I wouldn't have to ride as a "creeple" on the seat for pregnant women again.

Tuvarisch was disappointed that I had acquired this important document without having to give valerian in exchange, and Manfred had to change his view: the stolid Prussians weren't so undiplomatic after all. Bear Cub's family rejoiced with me and the lieutenant from the next room pestered me until I accompanied him to the welfare officers to get a free passage ticket like mine which avoided the detour through Camp Wegscheid.

And he came within an inch of ruining everything for me!

The welfare lieutenant asked all of a sudden, if he was with the Waffen–SS? He didn't say "Waffen–SS" but "forty–four," and everyone knew that that was how they translated the victory runes on our collar patch. While I calmly waved this silly question aside, the lieutenant said "Yes."

Then I put on a show of indignation, abused him at the top of my voice for having lied to me and left the premises under protest before they could ask me the same stupid question. The poor fellow came from Magdeburg and now had to take the detour over Wegscheid.

Meanwhile, the orthopedist had started on my temporary artificial limb. A veteran who had bitten the dust back in the Franco–Prussian War had bequeathed me his moth–eaten felt foot, while I was supposedly inheriting the lower leg from a famous fighter pilot. The knee joint, which was nailed on with huge staples, was a model from a patent application, an ingenious construction to be sure, but—as it soon turned out—very delicate. The thigh shaft was definitely worth seeing and unforgettable: a hollowed–out tree trunk, on the outside roughly carved into a dodecagonal shape with a hatchet, and not yet freed from the bark in all places. Aided by the stomach and shoulder straps and supported by the crutches, I could stand upright with it and even walk a couple of steps.

I didn't remove the artificial leg again, because I was in a hurry to get out of here before the welfare lieutenant got the idea of asking me whether I, too, had been with the forty–four. Wearing my improvised leg, and with Bear Cub as my baggage handler, I secretly disappeared from the hospital to occupy my new, furniture–laden private quarters in the boxcar, which was standing on a side track. There I practiced walking, and Bear Cub's family noted each bit of progress.

One night I had a great surprise.

First I dreamed that an American general was running through the hospital, loudly calling my name. Fists were pounding against the doors. When I awoke the calling continued, and someone was pounding against the door of the neighboring car. Bear Cub and her parents had also awakened and were listening. "Lieutenant," Bear Cub whispered, "someone is looking for you!"

Who could be looking for me here? No one knew I had changed living quarters—yes, someone did, the lieutenant from the next room.

Bear Cub opened the car door a tiny crack to check the lay of the land. "A single man," she reported, "in civilian clothes, with rucksack—not a Yank and not a railway official."

He came to our wagon.

"Who are you, what do you want?" asked Bear Cub.

"I'm looking for my brother," I heard him say.

It suddenly hit me, like a bolt from the blue, that all this time I had been totally occupied with my own problems, and had scarcely given a thought to my brothers. Somehow I had taken it for granted that they were all still alive, except Rainer, who was missing at Stalingrad, although at that time nothing at all could be taken for granted. Rase must have turned up at Lore's farm and told them that I was on the verge of starving to death. Klaus, who had last been captain at an artillery school, must somehow have reached home and paid his respects to Lore's kitchen at the first opportunity, heard all the news about me there from Rase,

got hold of a couple of wild pigs, brought them to Linz, combed all
the hospitals, and got the tip from the lieutenant in the next room.
After all, he'd been a Boy Scout before he became troop leader.

It was midnight and just like Christmas. Klaus put his rucksack on
the table and unpacked: strong, coarse rye bread, real, dark, aromatic,
and already ground coffee beans, chocolate, sausages, butter, no wild
pigs, but nonetheless Christmas in the middle of August. Twelve hours
later we were still sitting there with our unwashed coffee cups, clean–
scraped sausage skins, thoroughly degreased butter wrapping paper, and
a tin can full of cigarette ashes, in which the stubs and the stubs of the
stubs had been smoked down to the last molecule of tobacco.

The next morning American military police escorted our transport
leader away. Who would have thought it? He *always* went in and out
of the American departments, joking with them as if he were one of
them, acquiring straw and food for the emigrants, organizing papers
and formalities, was always out and about and the soul of the emigrant
train, which by now had grown to fifty cars. But then his five–year–
old son had had a conversation with one of the Yank soldiers:

"Are you a soldier?"

"Yes."

"Are you a brave soldier?"

"Yes."

"So is my Daddy; he was in the Waffen–SS, but I mustn't say that,
it's a secret, do you hear?"

And the Yank brought more brave soldiers to visit the boy's Daddy,
and he thought it was quite in order that they took him along, so that
the brave could be together.

So, Klaus thought, it would be far better if we travelled on ahead to
prepare the quarters for Bear Cub's family in Verden. Klaus was amply
provided with papers. He had come to Linz from Bremen with discharge
papers, and was travelling from Linz back to Bremen with discharge
papers. For me he had discharge papers in the name of Hans Wallner.
Except for the imaginative signatures—if they could be read at all—
everything was authentic. They had been acquired by the British sergeant
who later married my sister.

"That's right," Klaus was saying, "now you must finally rethink.
Everyone else is rethinking too." If the essence of evolution consists
in the development of creatures towards better and better adaptability,

the Germans are *truly* the crown of creation. After 1933 one could have believed that all previous elections must have been fixed, since over ninety percent of all Germans had put their money on Hitler, and yet they couldn't testify to this because they were civil servants, or had superiors who wouldn't have been pleased about this—which actually was not the case at all: the superiors only acted as if they wouldn't have been pleased, because they too were civil servants or had superiors who . . . and so forth.

And now they all had a common scapegoat, who, unprotestingly, had to take upon itself all the excrement of human misbehavior: the SS. I wasn't the SS; Meier, Mueller, and Kunze weren't the SS; we were the decent exceptions. The SS was an anonymous nonperson, a devil with a Nordic angel face and cruel hands, with a death's head and cloven hooves. If another bridge were senselessly blown up, an innocent person arrested, a bicycle or silverware stolen, the matter acquired a veneer of credibility if someone said, "SS"—and then eyebrows were raised as if it had been Satan. To have suffered under such beasts in human form brought you close to achieving that anti-Fascist qualification which was indispensable in order to be licensed by the occupying powers as a journalist, politician, or businessman, or to be tolerated as a civil servant. Due to my dislike of indecency I was now against having been against the regime, if only not to belong to the indecent.

Under the illusion that the trip home would be the same thing as the trip to freedom, we squeezed into a passenger train going west. Austria was by no means properly aware yet of its good fortune in finally being free of Nazi tyranny and independent once again, because it still did not have its borders under control. Instead the control was exercised at Plattling railway station. An American cordon marched out to both sides of the platform, and from a loudspeaker a voice crackled, "All male persons expose their upper left arm. Anyone leaving the train will be shot."

The witch–hunt didn't seem to stop. No one left the train. No one in the compartment said a word, because everyone was waiting to learn whether the others would say, "The swine" or "The poor swine," so that they could join in with the proper refrain.

Klaus whispered in my ear, "Faint!" I fainted and he caught me, dragged me to the door, opened it and shouted, "Orderlies! O–o–orderlies!'' A sentry rushed up with his submachine gun pointed at us. Klaus held my official notice of discharge from the hospital under his nose and told him in broken English that I was badly wounded, leg missing, typhus, Red Cross. The sentry held the paper still closer to his eyes so that he would be able to understand the German text better. Other people came up. Klaus rolled up my trouser leg until the monster of a tree trunk was visible, so they carried me to the Railway Mission[*] and left me in the care of the nurse there. Klaus had to go back to the train.

The nurse was very experienced and knew how she could best help me. She went out into the street and returned ten minutes later. Outside there stood a car, an Adler Trumpf Junior with red leather upholstery. The driver was wearing a forest warden's uniform. Chief forest ranger. How enviable he was, being able to speed along nearly empty roads with a civilian car at seventy kph. True, the car clattered and bounced along the neglected cobblestones, but the red leather upholstery alone imparted an atmosphere of peace, freedom, and well–being. Four years later I bought my first car. It was an Adler Trumpf Junior, but then it wasn't possible to get red leather upholstery.

I learned that there was a prison camp for the Waffen–SS at Plattling. There were continual escapes, which necessitated the train searches. No one wanted to spend twenty years in exile.

"That's your train," said the chief forest ranger, putting his foot down on the accelerator. Was Klaus in the train? Did he realize that I was in this car that was jolting along the road alongside the train? Had he asked about me at the Railway Mission? Naturally the forest ranger knew why he had to take me to the next railway station, but he didn't speak about it. He still kept one foot in the tried and tested nationalism of the community, but with the other he already had a toe–hold in a privileged function normally given only to tried and tested anti–Fascists, so he wasn't quite sure to whom he should express his sympathies. But the re–education campaign that was about to begin on a vast scale would surely not be long in bearing fruit among us adaptable Germans.

Klaus was standing on the platform with our few pieces of luggage, looking about helplessly, when I reached the platform just in time to

[*] Charitable organization for helping needy railway travellers.

see our train chug off. We laughed about our successful ruse and decided first of all to pause here and acquire food coupons on our discharge papers.

In real high spirits we stumbled into the town hall, where Klaus laid our discharge papers on the counter and explained that we had just been freed from prison and were terribly hungry. The civil servant took the papers, studied them carefully, and said, "One moment." He went into an adjoining room that said "Police" on the door.

Oh, oh! What did that mean? Klaus felt in his pockets and said, "Let's get out of here on the double!"

Instead of handing over both our discharge papers he had handed over the papers that said that Gunther Weber had been discharged once from Bremen to Linz and once from Linz to Bremen. It would certainly not have been so simple to give a plausible explanation for this.

We separated after agreeing to meet again at the freight depot. We were well supplied with papers, since I had my real transfer paper and Klaus was travelling as Hans Wallner, who was discharged from Linz to Bremen.

We met up again among the freight cars. A locomotive was steaming at the front of a row of cars. From one of the cars someone called to us, "If you can play skat I still have two places free."

We could play skat.

14

"How important such details can be at times," said Jeanette. The air smelled as if it were wafting over dry undergrowth, as it did back then, and the calm was filled with thousands of chirping crickets, as it was back then, on that Sunday late in May, eighteen years ago. On account of the heat I had already begun my duties at 5:30 that morning and was continuing late into the evening, after a long midday pause. I had adapted to the rhythm of the local population. At midday there was no one to be seen on the road—then or now.

Now, in the heat, I was drawn to water, but water was scarce in Montboyer. Jeannette and I got into the car and opened all the windows.

"Where are you driving now?"

"To the Dronne—was it called the Dronne, where we went swimming that time? We had to cycle more than ten kilometers, Monique, Toni, and the two of us. We met at the Tude bridge so that your parents wouldn't know."

"We borrowed one bicycle from Madeleine and the other from Monsieur Réau, do you remember?"

"Have you learnt to swim in the meantime?"

"No. There's no opportunity for that for miles around; a swimming pool will be built soon in Chalais, but I think I'm already too old to learn."

*   *   *

Never would I have dreamed that one day, tired and shattered from the years of fighting for the Fatherland, I would have to sneak back to this Fatherland like an escaped prisoner. Although I had associated home with peace and security, this proved to be an illusion with every kilometer that brought us closer to home.

Uncle Theobald, Erika's uncle, with whom I had had such a nice chat at Klaus and Erika's wedding, was the first to give me a foretaste of the enthusiasm with which we homecoming warriors would be received. Our freight train stopped somewhere in the Harz. Klaus suggested that we drop in on his cheerful Uncle Theobald. He was a stationmaster, a Party member, as he often liked to emphasize, and proud of his in–laws, strapping fellows that they were, decorated front officers, lads that he and the Fatherland could be proud of and whom he was glad to count among his relatives. In the Waffen–SS, no less! We simply had to go and spend a couple of days with him and regale him with all our experiences. We imagined how pleasantly surprised he would be, and how he would spend a couple of days with us so that we could relax and tell him what we had been through. He would be glad that we'd been spared.

However, it wasn't the pleasant surprise that kept him from closing his mouth, which was hanging open in astonishment: it was fear and horror. Of course, he'd been a Party member himself, even if only a little fellow–traveller with a very small post, and that was only so that he could make his lucrative living. Now here he was, laden with debts and worries. Besides, everyone knew whom his favorite niece had married, as he'd proudly told them, his in-laws were in the Waffen–SS, the bravest of all Germans. And now it would get around that his fancy relatives had sought a hiding place with none other than him.

We got precisely one cup of coffee and a fifteen–minute sermon about the changed situation and the noose that hung around his neck, which was being tightened by Communists and other such types, who wanted to take over his position at the railway station. He absolutely did not want to know anything more about where we came from and where we were going, and didn't even take along a light when he stealthily herded us out through the rear door into the dark night, over wire fences and the remains of walls. But first we had to promise him that we hadn't

Hans Woltersdorf   145

visited or seen him, and no doubt he would have liked to ask for his cold coffee back too.

"You look like a rogue," said Klaus, when it was light again; he insisted that the first thing I do was get my hair cut, as if this were the reason the uncle had sent us away like that. The people in the little Harz village waved at me in a friendly way, as if we were old acquaintances. A farmer even stopped his horse and cart next to me and said, "Well, Karl, are you back again? Does Maria know you've come? Do you want a lift?"

"I have to go to the barber first," I said to play along, and the farmer understood—of course I didn't want Maria to see me looking so untidy. Who was this Maria? Who was this Karl?

Even the barber said, "Hello, Karl," and blustered on with the latest village gossip, who had fallen and who was missing, who had returned home and with what wounds, and—thank God—he didn't let me get a word in edgewise. He had already heard about my leg from Maria, he said, but I'd got off lightly after all. And so I learned that I, Karl, had at some time been billeted here in the village with some unit or other. I was a sergeant and had gotten engaged to Maria, the farmer's daughter, shortly before my transfer east. In any case I, Karl, was not in the Waffen–SS, and I tried to imagine whether Maria was blonde or brunette, heavy or thin, tall or short. Would she realize that I absolutely was not Karl? The war's end had changed people a lot!

"I'm absolutely not this Karl," I said as I pressed the barber's sixty-pfennig fee into his hand. "You must be mixing me up with someone else."

"But, Karl . . ." He looked at me indignantly at first, then penetratingly, and at last he seemed to have understood: Aha! Met someone better in the meantime, now leaving Maria sitting there . . .

One hundred sixty kilometers and two days later saw me sitting at our final station, fifteen kilometers from Lore's farm. Klaus had gone ahead on foot to announce my arrival and organize a carriage from the farm to come and fetch me. A real mass migration came streaming through the station every time a new train arrived, with trolleys, crates, baskets, and cases. Some came from the East, and here they were either stopping or resting from a long, harrowing escape. But the locals, too, were on their way, acquiring, organizing, bartering.

Sometimes I thought I saw familiar faces, but finally I became engrossed in the thought that each face, each figure, each movement triggered off an association with something familiar. But there was Lissa, Lore's schoolmate and my dance–lesson partner.

"Lissa!"

The joy and surprise at seeing me again darkened immediately. Whenever I had come home on leave she had insisted that I go out with her at least once, to our favorite cafe or even dancing.

This time she didn't insist on going out with me.

"I wish you all the best, really, all the best."

Dusk was already falling when the carriage arrived from the farm. Klaus couldn't come along. The mere fact that he, as my brother, had turned up on the farm had attracted attention. Even Lore couldn't come; that would have been still more suspicious, the farm manager told me. And I shouldn't give myself any illusions whatever, as the SS had a bad reputation here. Even though at the railway station in the neighboring town they had kept back the British advance for ten days with an 88mm antiaircraft gun, over there they had superfluously blown up another bridge, and yonder they had energetically defended yet another town. I should just see the cemetery where they had their positions. Totally laid to waste. There were over fifty dead, mostly British. And a Hauptsturmfuehrer always had a girlfriend around. This just wasn't done! The Hoppe family was missing a radio and all their table linen; we were missing two bicycles. "SS," the manager said, raising his eyebrows; and my father–in–law had nearly been arrested and stuck into a concentration camp, because he supposedly let out information about the position of a V-2 launching pad.

The manager tried out his entire denazified routine on me. True, he'd been with the Storm Troopers, even before 1933, but then he'd built up the Cavalry Storm Troopers, which really were nothing more than an organization of cavalrymen in Storm Trooper uniforms. After all, without uniforms there wouldn't have been any organizations any more. And he'd only organized the Cavalry Storm Troopers because of my father–in–law's stud farm, that was all. And everyone could testify to how well he treated the work forces, including the workers from Poland, France, and Yugoslavia. For the sake of the prisoners of war he had risked so much that was really forbidden, I should know that myself— although I knew only that he had become a soldier already in 1938 and since then had spent only his leaves at the farm. But in this "indecent period" he had always remained decent, for when it all came out about what the Nazis had done, then he felt it safe to say that he had actually always been an anti-Fascist. On that account he had recently felt bound in friendship with the veterinary surgeon who had spent four years in a concentration camp. Of course, he'd done some stupid things, this vet, sexual offenses with little children and so on, but a person really can't help it if they're inclined that way. In any case the vet now belongs to the Denazification Committee, a decent chap, certainly not fulfilling his function with thoughts of revenge. On the contrary, he'll gladly turn a blind eye in exchange for a couple of sausages, two blind eyes for some butter as well. Maybe he could even be useful to me, this vet; not yet, but later, when more dust had settled—

I simply couldn't bear this slimy farm manager. I had found him unpleasant even before I got to know him, back in 1938 when he was going into the Wehrmacht and his big going–away party prevented Lore from turning up on our date, as if his party had been more important to her than our rendezvous, which we could, in any case, have only once a fortnight. What could his vet denazify about me, considering I was only seventeen when the war began!

The late summer night was mild. The barking of dogs spread like wildfire before us from farm to farm, as if announcing: he's coming! The cows in the meadow said a friendly moo and the horse snorted and clopped along the road. The shafts creaked and the crescent moon shone from behind the row of birch trees. At the time of our wedding a year ago, and even before that, when I had come home on leave, the carriage fetched me and Lore sat next to me, the moon shone between the birch trees, the dogs announced our arrival, and the cows mooed. In the icy winter nights at Avratin or Isiaslavl I conjured up dreams of this birch–lined road, the crescent moon, and the carriage with the clopping horse that conveyed us to a peaceful paradise.

But the manager—this innocent Nazi—talked endlessly. Personally I have nothing against the Waffen–SS, he emphasized, nothing whatever; after all, he knew them from the Eastern front and Italy. True, they were always better equipped, the Waffen–SS, but they also got quite a bit done, that you had to admit. No, front soldiers have nothing against one another, and to prove that to me he suggested we call each other by the familiar *du* and told me trivial stories in which his men called him "Herr Lieutenant," so that I would realize that he, too, had been a lieutenant and was thus on the same level as I. Then he reflected out loud on what would be the best thing for me to do, and concluded that his best advice to me was to present myself to the British. Voluntarily. And my father–in–law, with whom he had spoken in great detail about this, was of the same opinion.

Voluntarily. Just as at the outbreak of the war. Upright and courageous, as befitted us, I should go and say, "Here I am, reporting for the twenty–year exile with which we've been threatened." Good advice from those old warriors who had so enthusiastically led those of us who spent our puberty in transition from the Weimar Republic to the Third Reich, who believed what splendid times we were headed for, what satisfaction it would be to burst the chains of Versailles under so great a Fuehrer, to repossess the demilitarized Rhineland, to get back the Saar and Austria, to free the Sudetenland and vanquish the megalomaniac Poles, who were senselessly murdering ethnic Germans. And now I should take all the blame upon myself, become the nation's garbage can, into which everyone, having purified himself, could shake off the scum of the collective shame with which all Germans were burdened, because the dragon required its victim. And the more tattooed men they threw to the dragon, the less he demanded others.

It made you want to vomit.

In order not to arouse any suspicion—and he only meant well for me—I had to get out one hundred meters before the farm and let him drive on alone. I had already learnt to creep along in secret as a Cub. Going around behind, past the chicken coops, and announced by angry clucking and furiously yapping dogs, I reached the straw carpet of the stable and from there made it into the laundry room.

It was a parody of the return of Odysseus.

"And Lore?" asked Jeanette.

Lore found it far more humiliating than I did, and we became sworn conspirators, attempting to shape our future ourselves, not asking for anything more, no help, and above all no well meant advice. If I were illegally living on borrowed time, then what lay ahead of me ought to be no more than an interesting challenge compared to what lay behind.

So often it is the little chances that decisively influence the course of a life: chances that bring forth life, chances that destroy it or preserve it. No wonder complicated scientific theories maintain that chance is the mother and the father of all things. Everyone can find these theories confirmed a thousand times over in his own fate.

However, it can be contested whether chance is not merely a comfortable excuse when the chain of cause and effect can no longer be followed, or when results cannot be predicted from the wealth of influences and events; it is still precisely the unpredictable human being, with his spontaneous whims and ideas, who engineers these chances. But if the course of human events is somehow steered or directed, whether by God or by natural laws, and if this evolution has a purpose or a meaning, then chances are, of their very essence, meaningless. Whether and how one ignores or seizes the beckoning of Fate is as different as are humans themselves.

Then came Aunt Adele, or rather what was left of the woman who had once been so happy, so in love with life and ready for a joke. She was dressed only in an underskirt and had tied up the rest of her earthly belongings in a handkerchief. She had made her way from Koeslin, and what she was able to say, tearfully and racked with sobs, transported us back to medieval horror stories of abduction, murder, plunder, and rape, of human game delivered up defenseless and without rights to frenzied, drunken bands of soldiers, with no other choice than to suffer, take one's own life, or let it be taken. There are limits to the describable, and beyond is a transcendental realm that is just as unreal if described with normal vocabulary as is *Aida* if one were to try to give an impression of it without using music or lyrics. Only in these first hours did she speak about it; after that I never again heard her speak of it for the rest of her life. And why should she? For the dialectician of re–education these events were merely the revenge that could be expected for German crimes, and for those trained in such explanations, experiences like Aunt Adele's had the air of failed group sex.

After ten days Aunt Adele had once again recovered something of her former composure. We hatched plans. Aunt Adele wanted to go to the Rhineland, to see whether her brother and sister were still alive. To the Rhineland! That was a place which until then I had travelled through only fleetingly, a place where no one knew me and into which I could disappear. I would accompany her as far as Bonn. There she would refer me to a friend of hers and there I could study. Not I, naturally, but someone else by the name of Horst Werner, whose existence would begin from today onwards. I typed out a new certificate, according to which this former Lieutenant Horst Werner was to be transferred from a hospital in Linz to a hospital in Bonn. I painted in the stamp with red drawing ink, and even Robert E. Carr would have recognized the signature as his very own. Then, to be on the safe side, we also fashioned a discharge certificate with a whole new past for me, and we searched a Western story for typical American names for as many signatures and stamps as possible, which we transferred from authentic documents with the assistance of boiled eggs.

And Lore would follow as soon as I had firm ground under my feet: she would follow as Mrs. Werner. The railway trains still had special compartments for the severely war–injured, and Aunt Adele would come in as my companion; if she didn't get a seat, we would take turns.

At the crack of dawn Lotte, the coach horse that had been spared from war service, took us to the station, to the start of an exhausting future that, again through chance, turned out completely different from what we had pictured.

15

We retraced our cycling excursion along the thickly overgrown bank of the sluggishly flowing river. Even Jeanette had not been here since then; water and swimming were not for her. That time when we—Toni and I—got the idea to go out swimming, she and Monique didn't even own swimsuits. They sewed together a couple within hours so as not to be killjoys.

Her memories were quite different from mine. She showed me a place where we had stopped first, since the water was very calm here, exactly right for nonswimmers, and the bank was more densely overgrown, dense enough that one could hide in it; after all, they were very embarrassed in their swimsuits, not only because of their briefness but because of their white skin, and besides—they were half–naked! And they certainly did not want to expose themselves to the blazing sun. We had even argued, she maintained, because Toni and I were looking for deeper water for swimming, and more sun. I remembered nothing about this.

But there was the open spot on the bank, and the small boat was still there, but it was a different one, somewhat smaller and more brightly painted. The stake to which it was fastened and on which we had hung up our clothes was still the same.

We got out, looked for a shady spot, and sat down. The island was there, too, but Jeanette insisted that she had never gotten into the boat, because Toni had rocked it so much that she was afraid. I must have been wrong when I maintained that she and Monique had clung to me. Our memories coincided only in that Toni and I had swum to the island and left them behind, alone. The island was shady and we had called over to them how lovely it was there and why didn't they come too, and we had made fun of them because they couldn't swim and wouldn't dare to get into the boat either.

"We were really furious," Jeanette said, "and we swore: *'Vous êtes méchants! Bêtes! Filous!'* Then we put our clothes on, got on our bicycles, took your bikes along, and rode away, fifty meters on. We watched you from there."

No, Monique had not put Toni's jacket on and threatened to go into the water with it; it was his trousers. They were too long on her, even though she had rolled up the legs four times, and she had looked like Charlie Rivels in them. Jeanette laughed in amusement at the memory. "And when you came back to the riverbank we crept up and attacked you like Indians."

Right, it had been something like that. Then a tussle ensued, during which we got the clothes off them again and they squealed like pigs. And that aroused the curiosity of the boat's owner, and he came just as we had made peace and were making up. What must he have thought, Monsieur Roquebrun?

"You knew him?"

"Oh yes, that's why it was so awkward. He owns the old mill farther upstream and his ladies are good customers, friends of mine now. We must absolutely visit them later."

Of course we would visit them some time. Three or four years later we did so. My niece, Klaus's daughter, spent part of her holidays there. They gave a huge party. Forty or more people were there, including many children, one of whom was a guest in our house for a number of weeks, Philippe, a nice, well brought–up boy.

"Are you still called Horst Werner?" Jeanette asked.

"No."

"Did you study? What did you study? Did anyone discover that your name was false? It must have been difficult for Lore to go along with that."

*　　*　　*

Before Aunt Adele disappeared behind the French demarcation line, incommunicado at first, and before I made my way to a hospital in Bonn in accordance with my American certificate, she introduced me to an old friend of hers. Her name was Meta Pfaff, and she owned a miraculously undamaged house in the civil–servant district of Bad Godesberg. She was a spindly bundle of nerves and suffered from an insatiable, ravenous appetite. And so when Aunt Adele whispered to her that I had a magnificent farmhouse in the family she realized what charitable ambitions she had and dragged me along from one good friend to another, and to them too she whispered something about a farm that could be an inexhaustible supply of fat and meat. With each friend the supply grew larger until, by the time we reached the widow Moll, it was finally large enough to get me a promise of two rooms with use of the kitchen.

All my possessions could be accommodated in one not–very–bulging rucksack, which contained among other things four tins of food, which forthwith occupied a conspicuous place of honor on top of the clothes cupboard and exerted a magical power of attraction on Meta Pfaff and her wide acquaintanceship.

Lore's arrival was eagerly awaited, not only by me but also by these others, who hoped she would bring the milk and honey of Lower Saxony with her and invite the starving masses to the orgies. We, Mr. and Mrs. Werner, became guest stars in the diverse coffee circles and also received regular invitations to the unforgettable cultural evenings at Professor Althoff's, who earned his coal by charging an entry fee of one briquette per person or one–and–a–half for a married couple. In exchange we had the honor of hearing the singing voice of his seventy–year–old wife who at least by her bearing, gestures, and ferocious breathing technique still gave some idea of how she must once have shattered the Dresden Opera. The Professor himself accompanied her at the piano with the most unique flourishes of his hands and arms.

Naturally I had immediately applied to study while I was still in hospital in Bonn. The choice of fields was limited to philology, and barely one hundred places were available, for which there were around two thousand applicants. Consequently a sorting–out process was necessary. The one–armed professor had an informal but searching discussion with me about all the great men of recent history who, at least because of their Christian convictions, would have been anti–Fascists had they lived in our time and been able to choose whether to be pro– or anti–

Fascist. Had he known where and under what circumstances we would meet again a few months later he could have spared himself this silly fuss, but the outcome was that I quite legally joined those elect on whose democratic convictions the new academic Germany could be built. And so at last it stood in black and white on my self–fashioned discharge certificate that I was a student.

Unlike Lore, I had soon become so accustomed to my new name and my new past that I wouldn't even have turned around if someone had called my real name. Moreover, as a result of a thorough examination of my physical condition I possessed an authentic Severely War–Disabled Certificate that certified me as eighty percent severely war–disabled and entitled the other twenty percent to use the tram between Bonn and Bad Godesberg free of charge. Along with this I was allowed to be measured for a proper artificial limb at the state's expense. The soldiers of the Waffen–SS were cut off from any orthopedic care, as well as from any war–disabled pension, so that those who hobbled along on crutches and one leg were suspected of belonging to the underprivileged tattooed class.

By this time my list of sins, represented by document falsification and unauthorized claims on constitutional privileges, must have added up to several years' imprisonment.

An increasing source of annoyance was my unplaned tree–trunk limb with the ingenious patent model at the knee joint. It was happening more and more frequently that my lower leg remained bent backwards in the middle of the shopping street and would not swing back down again, either on its own or when forced. I don't know what the normal–legged population must have thought when I hopped past them, my leg sticking up backwards at a right angle, into the nearest doorway in order to pull down my pants. I always had a screwdriver and a square end wrench in my trouser pocket, and only when I began to potter about with these did the impression of being an exhibitionist fade and give way to a desperately oblivious curiosity. Least pleasant of all were those women who, on becoming aware of the tree stump that my under-pants had exposed, felt obliged to express their sympathy with a voluntary donation, such as a dispensable bread coupon.

And one day Klaus stood at the door. He had learned that I had gotten hold of a student place and he wanted one too. Naturally he couldn't be my brother, but, at best, a distant cousin. I took him to the one-armed professor, who happened to be in a good mood just then and, on the basis of my recommendation, had no doubt whatsoever that my distant cousin would be a good democrat. And so he got a fold–away seat in the lecture theater, while the widow Moll, fearing that he, too, might want to use her kitchen, secured him a room elsewhere in Bonn.

Although everything had gone smoothly until now, my student status and our accommodations were assured, and we mixed with a totally harmless circle of unsuspecting middle–class people, our thoughts were very much concerned with the problem of the future. For me this temporary arrangement was, in any case, a better alternative than prison or exile, but Lore found it very oppressive to have to live with unborn and unchristened identities, because sooner or later it would cause immense complications. If our hide–and–seek game should ever be uncovered, the course of studies completed by Horst Werner would have been a waste of time, for a subject that someone has only in their head but not on paper is of less use than a course of studies completed on paper but not in the head. She made a list of all our punishable shady deeds: we claimed food coupons for nonexistent persons; I received a war–disabled pension, although only forty marks, which I had indeed earned but not merited; they made me an artificial limb to which my missing leg, but not I, was entitled; and the list of fake certificates, papers, and documents continued to lengthen.

In the midst of these reflections there suddenly came a telegram requiring Lore to come home without delay. Since no reason was given we imagined that all hell must have broken loose somewhere. Three days later Pauline, my mother–in–law, arrived to take Lore's place in my household. Pauline was the only true anti–Fascist in the family, the only one I had heard curse about Hitler, the local group leader, the senseless two–front war, or the hot–pot Sunday. But now, when all the former Nazis seemed to have developed cases of amnesia about their recent past, she did an about–face and came out against the idea that I should give myself up voluntarily.

Lore had to come because I was being sought. Since people quite often turned up at the farm who could have been taken for me because of their looks, some frustrated resistance fighters felt obliged to make up for lost time by denouncing me: the officer from the Waffen–SS is there!

I was quite honored that on my account the British turned up one evening with four tanks and a reconnaissance company, surrounded the farm, and then initiated a comprehensive action in which they first arrested the flaxen–haired milker who had just escaped from Silesia and then took away the farm manager as well. Within the next few days the two of them would surely come to an agreement about which one of them was I. Wasn't the manager right, though, in advising me to give myself up and thereby spare him this bit of bad luck! In addition, my father–in–law had aroused suspicion by barricading the house, for a few weeks earlier Polish freedom fighters had attacked the farm and plundered and taken what they could carry and what they could load into a cart. This hadn't been an entirely bloodless event; Pauline, the only brave one around, was badly knocked about and still had a thick scar visible on her head. And so now, at yet another approach of an armed force, my father–in–law feared that the Poles had come to finish their business, though in view of the superiority of the tanks he soon gave up his defense. The British wanted no jewelry and no valuables, only me, and they took the milker and the farm manager away as substitutes.

When the error came to light they returned and asked for the SS wife, since wherever she was, I could not be far away.

"Where is your daughter?"

Pauline gave a statement that to the best of her knowledge and belief her daughter was with a girl friend in Hamburg and, at their request, she gave them the address.

Then we got an urgent telegram, for the Tommies would realize sooner or later that the daughter they were running to earth in Hamburg was not the SS wife but her sister. Pauline escaped a possible dressing–down by travelling to Bad Godesberg, while my father–in–law, a histrionically totally untalented Lower Saxon, was left to explain, "Oh! You meant the other one! She was just out in the neighborhood."

Since my coffee circle was naturally interested in why Lore did not come along to the next party, I had to lie to them in complete detail about what had happened. We were in Cologne to meet an acquaintance, and Lore had sprained or even broken her foot in a pothole. Our acquaintance, a physician from Hannover, had taken her to Hannover straight away in his car. There she lay, in a convalescent home, poor thing.

*   *   *

One day at the end of January 1946, what had always been in the air, and which would happen with no explanation, finally happened. I was just on my way back from a new certificate forgery at the town hall, where I had been claiming our food coupons and Mrs. Moll's pension, when I noticed a familiar Adler Trumpf Junior in front of our house. No, it wasn't the head forester from Plattling, but the police, as the lettering on the trunk proclaimed. A man was leaning on the front garden fence and looking up and down the street.

I was, indeed, absolutely certain that I had done nothing *new* that was forbidden, but who doesn't quickly search his conscience when he sees a policeman waiting in front of his door? If I were simply to go by everything would be all right; I would be warned, could secretly pack my things, and turn up again somewhere else, in order to disappear again. But my conscience was so clean and my curiosity so great that I wanted to chance it, and so I turned into the front garden.

Immediately the gentleman lifted his head and asked, "Are you Mr. Werner?"

Whether I said yes or no I could have been accused of lying, and so I lied, "Yes."

"Is your brother here too?"

Whoops! That was surprising. Why was he asking about my brother? I had told no one anywhere around here that I even had a brother.

"My brother? What makes you think my brother could be here?"

"That's just how it is," he said. "Is he here or not?"

"As you see, no one is here except me," I said. "What about it?"

"I'm just asking."

"And I've answered you truthfully. Satisfied?"

"I am, but what good is that! I must ask you to come along."

"Where? To the police station?"

"Yes."

In considering whether I should now put on a show of indignation or say nothing at all, I chose a friendly middle road. "I certainly don't understand your reasons, but will you please allow me to bring the widow Moll her pension and her food coupons?"

"Please," he said, walking ahead of me. Pauline opened the door and the man addressed her as Mrs. Moll. He had obviously already questioned her, for she was standing there red as a beet.

"I really have no idea what the gentleman wants with me, Mrs.

Moll,'' I said to Pauline, ''but it's surely a misunderstanding that can soon be cleared up. Meanwhile, here are your food coupons and your pension.''

I never again entered the apartment in Bad Godesberg.

This time I wasn't so able to enjoy the ride through the city in the Adler, because I had to comb through my most recent past for some gaps or tactical errors that could have drawn attention to Klaus as my brother. But why would anyone want Klaus? Because he was once a troop leader? And besides, if he were my brother his name would be Werner too. However hard I tried I could make no sense of the matter, and the gentleman with me uttered not another word until we stopped in front of the police station at the town hall.

Instead of interrogating me or bringing me before anyone, the police officials set in motion routine machinery in which scarcely a word was spoken. They emptied all my pockets down to the dirty handkerchief, and even recorded the torn–off trouser button. ''One envelope, un-opened.'' Thank God: because in it were two blank forms with stamps and signatures from my local registration authority, which Pauline had brought me to prepare a notarized copy of my high school diploma. I had to sign a receipt that everything had been put, according to the rules, into a closed and sealed envelope, which caused me to commit forgery before the very eyes of the police.

When I politely asked whether anyone could explain the great interest in me, one of the officials explained that they didn't know either, because it was all happening by order of the FSS. I hadn't heard the ''F,'' and in astonishment asked, ''SS?'' He then explained that FSS was the abbreviation for the British Field Security Service.

They led me to a large cell, where I had to remove and surrender my artificial leg. In case I should try to escape.

''Disgusting!'' cursed the two men in their mid–fifties, who did not at all look like jailbirds. They had laid a profusion of slips of paper on the table in front of them and were writing lots of mathematical formulas on them. ''Or are you a criminal?''

''Not that I know of,'' I said, ''but these days who can say that with any certainty?''

''Were you a Nazi?''

''I never had the time for that. When the war broke out I was seventeen and became a soldier; could you be a Nazi already at that age?''

"War criminal?"

"Of course. If the war was a crime and I took part in it, I'm a war criminal."

"Why have they locked you up?"

"On the orders of the FSS, they said."

"Aha."

"And you?"

They were engineers, works directors in a carbon brush factory that employed many foreign workers. They had been denounced for maltreating the workers.

"Did you?"

"It doesn't matter at all."

"How long have you been here?"

"Four weeks."

"And? Have you already been convicted?"

"No, not even questioned."

It was certainly not boring here. After ten minutes they brought me a pencil and paper and asked me to write down my life history. The full truth. With pleasure! I breathed into Horst Werner a complete soul with pedigree: born in Crossen–on–the–Oder two years before my birth, since I had already made myself older so that my application to study would receive preferential treatment. I mentioned nothing about brothers or sisters, and why should I; after all, it was going to be my life history. Of course I was in the Hitler Youth, Marine Division. For my military career I needed fantasy less than I needed sound knowledge about units and their positions and deployment, but I spent most of my time in hospitals and was finally in the "Linz" Regiment.

While in the process of creating my autobiography I was disturbed by loud lamentations outside the door. Someone furiously roared, "Heil Hitler!" and someone else roared, "Hold your tongue!" This exchange was repeated a couple of times, then the door was pushed open, a man stumbled in, clicked his heels, raised his right arm and shouted, "Heil Hitler, you Nazis!"

"If you don't hold your tongue right now . . ." the otherwise good–natured policeman threatened, but the new detainee replied, "Heil Hitler, you asshole!"

He couldn't calm down, paced furiously up and down and hammered on the closed door. "Let me out of here! I don't belong in here, you, you . . ."

"Why don't you belong in here?" one of the mathematicians asked. "Weren't you a Nazi?"

"Never," he said, "but I'm becoming one now."

"If you weren't a Nazi, what were you?"

"A Communist. Everyone in Godesberg knows that I was a Communist functionary, even after '33."

"And then you became a Nazi, like most of the other Communists?"

"No, not I, never. The Storm Troopers locked me up after the burning of the Reichstag."

"For how long?"

"Three or four days."

"And after that? Did you become a Nazi then?"

"I never thought of it, no, never."

"But Communists aren't locked up any more these days; on the contrary."

"I'd thought so too. But back then I cleared off to Spain and fought on the side of the International Brigade against Franco."

"Then you're something of an active resistance fighter."

"And how! But the way our people dealt with the priests and nuns there, no. You know, my wife is a strict Catholic and she can stay one as far as I'm concerned. We have five children. But that was too awful; so then I went over to Franco's side and joined in, half–heartedly: they weren't so much better either."

"And then you became a Nazi?"

"Not on your life! I'd had it up to here and wanted to go home, and Franco's people gave me a paper confirming that I'd fought on their side against the Communists."

"Then you were rehabilitated and could become a Nazi?"

"No chance! Because of my experiences with the International Brigade they stuck me in counter–intelligence and thought I was an expert. But how much could I tell, what could I cause to happen! Nothing! I didn't feel like doing it either. I was a flop. Then they shoved me off to the Marines, where I was one of the mutineers already after the First World War, but they didn't know that."

"And so then you had a big career there? U–boats or something?"

"That's what you think! I wasn't even an able seaman; I had it up to here and went ashore in Bordeaux, ran off and joined the partisans; they were still the only sensible Communists in Western Europe. First they thought I was a spy, but then I showed them. As long as everything was still really tricky and dangerous I was good enough. But then France won and de Gaulle, who had something against the Communists, came back, and they decided I was a German Nazi and shoved me off to Germany, these assholes!''

"And then you started up another Communist Party here, right?''

"That's just what I planned. So, finally, I'd managed it, nothing more can happen to me, I thought.''

"Naturally, that's what you were predestined for!''

"That's right, I was pre—was always a Communist, but then some asshole somewhere fished around and found I'd been in counter–intelligence, and for that they arrested me.''

"And now you finally want to become a Nazi?''

"Yes. It's garbage, but when I think about it, the Nazis still treated me most decently, and now I'm being locked up with them; so now they'll have their way, I'm becoming a Nazi!''

Without being invited he studied my life history and saw that they had taken away my artificial leg in case I thought of escaping; this elicited further obscenities from him and confirmed him in his decision to become a Nazi.

16

"Why did they arrest you? Who denounced you?" Jeanette asked.

Thinking about this question had kept me awake the entire night.

There was nothing in my tactical behavior in the coffee circle, at the Althoffs' cultural evenings or anywhere else that could have aroused suspicion or given rise to a malicious denunciation. To no one had I divulged my identity under the seal of silence. Only Aunt Adele knew the truth about me, but she was cut off on the other side of the strictly controlled French occupation zone. Then I was annoyed that I hadn't asked the policeman to produce an arrest warrant, for it would have had to give the reason for arresting me! Or did they want to teach me a lesson and demonstrate that even in Nazi Germany arrests took place without warrants, on account of denunciation or even only on suspicion? Were they trying to replace one evil with another?

For breakfast they served me my artificial leg, and a guard stayed there until I had put it on, washed and shaved, and was ready to go. At reception I was given back the sealed envelope and had to sign that I had got back all my possessions in good order. The policeman from the car was there again.

"Am I released?"

He shrugged his shoulders and said, "First you must go to the FSS."

This was housed just opposite the redoubt. I had to wait in a little room with a bay window. The policeman closed the door and climbed a flight of creaky stairs. I was alone and the window beckoned as a neat way of exiting; but then I would never find out why I had been arrested. The telltale blank forms with stamps and signatures were still hiding in the envelope. I tore them into tiny bits and let them flutter out the window, and as the last scrap was carried away by the wind the policeman stood in the doorway again with an impenetrable official air. "Come with me."

An English officer lounged behind the desk, enjoying a chat with a rather unattractive girl. Her nose was much too large and under it was a bright red mouth. What an awful lot of lipstick! We weren't used to this yet, so that she spontaneously conjured up a picture of the kind of baboon whose erogenous zones are similarly colored red to intensify its sex appeal. German girls didn't—yet—do this, and besides, there was no lipstick for them then.

In the manner typical of those subalterns who try to acquire authority through authoritarian behavior, the officer let me stand there as if I weren't there at all. He did the same to the policeman. By exchanging trivial memories of yesterday evening with his girl he wanted to show us what insignificant little nobodies we were. This killed any willingness I may have had to compromise. Then, as if by accident, he took hold of a file that was so empty he couldn't even leaf through it. Unfortunately he didn't let me see what he was staring at in it.

"So, your name is Horst Werner," he said as a result of his lengthy study of my file; and since this wasn't a question I saw no reason to answer.

"Since when has that been your name?"

For years I had practiced not batting an eyelid when an explosion or a bang happened near me, just to show the men that such things couldn't frighten me. Did he only suspect or really know that this wasn't my real name? I didn't do him the favor of reacting and simply answered, "Since 4 November 1919—or maybe two weeks later, after I was christened."

"And so you were born with that name," he concluded and held in his hand the life history I had written yesterday. "In Crossen–on–the–Oder. Where is that?"

"On the Oder."

For an instant he looked as if he were about to become outraged, but then he assumed the role of a person who really doesn't need to ask, since he already knows everything.

"Where is your brother?"

The only question and the same question that the policeman had asked me, and which didn't take me any further. He was going to have to come out with some more, and so I said, truthfully, "Fallen at Stalingrad."

"Don't give me such rubbish!" he suddenly burst out.

"If that's rubbish," I said calmly, "then I'd like to know what is to be taken seriously at all these days. My brother fell at Stalingrad."

"Do you have more than one brother?" he asked.

"Yes."

"Where are they?"

"In order for me not to have to give you such a rubbishy answer again, you'll have to tell me which one you mean."

He looked at the file again, in which there was obviously something more than my life history. After some searching he said,

"The one beginning with K."

A merciful stork had bestowed on me two brothers whose names begin with K: Klaus and Kurt.

"Oh, you mean Kurt?"

"Kurt, who else?"

Now my grey cells were working at top speed. So, he only knew my brother's initial. Had someone who knew me better denounced me, they would have known the full name and they would have known that only Klaus could have played any kind of incriminating role. And so I had to feel my way further and told the whole truth: "Kurt is a prisoner of war."

Kurt, in any case, was of no interest whatever to the FSS or any denazifiers at all, a careless, casual nonsoldier; a lieutenant in 1940 and still one when the war ended. I last saw him in Isiaslavl near Staro Konstantinov.

The Tommy furiously slammed the file on the desk and yelled, "Don't lie! Your brother isn't a prisoner any more. Why are you lying?"

Then he looked at the file once more and asked, "Why is it dangerous that your brother is near you?"

Now it dawned on me. Aha, the post censorship? Someone in the family must have written to me and again given me superfluous advice.

My mother? Make sure nothing happens to you, turn off the gas once the milk has boiled, don't let the bath tub overflow. . . . That could have been my mother. Or my father–in–law? Damnation, I didn't want any more well intended advice!

But at the same time the Tommy had given me a clue for a plausible story. I assumed a sad expression and admitted,

"You know, that's so. With a good deal of effort I managed to get a student place. Only people with an irreproachable past get that. And then one day my brother turned up. He had escaped and wanted to hide out with me. You know yourself how strictly it's forbidden to take in escaped POWs. I would at least have lost my student place. And so I had to send him away, which he couldn't understand. Or should I have denounced him?"

He didn't want to expect that of me and he asked brusquely, "What was your brother?"

"A lieutenant."

"What else?"

"First an advance observer, then an artillery officer. I don't know what else."

"What was he before that?"

"A pupil taking his college entrance exams. He was nineteen when the war broke out. What should he have been before that?"

"And then why is it so dangerous for him to be near you?"

"As I said, because I can be punished if I hide an escaped POW."

"That can't be the only reason."

"Under Hitler we became used to strictly obeying rules and prohibitions, and I assume that you don't take such prohibitions lightly either."

"And where is your brother now?"

"I don't know. He couldn't accept that I was sending him away; he found it unfair, unbrotherly. We quarreled and he left in a huff."

"Where to?"

"He wanted to study as well. He may have gone to Goettingen or to the East Zone, in the region of Crossen. They aren't so awkward about POWs there, I believe."

"You know that very well," he persisted.

"No, I don't know."

"You just don't want to say it."

"I advised my brother to let himself be properly discharged, but he was afraid of being sent back to France again."

"And he was afraid of that?"

"Would you go behind bars voluntarily?"

"Behind bars! Now you've given yourself away. So your brother is a war criminal!"

"A war criminal, don't make me laugh!"

"Then where is your brother?"

"I don't know. Maybe he'll write to me, then you'll find out—presumably sooner than I."

"You don't think we're so stupid that we'll give you the chance to warn your brother!"

"How can I warn him when I don't even know—"

"Because you're lying!" he roared. "You're all lying here. You know that very well. And now clear off."

"Home?"

"No, to prison!"

"What am I supposed to do there?"

"Think about where your brother is."

The policeman took me by the arm and led me away; he knew his superior and knew that he couldn't be fooled with. I saw how he shook his head, deep in thought, as we descended the stairs. Apparently this was all painful for him, very painful.

"And you do the dirty work for people like him?" I reproached him.

"What can I do! I'm a detective. I was a Party member and even a block leader. If I refuse they'll lock me up, and then maybe someone else will come, a Communist, who's much worse."

Yes, what could he do! The same as he had always done. Carry out orders, regardless of exactly who was giving them and without thinking about whether they were just or sensible.

"Can I do something for you?" he asked.

I sent him to my apartment to get toilet articles and other such things that one needs in prison. Maybe a few more cigarettes, and he had to tell the widow Moll what he had witnessed here, so that she wouldn't think I was a criminal. He did this all carefully and surprised me with several packets of cigarettes which Meta Pfaff's coffee circle had collected for me.

"Julien was nearly two years old then," Jeanette said. "I had already returned to Montboyer from Paris. We both had our problems then, you and I; that was the price we had to pay. But I don't regret a thing, and I'm glad you're alive, even as Horst Werner.''

Meanwhile we had untied the boat and were rowing along in a leisurely manner. The island had become overgrown by high shrubbery. Jeanette let her feet hang down in the cooling water and looked at her watch.

"Is it late? Do we have to go home?"

"For me there's no time to keep track of today."

"And it's Sunday anyway."

"Oui, une très, très belle journée!"

We helped each other out of the boat, and she asked to stay here for a little while longer. We leaned against the car and looked back at our bathing spot.

"Did they lock you up only because you couldn't say where your brother was?"

"Yes, they gave me no other reason."

"Did they release you soon after? Were you able to go on with your studies?"

"No."

"And your brother Kurt?"

"At that time he actually had escaped from being a French prisoner of war."

"Then you were telling the truth."

"Yes, but I wasn't aware of it as yet. I first learned of it much later."

"In that case you were precognitive, a seer," she laughed. "And what happened next?"

From Bad Godesburg I was transferred to a simple cell in the Bonn Prison. A plank bed, a bucket, and bare walls on which the previous occupants had carved notches to mark the passing of the days. Single cells are dreadful! The things that go through your head! If I had committed some crime I would have had to reckon with being caught and punished according to a proper law and would have been prepared for a prison sentence. That there were people who wanted to get revenge on the Waffen–SS, all right, such a thing could only be expected of primitive peoples, but not of the British, who are known for their fairness. But my official offense was not being able or willing to say where my brother was. Such tyranny gave me a sense of foreboding. I thought of Lore and Pauline and hoped that they would wait quietly and not get involved. I thought of Klaus, who certainly suspected nothing, and would perhaps visit me again in the next few days and thus fall into a trap. I had to warn him.

My guard had long since become insensitive to it all. "A crazy time," he thought. "In the last months of the war I no longer understood why they were locking up this person or that person, and now I understand it even less: honorably retired generals, professors—and you, because you don't know where your brother is."

"Would you do me a favor?"

"As long as you don't directly ask me to let you escape secretly."

"Nothing like that. But I really must have my new artificial leg, which should be ready around now. At Koenigstrasse 2."

That was where Klaus had his room. The artificial limb workshop was a few doors down in a side street. Klaus would send him on there. I knew that the leg would really not be finished for two months yet. The guard did me the favor and returned without the leg. The address hadn't been correct. "But a man lived there who knew you and gave the right address."

And so Klaus was warned.

I stayed only a week in solitary confinement in Bonn; I was just beginning to get used to it. It is strange: a person is not capable of getting used to chaotic confusion, even if such a condition has its more pleasant side; but as soon as rhythmic, precisely punctual patterns are introduced, when a person knows exactly that the guard is coming any minute, in ten minutes there will be a walk in the courtyard, half an hour after awakening comes the coffee, at 10 P.M. the lights go out— then one's existence becomes urgently self–evident, and one reacts inwardly only if one of the expected phases is omitted or even only delayed. The rhythmic order turns the initial uncertainty into certainty.

With thirty other detainees I was loaded into a van. None of them looked like criminals. The man next to me was a former major–general in the Storm Troopers, who sketched this entire arrest routine with Rhenish humor. For hours we drove through the expanse of ruins that had once been the Ruhr District, through cities that had only their bones and eye–sockets left to show, like gnawed–away skeletons. The naked chimneys rose out of the ruins like crosses on graves, and children in much–too–large camouflage jackets and women in shapeless uniform coats with head scarves for hairdos crawled like rats out of the rubble. The feminine element was still there and ten years later was able to put itself on display much more frivolously.

What an uncritical being the intelligent, critical human individual basically is in his immense adaptability! Within a single generation we enthusiastically embarked on the First World War for Emperor and Fatherland, bled to death in the entanglement of matériel battles, followed a backyard poverty or a mad craving for pleasure in liberal democracy, fought one another in a multitude of factions, once again threw ourselves into national tasks with National Socialist idealism, redeemed ourselves from an economic grave, and swung from success to success at a breathtaking pace, only to sacrifice all our economic, social, and ethical achievements to a war against half the world.

Just yesterday these people were prepared to defy an enemy who broke all written and unwritten rules of war to wage a war of annihilation against their homes, their kitchens, chairs and beds; who drove them into their cellars night after night, where they were buried alive, burned, smothered, and killed, and first lived through all the tortures of hell and met fates that would forever remain unknown, because the victims had taken their testimonies with them to the grave. Now they were there again, like ants, ready to help, to work, to worry, to obey, to hope, and once more to adapt themselves to the view that the victims were really the guilty.

The people waved to us, furtively, to be sure, but with their will to live obviously unbroken. Stress with its inevitable diseases, to which they ought to have been subject in these exhausting times, passed them by without a trace. They were still sound in mind and body; they did not crave health cures and hospitals. Despite the superhuman achievements that the war had demanded of them, they were throwing themselves into hard work not to rest until once again they achieved a miracle, an economic miracle that eclipsed all their former European opponents. Only then, in the peaceful and liberal comfort of their beds of affluence, would the children of this economic miracle be overcome by stress and fill the hospitals in greater numbers than the soldiers ever did.

When would the next person come along and persuade the Germans to march like lemmings to their own destruction, convinced that of their own free will they were sacrificing themselves in a senseless battle, or gradually degenerating in a state of continuing peace and prosperity? If it was so easy to turn obedience into blind obedience, discipline into uncritical submission, truth into lies and lies into truth, duty into stupidity, and the Fatherland into a nation of criminals, then the human individual, as crown of creation, has less character than the wolf or the snake, who, unwaveringly led by their certain instincts, always remain what they are and do neither good nor evil.

It was a damp, chilly day. We disembarked in an enclosure of barbed wire, corrugated iron huts, and tens of thousands of people, an internment camp near Recklinghausen. Freezing and standing in the mud, we waited to be dealt with.

A Tommy tapped me with a stick, which was supposed to mean, "Follow!" I followed, slowly and clumsily, to where I was supposed to think about whether I didn't know where my brother was after all.

There were only amputees, cripples, blind and injured in the special barracks. A one–armed man was tipping coal into an iron stove, and a tall blond fellow hobbled over to me, smiling mischievously. "Man, where did they catch you?"

I looked at him as if he had just offended and insulted me. Who was he? Who was he? No one dare recognize me here!

"Don't you remember? Baraque Fraiture, the armored crossing, where Rosenbaum lost his leg; the Battle of the Bulge."

I looked at him helplessly. Of course I knew him. He was the lieutenant from the Reconnaissance Division, with whom I'd—and then he said it.

"We sat in a hole together and made a little fire out of mortar gunpowder pellets. It was like a miracle: for some reason or other we left our hole for just two minutes, and just then it was destroyed by a bull's–eye."

"Bull's–eye? Where?"

"You were the leader of the Fourth Company!"

"Which Fourth Company?"

"DF."

"DF? What's that?"

"Good heavens: The 'Der Fuehrer' Regiment! Were you injured in your head? Forgotten everything?"

"Not at all, my head is in perfect shape. I know about the Battle of the Bulge from hearsay, and I was never in that regiment."

"You are joking!"

"You're not the first person to mix me up with someone else. Just a few months ago the people in a village in the Harz would have sworn an oath that I was someone named Karl and engaged to a girl called Maria. I guess I must look like every other German."

"What's your name then?"

"Werner, Horst Werner."

"The fellow from the Fourth was called something else, he had a longer name." He reflected a moment, then whispered to me, "Were you maybe at Oradour? You can tell me. Here is a man who was at Malmédy and no one has discovered it yet."

"Not at all," I said. "I was in the Schweinfurt antitank unit and finally in the Linz Regiment."

I felt a bit of a traitor, but he would surely understand that I had to continue to play my role consistently.

"Why are you here, then?"

"I don't know exactly. They're supposedly looking for my brother."

"Was he a Nazi big shot?"

"No way. He was a totally harmless artillery lieutenant."

Meanwhile a thick cluster of people had gathered around me, the new guy, and the tall blond fellow—now I remembered his name, Bloser!—introduced me: "Listen, folks, here is someone who has lost his way. He was no Nazi, not with the Waffen–SS, hasn't even any Nazi relatives and is obviously a mistake of the Allies."

"I can confirm that," said a one–armed man with unkempt hair as he proffered his hand. Someone else who knew me? Who was he? He was too small for the Waffen–SS. Then it hit me like a ton of bricks: he was the philosophy professor who had, after a thorough examination of my democratic convictions, found me worthy of occupying one of the few student places in Bonn.

"Why are you here, Professor?"

"Intelligence," he said, "I was in counterintelligence."

"And that's enough to be locked up for?"

"As you see in your own case: God's ways are inscrutable. Do you play chess?"

"Yes."

"Being able to play chess is just as important here as having been a Nazi."

"What actually happens here?" I very much wanted to know. "Are we denazified? Do they hold legal proceedings?"

"Nothing," he said. "Most of the people have been sitting here for many months without any notice whatsoever having been taken of them."

No one appeared surprised by my suspicious innocence, especially since no one, or everyone, had to feel guilty according to the new criteria of guilt. So I was advised to arm myself with a good deal of patience for the coming years and tighten my belt. For all of us the advantage was that here we could no longer be arrested unexpectedly.

17

They found it scandalous, incredible, outrageous, unjust, that I, the harmless, innocent, insignificant nothing, was ordered over the loudspeaker to report to barrack number fourteen for questioning on only my fifth day there, since a thousand others, whose positions would have deserved far more attention, hadn't had this honor even after six months of waiting. They had spent much of their time preparing what they would sling at their interrogators or what they would play down.

The name Chryseels was on the door, and on the other side of the door sat a red–haired, freckled Belgian First Lieutenant, who could just as well have been with the Belgian Langemark Voluntary Brigade. I immediately found him disagreeable, and not only because he kept me standing and waiting for a quarter of an hour in order to devote himself completely to sharpening a pencil and unwrapping a piece of chewing gum. Without even having deigned to look at me first, he finally said, "Mr. Werner, you must think you're very clever, but you're quite stupid. I'm going to prove that to you."

It was tactically unwise to think I would break down after this disqualification. Had I, in view of the frank confessions of Bloser and others, considered laying my cards on the table now, this red–haired man was challenging me to take up the gauntlet and to find out which of the two of us was really the stupid one. He had my self–made Wehrmacht discharge paper lying before him and was looking at the reverse side, which had mainly authentic stamps and signatures.

"As I see it, you've been claiming food coupons for two people."

He saw quite correctly.

"For you and your wife, correct?"

When I didn't comment on that either he acted outraged. "That wasn't your wife, but your brother! You claimed food coupons for your brother, will you deny it?"

"Yes."

"So you admit it?"

"No. That is, I do deny it. Your people will certainly have searched my apartment and found my brother's women's clothes."

"That was camouflage."

"Then your people will surely also have asked the other occupants of the house whether my wife is my brother or my brother is my wife."

"Where is your brother?"

"I don't know, and if you keep me here I'll never find out, either."

"You know very well where he is and you won't tell us, which arouses suspicion, because if your brother wasn't a Nazi, as you insist, you would tell us where he is. But you are welcome to think about it. We have time: five weeks, five months, five years. Go and think about that!"

When anyone returned from an interrogation even the meager midday soup was interrupted: no one wanted to miss a word of what the interrogatee had to report, for everyone wanted to evaluate the interrogators' tactics for themselves. But what I had to report was even thinner than the soup.

The inmates had been cut off from the outside world for months and were not allowed either to receive or write letters, or to read newspapers or listen to the news. The new arrivals were the only source of information about what was going on in the outside world. In this soil, fertilized by lack of information, the rumors and slogans grew like weeds. The daily soup of bird seed—"not suitable for human consumption," it said on the paper sacks—was just as meager as the news and increased the hunger for both.

This hut with its seventy occupants swarmed with great names from science and industry. A quarter of the inmates were high–ranking professors and scientists. Another quarter were representatives of the iron and steel works, the linen and textile industries of Wuppertal, Solingen steel products, the metal factories of Velbert, the Krupp factories and other world–famous brand names. The rest consisted of leaders of the Hitler Youth, Storm Troopers, Gauleiters, diplomats, intelligence officers, and a few from the Waffen–SS, among whom were two Dutch volunteers, both double amputees, who ate their bread dry and devoured the butter pat in one go. Every day they expected amnesty from their queen, since her German–blooded prince consort had himself once been with the SS.

No wonder our hut developed into a cultural center, especially since we were excused from outdoor work and morning roll call. The blind poet Hymen recited from his *Letters to a Lady in Mourning,* and Heinz Steguweit composed his daily verse, which was read out each morning. He had a note pad filled with prepared rhymes: mouse, house, Klaus, from which he put his verses together like a puzzle.

The first adult education center was born here. Here you could learn all the languages of Europe, including Latin and Greek, or study law, economics, philosophy, even general medicine. Participation cost a quarter of a slice of bread, and anyone who could contribute a cigarette got a week's credit.

Only five days later I was summoned to another interrogation, which made me definitely unloved. Chryseels smirked triumphantly and held in his hand the document which transferred me from a hospital in Linz to a hospital in Bonn.

"Have you looked at this closely?" he asked craftily.

"I know what's written on it."

"And the stamp? Have you ever looked at that closely too?"

My blood pressure rose slightly, and if lie detectors had existed then, one of them would have been jumping up and down for joy. I merely shrugged my shoulders indifferently.

"How does one write 'public'?" he asked.

I spelled it out. "P—U—B—L—I—C."

"And what's written here?" He had jumped up and slammed the paper down on the desk in front of me.

I read, "P—U—P—L—I—C."

"The stamp is a fake," he said sharply. "How primitive, stupid, ludicrous, to work with fake stamps."

He was right about the stamp being wrong, but it wasn't wrong in that sense; because this mistake was just about the only thing on the stamp that was authentic.

"Do you think that all Americans would immediately notice a misspelling of 'public'? Maybe the people there in Linz still haven't noticed this mistake and are still using this stamp. If I were you I'd notify them."

"You can rely on that," he said, but no longer seemed so certain of his triumph. Instead he asked once more whether it had occurred to me meanwhile where my brother was, and if not, he had plenty of time, five weeks, five months, five years.

When I returned to the hut all hell had just broken loose. A thirteen–year–old Cub from the camp for boys (who were suspected of being werewolves) had climbed over the three–meter–high fence so that he could visit the grown–ups. This was all the more annoying since one of the Cubs had disappeared a few days earlier. On his bed there lay a note that said, "I am now a democrat. Democrats don't have to stay in the camp any more. And so I have let the camp commander drive me into free democracy in the trunk of his car. Heil Hitler, comrades!"

Now a Tommy was driving this other werewolf cub past our hut, hitting him with a stick. This aroused the indignation of the paraplegic officer from the police division, so that the guard desisted from striking the boy and threatened instead to bash the ex-policeman, whose name was Keller. So, once again indignation was aroused, in all the hut occupants this time, and we formed a protective wall around Keller. The Tommy contented himself with the curse, "Fucking Nazi! Bastard!" and hurried away to fetch reinforcements. Reinforcements came in the form of one officer and three men who now made the mistake of getting involved in a discussion with us.

Ulrich Graf, an expert in international law who spoke excellent Oxford English, raised the tone of the discussion by correcting some of the officer's nuances of expression, whereupon the officer slung the name "Bergen–Belsen" at him in reference to the subject of treatment of prisoners. At hearing this word, our one–armed boilerman felt obliged to intervene. "What do you want? I was in Bergen–Belsen!"

Suddenly there was deathly silence. For the British, who had liberated this concentration camp, Belsen was living proof of Nazi cruelty, concentration camp mass murders and SS brutalities at their worst. And here was someone who claimed to have been in Belsen. If he was there as a prisoner he did not belong here; if he was there as a guard he should have forfeited his life, he ought to have been lynched long ago. Until then no one had known what this outsider in our academic midst, the usually coal–black boilerman who very skillfully kept our iron stove functioning, really was doing here. Now it came out. Graf translated for him.

"You're responsible for all those deaths," he roared at the British officer. Graf didn't translate that, but instead asked him to tell his story coherently. He was a prisoner in Bergen–Belsen for two years and the British had freed him. Before that, however, he was a guard in various concentration camps and wore the infamous death's head on his collar patch. Earlier he had been a Communist.

As far as this honest and usually unemployed agricultural worker from the Ruhr district was concerned, Communists and unemployed Nazis belonged in the same pot. If they didn't have different uniforms and flags you wouldn't be able to tell one from the other. What he had to defend was not one ideology or the other but his idea of order and discipline. He thought he had the opportunity to do this when he was offered a position as concentration camp guard. His task was to bring a semblance of order into the chaos of homosexuals, black marketeers, gypsies, Jehovah's Witnesses, pickpockets, Jews, and hack journalists. Whatever else they may have been and for whatever trivial reasons they may have been locked up, for him most of them were disorderly, slovenly, undisciplined, crooked swine who needed to be got into shape. And if you saw it that way, then you had to hit out, give these swine a kick in the ass. The other guards had done this too, but he was the one who'd got caught. And then there had been a law from Himmler, a theoretician who hadn't a clue about practicalities: an SS man who so much as touches a prisoner is worth no more than the prisoner and deserves to be locked up as well. And so the boilerman became a prisoner, spent two years as an outcast among outcasts, and the arm that he had once used in punishment withered. One of those whom he had once kicked in the rear had seen to that. An eye for an eye, an arm for an arm.

A simple man, our boilerman, always beefy, always blustering, un-friendly, and snapping, but he always threw his half–slice of bread at anyone who got on his nerves by complaining about the paltry food: "There, eat and shut your trap!"

And how was it at Bergen–Belsen, we wanted to know.

For most of the people it was a transit camp for new prisoners. Even up to the beginning of 1945, up to two passenger trains per week each carried two thousand Jews to Switzerland, where they were to be exchanged for German prisoners of war. "But then you came with your bomber planes, bombed all the railway stations to hell, shot up all the trains, attacked every truck on the road, shot the farmers in the field and the children on their way to school. Then no more trains could run, and the new prisoners arrived on foot from wherever, more and more of them, and couldn't leave again. There wasn't enough food any more, and the prisoners brought typhus and other diseases, and there were no doctors, no medicines, no form of care! They died like flies, including the guards; the situation got worse and worse, and what you saw when you liberated the camp was your own work, your guilt, you have it on your conscience! It stank like the plague. I was there. You can't tell me anything!"

Graf had to stop him, or he would have worked himself up even more. The officer had casually stuck a cigarette into his mouth. "So, you were in the concentration camp," he said, offering him the cigarette. The boilerman put his hand behind his back. He offered it to Graf, who didn't take it. He offered it to Keller, who didn't even look, and finally he threw it on the floor, trampled on it and left, without taking the boilerman or Keller along. When he had gone they threw themselves on the crushed cigarette and rolled a new Chesterfield out of it.

Chryseels' five weeks, five months, five years once again came to an end after five days. I was summoned for questioning again.

Chryseels had another new trick.

"We have arrested your brother, Mr. Werner!"

"Oh, that's great!" I rejoiced. "Since that was why you'd locked me up, now you can let me go."

"No, no," he countered. "We have interrogated your brother and he has told us everything."

"What has he told you, then?"

"Everything about you."

Now, there my conscience was clear, for I was certain that they had not found or arrested either Kurt or Klaus.

"Why shouldn't he tell you everything," I said, "since neither he nor I has anything to hide."

"You say that although you know that's not true. But the game is up. We know everything."

"So much the better. Then you can tell me what isn't true."

"That I would gladly hear, from you, in order to be sure that you're now telling the truth."

"But you have my life story, all my papers, the questionnaire with the 134 questions. Where have I given false information?"

"What's there is harmless, it doesn't interest us. We want to know about what you've hidden from us."

I was enraged. "But that's ridiculous! Naturally I haven't mentioned that I had the measles or whether my aunt was a Party member."

"You know very well what we're interested in, and I ask you: were you a Nazi?"

"If you could define more exactly what a Nazi is, I can tell you whether I was one or not."

"I should give you a definition of what a Nazi is? You're joking, surely!"

" 'Nazi' as a concept never existed for us. It was a swearword, but for what and for whom, can't you tell me?"

"But that's—don't you know? Are you just pretending to be so stupid?"

"But you've said yourself that I'm very stupid, and if you, on the other hand, are so clever, Mr. Chryseels, then you surely ought to be able to explain to me what a Nazi is. Was every Storm Trooper, every Hitler youth, every SS member, and every Party member a Nazi?"

"Naturally. That is, it also depends on their way of thinking and on what they've done."

"My way of thinking was already thoroughly examined when I applied to study, and if you want to know whether I denounced innocent people, locked up Jews or Poles, or even shot them, then I can say no with the clearest conscience. But if someone is a Nazi just because they did their duty to their country as a soldier, then I was a Nazi."

"You talk like all the others: everyone was only doing their duty. You're lying like all the others. And so I'm giving you time to think about it, five weeks, five months, five years."

In the mornings I studied economics with Professor Ruberg. I couldn't manage any more courses than this, because I needed the rest of my bread slice for myself. In the afternoons we played chess. A one–armed local group leader spent his days carving chess pieces out of firewood and gave them to the chess players. It was his way of learning to live with only one arm.

In the evenings my philosophy professor took me along to interdisciplinary discussions, which were the most interesting lessons of my life. The participants included prominent, world–famous physicians, neurophysiologists, experts in international law, historians, two atomic physicists, a professor of theoretical physics, philosophers, biologists, psychologists, and behaviorists; and yet it was a disciplined circle in which everyone was allowed to have his say, everyone wanted to learn from everyone else, and each person brought not his own vanity but only his specialized knowledge.

There were questions about truth and objectivity, about justice and the origin of life, about the meaning of life and the nature of feelings, the sole validity of natural–law causality and the theory of relativity, and whenever concrete results appeared to have been reached, new problems and new phenomena turned up which again questioned the result that was in the offing. I was allowed to join in and to request that the technical jargon be translated into generally understandable language, because it then first came to light what the technical language was really hiding, and I was also allowed to ask those stupid questions that are always the hardest to answer, and to which each person was able to contribute from his own point of view.

The story of Doetz and Timmermann, which I told them, gave the scientists food for thought that they couldn't finish digesting even in the remainder of their internment. They were both with me in a group of recruits: Timmermann, a sturdy brewer's drayman from Holstein, and Doetz, a high school dropout who had learned the basics of hypnotism from a village schoolteacher. He wanted to try out his skills on us, and we had to line up in front of him and fold our hands. Then he made some funny gestures and looked deeply into each man's eyes, and when he stated that we would not be able to unfold our hands again he was disappointed at how easily we were able to extricate ourselves from his hypnotic web—except for Timmermann. He could no longer unclasp his hands, not even with our really forceful help. Aha! Now Doetz came into his own and continued his experiment with Timmermann alone.

Soon he needed only to snap his fingers and Timmermann was in his power. Doetz misused his power at once. Whenever it was his turn for barrack room duty he snapped his fingers and indicated to Timmermann that it was his turn. And Timmermann swept, wiped, cleaned, and scrubbed with a thoroughness of which he was totally incapable when it was his real turn for duty. Of course we were envious and persuaded Timmermann that it was Doetz's turn and not his, and we held the duty roster under his nose and showed him in black and white that today, Thursday, was Doetz's turn for barrack room duty. One could otherwise speak rationally with Timmermann about everything, but not about this. He would damn well not be kept from his housewifely duties. And so we gave up.

Then Doetz did further experiments with him. "Timmermann," he said after having snapped his fingers, "this won't hurt, it won't bleed, and it won't leave a scar." Then he took his pocket knife and carved a wound nearly three centimeters long and one centimeter deep in the flesh on Timmermann's chest. We heard the slicing sound and made sympathetic faces, but Timmermann didn't turn a hair. It didn't hurt him and it didn't bleed, and the red line that was visible for a moment disappeared very quickly. And even when he pricked Timmermann with the knife in his highly sensitive tongue Timmermann was amazed by our agonized faces, while he himself felt nothing.

One day Doetz took a burning cigarette, held it before Timmermann's eyes and said, "Do you see this blank cartridge?" Timmermann saw it; just like those he carried every day. Doetz took him by the lower arm and stubbed out the cigarette on it, two, three seconds. We saw the embers drop down and waited for Timmermann to scream and furiously attack Doetz, but nothing happened: no pain, no burn mark, no blister, as if Timmermann had actually been touched there with the cool metal of a blank cartridge.

We got gooseflesh, but the sorcery got even more mysterious. Now Doetz actually took a blank cartridge, held it under Timmermann's nose and said, "An Eckstein." This was a very popular brand of cigarette. Timmermann suspected something bad, but before he could draw back Doetz had pressed the cartridge against his upper arm, for only a very brief second, but Timmermann screamed, hit him on the finger so that the cartridge fell to the floor, and rubbed his upper arm. Doetz woke him and asked what he had on his upper arm.

"Oh, nothing," said Timmermann. He'd got a little burn there. We saw the dark red spot that soon formed a blister. We felt rather uneasy after that, and even Doetz stopped his experiments, because he feared that one day he would no longer be able to control the spirits he summoned.

The scientists' feelings were no less aroused than ours had been at the time. One of the physicists tried to contest the story as incredible, but he was contradicted by the psychologists, the physicians, and the neurophysiologist. But the physicist insisted that it was impossible and he explained and described that even living skin, the same as nonliving matter, was made up of molecules and, in turn, of atoms, and that very specific physical or energetic conditions must exist in order to produce specific effects or reactions. He drew a model of an atom and described how electrons behave in the supply or release of energy, explaining that this was a matter of elementary particles and, consequently, of elementary behavior. Cause and effect can be calculated in advance, and that could be proved experimentally at any time. Consequently, it would be impossible for electrons to react to a heat–energy thrust when there had been no heat at all, nor could they react to cool metal as if they had received a heat–energy thrust. Even the other physicists agreed with him.

However, there were others who could give authentic reports of fakirs, Hindu priests, and other exotic people who pierce themselves with arrows without bleeding or scarring, and who walk over glowing rocks without being burned. They drove the sceptical physicists into isolation. Timmermann was burned because of false information, a lie, but he would not have been burned if he hadn't known the language and thus not understood the hypnotic rapport. Hypnosis, the psychologist said, shuts off only the critical consciousness, while the uncritical subconscious experiences the rapport as an authentic phenomenon with all the physical consequences. How could the deceived subconscious mind set off a chemo–technical process that contradicted natural–law causality?

This was the question, and this was the indigestible food for thought. The ensuing discussion, in which the neurophysiologist, the philosophers, and the physicists all had their say, was very stimulating; I found it fascinating and decided then and there to devote myself to this problem and find a solution to it. These highly qualified scientists showed me that at that time no solution existed for this complicated problem and that no answer would be found, no matter how thoroughly a person studied. Only a few years later I began, in what little leisure I had, to study what had been written about this problem and to write an exposition describing the problem and suggesting a possible solution. I finally had enough time thirty years later to let the seeds that were planted here ripen into an interdisciplinary answer to the still unsolved question.

This was all much more exciting than the hunger, the uncertainty, and this Chryseels, who kept summoning me for interrogation in a regular five–day rhythm.

"Now we've got you!" he said. He was quite light–hearted and first let me think for a while about where he might have me. He leafed through my papers as if he first had to study the extensive incriminating evidence once more, casting an observant glance my way every now and then, while I concentrated on counting his freckles.

Since I showed no signs of curiosity he let the bomb drop: "We have arrested your wife!"

"That's very gentlemanly," I said, "but what else could I expect of you?"

"Why didn't you tell us where your wife was?"

"Did you ever ask me? You were looking for my brother."

"Sooner or later we find everything out. But now let's check: where do you think we've found your wife?"

"In Hannover, I assume."

"Right, in the convalescent home. You see, we know everything. But for your peace of mind I can tell you that her ankle is nearly healed. She can be released in the next few days."

"Thank you for the good news."

"Your wife was sensible enough to tell us everything. We now know all about you."

"That's good," I said. "In that case you'll finally have realized that you've locked me up here with no justification whatever. Now, hopefully, I can go home."

"You don't believe me, do you? We know everything, and this is your last chance to tell us the truth."

"I know that you know everything." Suddenly as in a vision I saw the fairytale goblin dancing around and singing.

"Well then, let's have the truth!"

He was playing with the pencil and my papers, the food coupons, the student certificate, the war–disabled identification, and other authentic and inauthentic documents. I was really tired of this and would have been prepared to tell him the truth, but then this silly, conceited twit would think he had driven me into a corner. I was very stupid, were his words of greeting to me, and he was going to prove it to me. I was all too happy to establish which of the two of us was the stupider.

"Well, what is it? Do you finally wish to confess?"

"Yes," I said. "I'll tell you the truth now."

"Well then, please!" He took out the pencil.

"You're playing a ludicrous game here," I said indignantly, "because you've known for a long time that you've locked up an innocent person, but you don't have the courage to admit your error. Some propaganda or other has drummed it into your heads that all Germans are criminals, and now you hope that the Germans just need to have pressure put on them to make them confess that they were involved in some crime, and you thought that you could find some brown or black spot on me out of which you could make a crime, but you'll find nothing of the kind in me or in most German soldiers. Shall I tell you a lie to satisfy you?

"And one thing more, Mr. Chryseels: until now I was only a soldier, I never bothered with Nazi propaganda or with politics, nor did I have any reason to mistrust my government. But here I am, locked up with nothing but Nazis or with people you take to be Nazis, and I'm beginning to be interested in Nazi crimes and Nazi guilt, and I must confess to you that these Nazis are thoroughly decent fellows, neither idiots nor criminals nor uncritical fellow–travellers. Here I'm learning the difference between lies and the truth, but in a different way than you would prefer, and if I wasn't a Nazi before, then I'm becoming one now, the more so the longer you keep me here, because I'm beginning to feel very much at home among the elite that you've packed together here, even for five more weeks, five months, or five years."

Since he was still searching for words and was looking furious in order to let me know what sort of words he was searching for, and since I was still wound up I continued: "There's only one thing that's extremely unpleasant for me here, Mr. Chryseels. The decent people in my hut think I'm an informer whom you've planted here, because you summon me for interrogation every few days, while most of them haven't even been interrogated once, although some of them have held really high positions. They think I'm not being interrogated but giving regular reports on what I've heard there. I wish to eliminate this unpleasant suspicion once and for all, and to ask you either to leave me in peace or to produce some really incriminating evidence, but not to keep on playing this absurd hide–and–seek game and acting as if you know something that you can't possibly know.''

"Hold your tongue!'' he shouted furiously. "Everyone's lying here, no one is telling the truth, not even you!''

"Think just once, Mr. Chryseels, about whether perhaps those people aren't lying who have served you a dish full of hate propaganda, so that you're now looking for criminals that just don't exist to expiate crimes that have never been committed.''

"That's enough!'' In a rage he slammed the table with his fist. "We will find out the truth, including the truth about you, and if you feel so much at home here then perhaps we'll meet again after five years!''

My return to the hut was hardly noticed, since a heated discussion between Graf and the Flying Man had just flared up. This fighter pilot from the First World War and brigade leader in the Storm Troopers' flying division had discovered a comrade in the camp commander, who had also been a fighter pilot in the First World War. Ever since then the British were the best Germans to him. At every inspection he would clamp a monocle to his eye and humbly await the commander, who would ask, "Where is the Flying Man?'' the minute he entered the hut. Then names and war theaters would be mentioned and he got four Chesterfields which he smoked all alone, really all by himself. This just wasn't done! Usually if someone produced a cigarette a group celebration was held immediately. Everyone was allowed one drag, a deep breath and an "aah.'' But he smoked them all by himself, and not even in secret. And when the commander asked him—and him alone in the hut—if everything was all right or whether there were any complaints, he said, "All right, Sir!'' instead of complaining that the purging policy in accordance with the Morgenthau Plan was being practiced here by starvation and that our meager birdseed soup was, as the declaration on the sacks said, unfit for human consumption. After the "All right, Sir'' we began to crow and cackle loudly, but the Flying Man soothed the commander and assured him that this meant nothing and we were just boisterously silly.

The cause of the discussion between the Flying Man and the group around Graf was the appearance of some lawyers who were looking for defense witnesses in the forthcoming Nuremberg Trials. These lawyers had reported the existence of a huge abundance of complaints, claims, and accusations which would be judged under retroactively passed laws as crimes against humanity and human dignity, planning a war of aggression, conspiracy against peace, and so forth. A Control Council Law, No. 10, had been passed whereby all German crimes discovered during the war by one of the nations at war with Germany would merely have to be noted by officials, without any individual proof having to be provided. The most monstrous complaint, and one which was already considered as proved according to this law, was that five to eleven million Jews had been systematically murdered, mostly by hydrocyanic acid poisonous gas, a genocide of the greatest proportion. A commander of the largest death camp in Auschwitz was already supposed to have submitted a detailed confession.

Thus the heated discussion. The Flying Man was the only one who unconditionally believed everything, not because he knew anything about it but because he couldn't stand Himmler's whole clique and therefore considered them capable of all the crimes being laid at their door.

There were then some competent people in the camp who must have known more about these mass murders, the former legation counsellor Eberhard von Thadden from the neighboring hut, for example, who had headed the Jewish Department in the Foreign Office under Ribbentrop and Secretary of State von Weizsaecker. He had been mostly concerned with Jewish emigration and had negotiated all over the world without achieving generous immigration quotas anywhere, except in China. He told about the plan for a Jewish state, most likely in Palestine, which had fallen through because of the British position. Then Madagascar was considered, which again was occupied by the British. Finally they had agreed on a region in the Ukraine; but the stepping–up of the war situation no longer allowed this plan to be put into effect. He considered the assertions of mass murder to be out of the question, at least on the scale being claimed, since according to the official Koherr statistics nowhere near that many Jews had lived in Hitler's sphere of control.

Our boilerman, the concentration camp expert, when asked if he knew anything about mass murders with poisonous gas, said categorically, "A load of garbage!"

A director of I.G. Farben–Chemie knew that a large industrial center had sprung up overnight in Auschwitz; among other things the Buna Artificial Rubber Production plant had been erected there. Umpteen thousands of workers were needed, who were accommodated in many work camps, and in view of the lack of good workers, among whose numbers the Jews undoubtedly were, it would have been absurd to murder them instead of making sensible use of them.

Only the Flying Man provoked us to anxiety and fear and argued like a prosecutor that these claims of Himmler's atrocities were true. He unravelled a red thread that started with the first boycott of Jews on 1 April 1933 and led to the Jewish laws, the anti–Jewish agitation, and Crystal Night, and then to arrest and extermination. Graf, on the other hand, cited the worldwide call of international Jewry on 24 March 1933 for economic war against Nazi Germany until its destruction, to which the Jewish boycott on April 1st could be seen as a reaction. He spoke of a declaration of war against Germany by one Chaim Weizmann in the name of international Jewry shortly after the outbreak of the war, whereby according to international law the Jews in Germany and Europe would have had enemy status, and their internment would have been justified. The Flying Man called this nonsense, since the Jews hadn't had their own state and Weizmann was not entitled to make such a declaration on behalf of all Jews. He pointed to the many Jewish comrades of the First World War and cited Hitler's *Mein Kampf* and various speeches by Hitler in which he threatened to exterminate the Jews. Everyone who was observant, able to read between the lines to some extent, and not lulled by the loud *"Sieg–Heil"* ought to have been able to foresee the consequences.

Everyone like him, that is.

He was old enough to be my father, this Storm Trooper brigade leader, an influential man, anyhow, who now claimed always to have heard, read, and known that that clique which he himself had actively supported had committed such crimes or intended to commit them. He had not done anything to oppose them but had helped to train and encourage the youth, and inspire us to give our all for this just war. Now he wallowed in the consciousness of always having suspected or even known the whole truth. What kind of an irresponsible person was he! But if what he said were true, and if it had happened even under the protection of our uniforms, then God have mercy on us!

But Graf and especially the intelligence people, who must have been imagining things, considered it all impossible, and so this repulsive creature of a brigade leader merely left the stale taste generated by people who were ready to cry "Hosanna" and "Crucify him" at the same time, and who trimmed their sails to the wind even before they knew which way it would blow.

We shook off what it ought not to be because it could not be.

18

My neighbor in the next bed, the railway official, greedily and smirkingly devoured what I had to report about my interrogation by Chryseels, and urged me to persist in playing my role. By now, he thought, Chryseels would be ready to give up.

But Chryseels did not give up. In his obsessive five–day rhythm he called me to interrogation once more. In the hut I had let it be intimated to the other detainees, who were asking me about the reasons for my frequent interrogations and were far from being convinced of the truth, that I was being confused with someone else and that no one would believe that I wasn't this other person.

"How can one recognize the SS?" Chryseels asked me without any preambles, closely observing how I would react to this question.

"By their uniforms," I answered promptly.

"And if they're not wearing a uniform?"

Now I had to consider carefully how to answer. Attack is the best defense.

"Aha, now I know what you're getting at," I said. "Anyone who wanted to join the SS had to be a certain minimum height, 176 cm. I believe. And you think that because I'm 180 cm. I must have been in the SS? In that case I can assure you: in my unit there were many men that tall who weren't all in the SS."

"No, no, I don't mean that," said Chryseels. "Even if they weren't that tall and still wore no uniforms, you could still recognize them. How?''

"Oh yes, wait a minute! They're supposed to have a tattoo on their arm.''

"Which arm?''

"The left?''

"Correct, and what do you have there?''

"A scar,'' it occurred to me.

"A scar!'' Now Chryseels was getting quite excited. "I thought so. And what was there before?''

"Nothing. No tattoo, in any case.''

"And how did you get the scar?''

"Do you want to know exactly?''

"Yes, exactly.''

It was in Russia, in July 1941, east of Yelnia. Until then we had continued to advance, ten, thirty, or even fifty kilometers per day. Our division led the advance towards Moscow and we had penetrated farthest to the east. It occurred to me that if Chryseels knew anything about the war in Russia he would have realized that this involved the *"Das Reich"* Division, but he merely listened with interest without having made any connection.

We had to remain here without advancing farther, and watch the Russkies gathering in front of us, assembling more artillery, bringing up more tanks and new troops. For the first time we found ourselves on the defensive. The Russkies attacked with ever–increasing frequency, and in between attacks their artillery bombarded us ceaselessly with grenades. It was crazy the way they stormed over the coverless terrain, while we, having to be sparing with our ammunition, let them come close so that they were then senselessly and hopelessly mowed down by our machine guns.

They assembled loudspeakers and called over to us: "While you're bleeding here, the SS are making your womenfolk pregnant at home and locking your friends up in concentration camps. Desert! Give yourselves up! It's your last chance, because none of you will survive our attack tomorrow!''

And they attacked, with hordes of men and tanks, and they remained in front of our positions. This charade was repeated several times a day. Our ammunition was getting low. After two weeks we were finally relieved by a fresh if not yet so experienced unit. One hundred twenty–five knocked–out tanks lay in front of our division's positions.

At that time I was a motorcycle dispatch rider, and very busy, because our telephone connections were always being shot up. I think I can still count on my fingers the number of hours I slept in these two weeks. Even our food had to be shared with the Hiwis, the Russian defectors or POWs who were serving with us. A Hiwi assigned to me had tried to shave himself with my carefully–rationed tube of cheese and was cursing because it didn't lather. I couldn't care less, I just wanted to sleep.

Thus I missed the alarm and was awakened by Andreas, a tall chauffeur from Holstein. "Wake up, man, there's one!"

"Who? What? Where?"

A tank. An unusual monster whose like we had never seen before. Its silhouette loomed through a bit of wooded area. We found out later that it was a T–34 that was put into action for the first time here. Our 37mm antitank gun was no match for it. With this they could penetrate the front. And one of them was standing at the edge of the wood, about a hundred meters from us, aiming northward.

We had grown used to destroying tanks in close combat. I still had one hand grenade in my belt and Andreas fetched a one–kilo explosive charge from the trunk of the head vehicle. The tank's engine had been turned off. We sneaked up to it through the wood from behind. There it stood, the new T–34. My heart was pounding. Inside the tank voices and noises could be heard. Andreas crawled to the left side with his explosive charge so that he could lay it there under the track. I climbed carefully onto the tank from behind and approached the hatch cover. The voices stopped. Damn! How did one get this cover open? I braced myself against the turret with my thighs and tore at the cover until I realized that a bolt was fastened there with a padlock.

So, the crew was locked in. They couldn't get out if their situation became hopeless; they were riding in a sealed coffin: win or die! If only I knew some Russian so that I could make them realize that I wanted to get them out of there and they must give me some time!

Something hit my right thigh. Then I saw the thick, round thing that hung on a chain next to the turret. A dull shot rang out and I felt a blow. I quickly withdrew my thigh from the close–combat opening and held firmly to the disc that closed it. Now what? They pulled on the chain to close the hole again and shot through the opening a couple of times. My hand grenade was too thick to fit through the hole.

Then I thought of my flare pistol. It was loaded with a violet signal rocket cartridge, the signal for tank warning. I stuck the hand grenade into my belt, took out the flare pistol, and held firmly to the disc. Carefully I inserted the muzzle of the flare pistol into the hole. They would shoot us as soon as they saw something. And so, very quickly: muzzle in. They fired immediately, but I had the pistol out again already.

Now down below, near the tracks at the dead angle! Oh! I couldn't have known yet that the T–34 had a close–combat opening below as well, a shaft through which hand grenades could be dropped. Two pineapple hand grenades were lying under the tank and hissing.

"Andreas!" I could still shout a warning and raise my head, then they exploded. A blow struck my right foot, another my left foot, another my wrist, and another my left arm.

That was it. But Chryseels wanted to hear the rest.

Andreas shouted from the other side, "Cover! Explosive!" When the hand grenades exploded he had, in the heat of the moment, pulled the detonator on the explosive charge. Now this exploded too.

"Andreas?!"

Then he came crawling along with blood oozing out of many tiny holes in his uniform, and from every possible chink and hole in the tank there bellowed violet smoke. My pistol! I had leaned it against the track and a splinter had blasted a hole in the neck of the butt.

"Anything broken, Andreas?"

"I think all my bones are still in one piece."

"Mine too, I think."

Were they shouting? Yes, they were shouting, loud commands and shrill cries of fear. We lay to one side, ten meters away. Andreas had aimed his gun at the turret.

"They can't get out, Andreas, the turret is bolted from the outside."

"Scandalous! Can't it be opened?"

"I tried, but they shot me in the thigh."

"The chief said they were bringing an elite tank brigade from Moscow. Now I know how they make the elite."

Then there was a fearful thunderclap, as if the whole tank would burst. The turret rose a few centimeters, tilted to one side, and came crashing down.

These idiots! How can heroism be forced on people like this! If they had left me alone I would have cracked or shot open the padlock and got them out. Being a prisoner isn't fun, of course, but at least it's temporary. But to be sealed into one's own coffin with no hope of surviving, no, that's not war anymore, no longer the war that we had learned as the continuation of politics with other methods, such as a year ago in France with immediate ceasefire as soon as the goal had been achieved. The opponent is to be rendered incapable of fighting, we learned, incapable of fighting, not dead. Death is only a risk, not the goal. The wounded, I learned, are more useful than the dead, because the wounded need medication, doctors, and orderlies, and orderlies have no time to fight.

There was nothing more we could do here. We withdrew.

I couldn't get the men from the Moscow tank brigade out of my head. What a drama must have been played out in their coffin before they decided to commit suicide! Why did this warlike competition have to degenerate so grimly despite the playing rules of the Geneva Convention?

"Crazy fellows, these Russians," said Chryseels. "And this is supposed to have happened in 1941?"

I nodded.

"And that's how you got the scar on your arm?"

"Yes."

"A doctor will be able to tell whether your scar is really that old."

"Certainly."

"Go into the next room for a while!"

He telephoned. The doctor didn't seem to be particularly enthusiastic, because Chryseels had to assure him that it would only take a very short minute and that it was very important.

The doctor came. Brusquely and carrying the inevitable cane under his arm he plodded through the room. His bad humor was directed at the Belgian, whom he scarcely deigned to look at. I held my exposed arm up for him. On the lower arm, far from the tattooed place, was the souvenir from the hand grenades.

"That there?" He pointed to the scar with his cane.

"Yes."

Jerkily he turned round, clasped the cane under his arm again, strode straight past Chryseels, and before he slammed the door behind him he said, "Four years, yes."

"You can go too," said Chryseels, slightly more dejectedly; behind me he mumbled, "Crazy fellows, these Russians!"

I was summoned to Chryseels one last time. I went with really mixed feelings, because on the one hand I seemed to have won the duel with him, but on the other the consequences weren't particularly satisfying. Was it so advantageous to continue as Horst Werner?

Chryseels had assembled three of his colleagues. They sat there like a jury furtively sizing up the defendant and trying not to show too obvious an interest. And so they talked about trivial things such as bartering transactions with the civilians, places where radios could be exchanged for cigarettes, girls for chocolate, or watches for gasoline. Chryseels asked what they thought of me and, without looking at me, they thought that I really didn't look like a criminal, which wasn't saying anything since most criminals don't look like criminals.

It occurred to one of them that perhaps I understood French, whereupon Chryseels acted as if he had forgotten some more trivial questions. He leafed through my questionnaire and asked:

"What foreign languages have you learned?"

"Latin and Greek," I said.

"No English?"

"Only for two weeks, then there was a school reform. 'I am dipping the pen in the ink–pot,' I learned, but you can't use that very often."

"And French?"

"No. I picked up a bit in France, *'Bonjour, Madame'* and that sort of thing."

With effort I suppressed a smirk when I heard Chryseels recount how my previous interrogations had gone. It was a summation for my defense. I had never reacted with the slightest insecurity to any of his tricks, that they had arrested my brother or my wife and they had confessed everything. First he had thought that I was extremely cunning, but now he was convinced of my innocence. It was up to the others now to give their judgment as well. They studied my life history, the more or less false documents, and began a series of cross–questions:

Where were you on 2 August 1940? What was your commander's

name at that time? In what street are the antitank barracks in Schweinfurt? What was the name of the battalion commander of your Hitler Youth unit? In which county is Crossen–on–the–Oder?

I had never had a good memory for names, I explained, and had to think longer about names than about dates and places. I couldn't rattle off my answers as if I'd learnt them by heart, and I kept hesitating with the first names, while Chryseels and his colleagues were becoming less and less doubtful. In the opinion of the three others I was on the level, and they left the room.

Chryseels was now forced to give in, and he invented an excuse.

"We're looking for a Paul Werner; don't you also have Paul as one of your names?"

"No, there's no Paul anywhere in my family."

"This Paul Werner is supposed to have been a brutal concentration camp guard," Chryseels said, expanding on how difficult it was to find those who were really guilty, because they were all lying, no one had done anything and no one was a Nazi. And so unfortunately it sometimes happened that even innocent people were locked up, such as myself. But now he would see to it that I was released. After all, it wasn't his fault; if the British delivered a suspect he had to proceed on the basis that there were urgent reasons for their having done so.

"And how much longer will it be until I'm released?"

"You'll have to count on a few weeks."

"Oh no!" I moaned. "Then I won't get out in time for my second semester! Maybe they've already even given my student place to someone else in the meantime—maybe even to a Nazi." I cursed and complained that merely the fact of having been arrested would endanger my studies, because some mud always sticks. Chryseels promised to do everything he could to speed things up, and as real compensation for the injuries I had suffered he offered and lit me a cigarette.

I hurried back to the hut as quickly as I could, to let my fellow–sufferers each have a drag on it—except for the Flying Man, of course. "They've realized their mistake, boys! I'm going to be released as soon as possible."

Over the next few days they lined up at my bed to reserve space for a little letter in the hollow part of my artificial leg. They unscrewed the lower leg and stuffed it full of forbidden messages.

19

"I had no idea you were such a *filou*," said Jeanette. *"Le plus grand filou de la sainte messe de Montboyer!"*

She sat on the hood of the car and I leaned on it, and by now our shadows had grown so long that our heads were swimming on the water.

"When do you have to go back?" she asked.

"Tomorrow, midday at the latest."

"Already? But you'll come again some time, won't you?"

"I promise. But I have one more errand tomorrow. Is there someone who can teach Julien German?"

"The headmaster of Julien's school teaches German. Should Julien learn German?"

"Don't you think it would be good for him?"

"Oh yes, of course. He has a gift for languages. He's quite good in English. What would you advise him to do?"

"He could come to Germany—to me, that is, if he wanted to and if you had nothing against it."

"Of course he'll want to, and I? What should I have against it? He would have left home in any case. And what do you do in Germany? Did you finish your studies? Are you still called Werner?"

"No, I'm back to my normal self again and have built myself a factory. It started quite small and it keeps growing."

"What happened afterwards? You were released as Horst Werner, and then?"

"No, it all turned out quite differently—yet again."

At the moment there was considerable excitement in the huts on account of the host of complaints submitted by the Nuremberg defense lawyers. The man who had been at Malmédy could not calm down, because the things being claimed were not true, they were fabrications, crazy, dreamed up! He knew exactly what had really happened, but the lawyer advised him not to volunteer the information, because there were seventy–five men of the tank regiment already locked up who all knew exactly what had transpired there. It would be crazy to want to sacrifice oneself as well.

Another indignant person was Hamlet, who displayed himself as a virtual caricature of an adherent of the Waffen–SS code of honor, prepared to tell the truth and nothing but the truth, but not to take the disgrace himself. The Russians had charged that German planes had bombed a hospital in Gorki, a small city southwest of Moscow. No, that's out of the question, because the hospital was intact when he arrived there with the *"Das Reich"* Division. The division had camped in the hospital park, and the Russian planes came and dropped bombs on the hospital and the park. Hamlet was right up close when a bomb tore the left arm off Wim Brandt, the commander of the reconnaissance division. He was right, because I, too, was in the park, and in the hospital—which was intact—looking for an old blanket to put under my motorcycle saddle as the spring on the saddle was broken.

And I, too, had reason to get agitated without daring to do so, because I absolutely couldn't have been there—not as Horst Werner.

It was in the region of Staro Konstantinov. Again and again we met among the Russian prisoners people on whom we had been billeted only four weeks earlier. When the Russians occupied a place they recruited all the men who were at all capable of fighting and put them at the front after a short period of training. There were people there who had been imprisoned by the Germans as early as 1941 but were released to their homes in the Ukraine half a year later, not only for humanitarian reasons but also because there were not enough workers in these villages and the Ukrainians were hostile to Stalin. In any case most of the civilians were fleeing before the Russians, because their reputation as marauders and rapists in the anti–Soviet Ukraine had preceded them. We satisfied ourselves with requiring all able–bodied men in the places we occupied to leave their villages and head west. In order to emphasize this we set a deadline and threatened that after this deadline the men ran the risk of being shot.

This matter was under the control of my adjutant department, and so I deliberately did not mention on the placards we hung out who would do the shooting. But we never seriously planned to take any such punitive measures in this affair. The placards fell into Russian hands, and now they were claiming that we had shot civilians. That is not true, it is a lie, and I am very well aware of it.

And so now I was struggling with myself about whether I should go and reveal what my function was at that time, and thus my real name, in order to make myself available as a witness.

In the middle of this crisis of conscience the loudspeaker announced that I, Horst Werner, was to come immediately to Interrogation Hut No. 11. Everyone pricked up his ears when they heard "No. 11," because it was under the control of the dreaded Captain Factor, a professional criminologist who was known to work only on serious cases, usually with the result that his prisoners were transferred to Punishment Camp Four, a special camp for criminals.

Everyone who had packed letters and messages into the hollow space in my lower leg pounced on me, removed the artificial limb, unscrewed the lower leg, and fished the contraband out again. Then they said goodbye to me as if they would never see me again.

Although I had imagined Factor to be a sharp barracks watchdog, my first impression was that he was a few shades more pleasant than Chryseels, even though he wore a somewhat wider version of a Hitler moustache. Back then moustaches weren't necessary as proof of one's masculinity. One of our commanders had grown a moustache after the French campaign, and when our division commander saw him he said to him, "You still have lots of dirt under your nose; get rid of it!" That was on the tip of my tongue when I saw Factor.

Factor didn't bother with a demonstration of his power and immediately offered me a chair; he had even stood up and made a motion to adjust the chair for me. Consequently I considered for a moment whether I shouldn't come clean with him, but only for a very short moment, and then I was once again fascinated by the little game I had won against Chryseels.

"Have you found another fly in the ointment?" I asked.

"Several," he answered. "Do you know a Dr. Meyer from Hannover, Gummistrasse 44?"

"No." I suspected what was coming and made a face that had caused my basic–training commander to see red, because, as he said, I "grinned like a silly Tommy."

"Do you know an Erika Bee from Bremen?"

"Erika B.? Who is that supposed to be?"

"Not B., but B—e—e?"

"Never heard of her, an impossible name!"

"Do you know them both or not?"

"No."

"You're lying!" he shouted, slamming the table with his fist.

"I'm not lying!" I shouted just as loudly, because I knew exactly what I was talking about.

"But you get mail from them!"

"Oh, that's what it's about!" That was what I saw coming. They had continued to intercept my letters, and I could only hope that they didn't contain anything suspicious. "Mr. Factor," I explained, "all of my relatives live in the Russian zone. When they write to me they give the letters to someone who goes over the border to the West. There they post my letters under some fictitious sender's name or other, in Hannover, Bremen or somewhere else."

"Good, accepted, one to nothing for you. But what about Aunt Adele?"

Damnation. For a moment now I couldn't stop the blood from rushing to my face, and Factor seemed to have noticed.

"Poor Aunt Adele," I said. "She had dreadful experiences under the Russians." I hinted at all the things she had had to endure. "Leave poor Aunt Adele out of this!"

"Then you know Aunt Adele, don't you? And Aunt Adele knows you!"

"Fleetingly. I met her for the first time a few months ago. She's a godmother of my wife."

"Anyhow, you know her so fleetingly that she introduced you and warmly recommended you to various acquaintances in Godesberg."

"These days everyone has to help everyone else, otherwise you die."

"And Aunt Adele knows the truth about you, isn't that so?"

"What are you getting at?"

"Let's play the game so that I ask and you answer. So, let's be brief: either Aunt Adele has told the truth about you, in which case you have lied and have to be locked in Camp Four, or you have told the full truth, in which case Aunt Adele has lied and we have to lock her up.''

Blackmail! Infamous blackmail! What could Aunt Adele have said? Of course she knew my real name and that I had been in the Waffen–SS, but we had both prepared my documents for my studies under a false name. In doing this she had once again been the high–spirited aunt, full of funny ideas and practical jokes. Could she have been put under so much pressure that she had finally talked? Understandable in her position; after what she had gone through . . . and maybe her sister and brother, neither of whom I knew, had also persuaded her not to take any further risks. What could she have said that didn't agree with the life history I had written?

"Aunt Adele doesn't know much about me," I insisted. "It's understandable if she has said something that doesn't agree with my data! She may have mixed something up, something that hasn't to do with me at all but possibly with her son, who was killed.''

Factor observed me without moving or saying a word. And so I continued. "You know how it is: when someone is asked something they want to give an answer, even if they really can't answer the question.''

"Don't try to pull the wool over my eyes, Mr. Werner," Factor said, emphasizing the "Werner" as if he wanted to give me a clue. "If you continue to insist on what you've already said we'll lock Aunt Adele up here in the women's camp and confront her with you. It's up to you. We can have her here in a few days. One gets in here quickly but doesn't get out so quickly. You decide!''

After a pause he rang. A messenger appeared and, as far as I could make out, he was to fetch a new questionnaire, the one with the 134 questions. The messenger brought the questionnaire. Factor placed it on the table in front of him.

"Well, then, what's it to be?''

A damned shitty trick, this business with Aunt Adele! The first thing on the questionnaire was to write your name.

"Well," I said, "write down what Aunt Adele has said. Then we'll see.''

"I'll write what you dictate to me, and this is your last chance!''

In contrast to Chryseels he showed not the slightest uncertainty. A pro. For nearly ten minutes we haggled silently over the first letters that I was to dictate. Then he became impatient.

"Do you want to insist on your previous story? You just have to say so. It's best if you write it yourself, but quickly, I have other things to do."

He pushed the questionnaire and a pencil over to me and watched while I printed the first letters of my real name. When I had finished the name he snatched the questionnaire from my hand, read it and asked,

"What? Your name isn't even Werner?"

"Shit!" Angrily I slammed the table with my fist. "Then you've tricked me. One to nothing for you."

He laughed at the top of his voice. "Your name isn't Werner at all—that's fantastic! I would never have thought of that!"

"I think Aunt Adele—"

Still laughing, he waved my remark aside. "Aunt Adele lives in the French zone, so we couldn't simply go and investigate. We were only told that Aunt Adele would know you better."

Then he became somewhat more serious again, but in no way triumphant. "Tell me the truth: you were with the Waffen–SS, right?"

I nodded.

"All right, but how did you manage the business with the tattoo or the scar?"

I told him the story of how I got the scar in 1941 and about the sullen doctor who was called in only to confirm how old that scar was.

Factor slapped his thighs with laughter, then became serious again and asked, "Why have you been playing this hide–and–seek game?"

"The reasons ought to be well known to you. In the first place, as a former soldier or even reserve officer of the Waffen–SS I would not have been allowed to study; in the second place your Mr. Montgomery promised to send us into a twenty-year exile—"

Factor waved this aside. "You needn't take all of that so seriously. You Germans really pressed us hard, and it was sometimes touch and go. Understandable postwar hysteria."

"So far we've seen no signs that you don't take your orders seriously; on the other hand, you seem to be well on the way to practicing a law of lynching and revenge that would be expected only of the most primitive tribes."

Factor offered no objection.

"Thirdly," I continued, "your Mr. Chryseels greeted me with the words, "Mr. Werner, you must think you're very clever, but I'm going to prove to you how stupid you are." He quite simply provoked me to find out which of us was the stupider."

Factor grinned. "A good many crimes have undoubtedly been committed, and they must be investigated more closely so that the guilty parties can be punished. But if you weren't at Malmédy or Oradour I wouldn't know what could have happened to you."

"No, I wasn't there. I was in hospital at the time of the incident at Oradour. But later I asked people who had been there, and they had no reason to gloss over anything. I don't know how you would have acted if you'd been in the same situation."

"I don't know much about it," said Factor, "only that several hundred women and children were herded into the church and killed there. Is there any justification for that?"

"Not at all," I declared. "But do you also know how the women and children died?"

"Shot with machine guns at close range."

"Then the bodies would have had to have bullet wounds, but they didn't. There was a violent explosion in the church tower. None of our people was in the tower. The infantry company deployed there had neither explosives nor engineers. They could have neither prepared nor detonated the explosion. What has been established is that weapons and ammunition were found in a number of the houses in the village; that an ambulance was found outside the village in which the occupants, some of whom were shackled, were burned alive—"

"Let's leave it," said Factor. "This will come out at the investigation."

"Do you believe in all seriousness that such cases as this will be investigated fairly?"

"Are there no better reasons why you have been living under a false name?"

"Yes. When the Americans marched in front of our hospital in Czechoslovakia on May 8th and assembled the returning Germans I saw them shoot a Waffen–SS Untersturmfuehrer on the spot."

He didn't go into this, but asked me to sketch briefly which units I had been in and what action I had seen. Then he called some of his comrades over who were very familiar with the Waffen–SS; men who had been taken prisoner by the Germans at Dunkirk in 1940 or who were at Arnhem. They knew the names of commanders and officers and wanted to know whether these men were still alive. They assured me that they had no intention of tracking them down; they spoke respect-fully of them and praised the particularly fair behavior of the Waffen–SS at Arnhem. I didn't know whether to believe their flattery; I mentioned the generous gesture at Arnhem and said that neither Hitler nor the German people had wanted a war with England. They were prepared to agree with this; but they felt that Germany under Hitler had become a threat against all of Europe that had to be crushed. We discussed the Czech and Polish crises and the causes of the war, and they were interested in how we, as youths, had experienced the Third Reich. Factor said that he had studied in Germany at that time and could, in principle, confirm what I said. Half a year before the war ended he had been shot down over Germany and had hidden, likewise under a false name, with an old school friend, and thus could sympathize somewhat with my game of hide–and–seek.

I reproached them for the inhumanity of their bombing attacks on the civilian population, and we argued about who had started them. But before we could get into a serious squabble about that, they steered the talk back to the Waffen–SS and expressed interest in the real back-ground to our elite combat record, which they attributed to ideological fanaticism. But I was able to convince them that such fanaticism could scarcely be presupposed, considering that our troops were made up of volunteers from many countries of Europe. Instead I referred to the special leadership principle, which appeared to be completely new to them. The necessary qualification for an officer's career was not the high school diploma but exemplary ability, the true authority. Everyone who led a unit had to be the best man in his unit as well; not the uniform, not being in command, but example made the leader.

Our discussion lasted for hours. I was offered cigarettes and even cognac, but not at all in a patronizing way. We spoke our minds quite bluntly, and none of us was burdened by any form of a collective guilt complex. We agreed that every nation is entitled to strive for power and domination, and this gives rise to rivalries that could lead to military conflict. They did not claim to have carried on a crusade for morality and justice, but only to having played a political power game in which we had underesti-mated not so much England's military as its political strength. Now we had to come to terms with having lost the war, while England was in no way convinced that she had truly won it.

They spoke about the Teheran crisis, which was topical just then, and a possible military conflict with Russia, and I had to tell them all about my experiences in Russia.

At last it was I who had to remind Factor that my questionnaire had not been filled out yet. He passed it to me and said, "Just put a line through everything that's irrelevant."

"And now what's going to happen to me?"

"To Horst Werner, you mean?" Factor consulted with his colleagues, and at length they nodded in agreement. Then he rang for a messenger who returned with an envelope containing all my more or less authentic papers.

"The problem," said Factor, "is that we can't hold both of you here, because then one person would be missing at roll call." He passed the thick envelope over to me. "The only possible solution is to release Horst Werner today and to take you in as someone new instead. Keep the papers as a souvenir. Can I do anything else for you?"

"Oh yes," I said, not really seriously. "See to it that I get out of here as quickly as possible, because I'm among nothing but Nazis and am on my way to becoming one of them if I have to stay here any longer."

After hesitating a moment he gave me his hand and said, "All right, if you cooperate you can be out in four weeks at the latest." He told me how I would have to cooperate. At the moment the only people being released were those incapable of remaining in the camp. Considering my many injuries, typhus, and so forth, it must be possible for the doctors in my hut to make me incapable of remaining in the camp. Then he gave me the rest of his pack of cigarettes. "For your comrades," he said.

And so I approached the hut, provocatively smoking a cigarette. The guard at the door called out, "He's coming—and he's smoking."

Five hours' interrogation by Factor, this must be good for at least five years' imprisonment! At last, for once and for all, a real Nazi criminal, and a wolf in sheep's clothing at that! But that I came back enjoying a cigarette—that irritated them. They were bursting with curiosity, but I let them fidget, let them take deep drags on the cigarette, and when the last crumb had been extinguished I took out the next one, and then another, and then another. But in the end their curiosity was greater than their craving for tobacco.

"What's happened now, tell us already!"

"As promised: Horst Werner was released today." I produced the thick envelope with all my papers, they examined them and confirmed, "It's true, he's had all his papers handed back to him."

"But they're all falsified," I explained, to everyone's confusion; and I described who had been admitted as a new entry and would occupy my bed from now on. When Bloser heard my name he came limping over to me, landed me a straight left, and said, "You sly rascal! Then you were at Baraque Fraiture, you even led the Fourth Company!"

He was now my new witness; for the Hitler Youth battalion commander badgered me with the question of what name I would come up with next time, while Hamlet, custodian of our elite code of honor, was indignant that I had deceived my comrades, a deserter, a rat who left the sinking ship. He no longer spoke to me; nor did the Flying Man, who had previously regarded me as one of the few non–Nazis, with whom one could put oneself on a par. Otherwise, I had now become deserving of internment, and the philosophy professor said that I would just have had to wink an eye and he would have given me a student place, even without testing my trustworthiness.

No one, however, was prepared to believe that they could, without hesitation, once again entrust me with their letters and messages in view of my impending release within the next four weeks. That would be the biggest joke in the camp! No occupying power would take kindly to being led around by the nose for weeks. No, I would surely be the last person to see the gate of the camp at Recklinghausen close behind them. Even when I shared out the last of the cigarettes, with a greeting from Captain Factor, my credibility did not increase. Hamlet declined to profit from this blood money, but the others didn't care whether I had got them as a gift or swiped them.

I was to submit voluntarily to having my fortune told with cards, by an expert, of course, the town party leader from East Friesland. Here, cut off from the outer world, fortune-telling was the only source of information about past or future events. It was a way of finding out whether someone was about to get a parcel from their relatives or an important bit of news, whether this news would be good or bad, whether someone would be transferred to another camp or even released. The jack of hearts and the queen of diamonds were particularly important positive signs, as was the ten of clubs, but of course it was the combination with other cards that was decisive, and interpreting this was a science in itself which no one had mastered as well as the town party leader. The price for consulting this forerunner of the modern computer was, naturally, a quarter of a slice of bread, but thanks to my gift of cigarettes from Factor I now got my fortune told for free. But what our local oracle read into the ace of clubs, seven of diamonds, and ten of clubs was enough to shatter any confidence in fortune–telling with cards, for it indicated that within a short time a change of place awaited me. Some experts tried to interpret this as a transfer to Camp Four, but the queen of hearts lay in such a way that it could only mean release from the camp. Until then the party leader may have obtained many a slice of bread with his, thus far, trustworthy predictions, but from then on his skill was no longer worth a crumb.

The most important road I took led me to the commission that was gathering and sifting the evidence for the Nuremberg defense lawyers. Among the legal beagles, historians, and senior civil servants in this commission was Walter, by trade a doctor, dentist, and company commander in a Muslim division, someone who knew everyone and everything and whom we named Yebemtibocka, because he used this ugly Muslim swearword in place of the more common local word, "shit."

Now I had no particular difficulty in changing back from Horst Werner to myself, the adjutant of the Lex combat group. I described the case of the alleged shooting of able–bodied civilians near Staro Konstantinov.

"And you want to testify to this?" asked Walter.

"Yes, that's why I'm here."

"My God! Just keep away from that and don't say another word about it!"

"But what I'm saying is true, it's the whole truth."

"And if it's true a hundred times over the prosecution will trot out hundreds of witnesses to testify that you did shoot the civilians. And what do you think will be left of your truth then!"

"But no one can conduct a legal action that way! And besides, I'm volunteering to testify to this. I would never do this if there were the slightest indication that the prosecution was right."

"The indictment already refers to a whole row of witnesses who swear to the accusations. As a voluntary witness you will immediately be arrested, handed over, and ceremonially shot, along with your truth and your good conscience, and from then on your family will have a relative who was executed as a war criminal.''

''But then it would be completely pointless—''

''You've said it, and now it would be best for you to forget this story and tell no one that you as an adjutant, whether with or without orders, were responsible for this shooting.''

''But no one was shot!!!''

''You know it, and I believe you, but neither of us can prevent a crime that never took place from going down in history. It wouldn't be the only time, the first time or the last.''

I no longer understood the world, because at that time I still had no idea how the world really is. And whenever I heard about the discovery of yet another German crime I had to think of Staro Konstantinov.

20

"Consult Professor Schulz from your hut," Factor had suggested. Schulz was a well known scientist. Walter, too, Yebemtibocka, contributed ideas on how I could feign illness before the English medical committee. In line with the Hippocratic Oath, which binds them to heal, the two medical men would, just this once, make me as ill as possible.

Ten minutes before I was hauled before the medical committee, Schulz pumped me full of quinine, so that my heart was hammering like a machine gun. Walter disinfected his razor blade and made a slit in my gum. "Suck hard," he advised, "so that your mouth fills with blood!"

And so, trembling wretchedly, I stood before the three doctors, who from experience started with the prejudice that all release cases were fakes. In accordance with my instructions I coughed blood so that the doctors increased their safe distance and allowed Schulz to take over the presentation.

"Grenade fragments in the lung," Schulz explained, showing them the scar on my back with a doleful expression, as if he too were suffering from it. "Amputation of the left thigh," he explained superfluously, as they regarded with amazement the unplaned marvel that was my artificial leg. "Done in an improvised fashion in the last days of the war, with severe phantom pains as a result."

Now that he was saying it, I could feel them.

He commented on my racing pulse, along with the typhus, with a wealth of Latin vocabulary that I could place neither in Livy nor in the *Aeneid,* and the scale on the blood pressure gauge was scarcely adequate to measure my atmospheric high pressure. Schulz also took off my right shoe to show that the ball had been pierced by a grenade fragment, so that I couldn't walk at all on my left side and only a little on my right.

The three members of the medical committee looked really serious, and would have preferred to send me home immediately, before I brought the good reputation of the internment camp into discredit by a premature death behind barbed wire. But first Factor had to allay any doubts about my successful re–social–democratization, in writing. And then, of course, the administration!

Once again all my hut–mates fell upon me, dismantled my artificial limb, and stuffed every nook and cranny of it with letters and addresses, so that I began to fear whether the extra weight of these love letters would cause the lower leg, which was temperamental anyway, to stay bent backwards at ninety degrees right in front of the camp gate and thus cause the guards to want to fix it for me.

My dear companions in suffering gave me the objets d'art, chess figures, spoons, and other souvenirs they had hand–carved and polished during their weeks of leisure, which somehow and somewhere contained addresses to which I was to send greetings. I had no idea what sort of risks I was hauling around.

On top of all the secret messages they laid a collection of the latest porn verses, which I could use to bribe the inspectors in case they decided to unscrew me. All the medical people had contributed to this community epic, and the higher their rank in scientific circles, the more ribald was their humor. Even Walter had let off steam this way, and Graf retained the option for an English edition.

Factor kept his word. At 10:30 A.M. I was to report to the administration hut for release. It was May 22nd. Shortly beforehand Walter cut one more slit in my gum, so that I could conjure up my impressive pulmonary bleeding in case of a too–intimate body search.

There were five others there. The inspectors came, tore open my bundle of souvenirs, and found Horst Werner's personal papers among them. Needless to say, that was something! Since I wasn't in the mood for explaining in detail yet again why I was smuggling my predecessor out of the camp, nor for losing a lot of blood in the process, I simply referred them to Factor. They hurried away to him and returned, having been put in the picture. Factor accompanied them and looked over towards me.

Then my body–searchers discovered the artificial limb. Aha! They pulled up the trouser leg and tested whether the limb could be taken apart.

Immediately blood gushed from my mouth on to their hands, and when they looked up at me indignantly they saw my vampire face and let me be.

Four sentries accompanied me to the gate—not because they were afraid I might break out, but to prevent me from breaking down before I had left the camp.

The gang in my hut had tied a white undershirt to a pole and were waving it to celebrate the arrival of their wandering post office on the other side of the barbed wire, while Factor was still standing in front of the administration hut with both hands in his pockets so that he would not be tempted to wave.

Our debates were still going through my head, and they accompanied me through the ruins of Recklinghausen into freedom, which I entered with as much uneasiness as I left the past behind. All our former values of fatherland, comradeship and chivalry, discipline and duty, achievement and order, had been condemned; for they were the roots of those evils from which tyranny, oppression, and crime had grown. The logical conclusion of the postwar generation was that those who had uncritically followed a Pied Piper had forfeited their claim to authority, especially parental authority. If their former ideals of obedience, discipline, and order were the causes of the chaos, then the opposite must also have the opposite effect. And so they opposed every system of order, while the ever–new ideal of freedom affected primarily the lower instincts and found fulfillment in beat, bed, and hash.

I was a member of a criminal organization and thus per se, by judgment and by law guilty, and at the County Court in Recklinghausen was given only the opportunity to prove that my guilt was very slight.

The judge was in a bad mood, not only because he had to cope with this new and curious conception of legality, but also because he, himself a former Luftwaffe officer, was having to pass judgment on comrades.

"Don't talk to me about justice or injustice," he said to me right after my initial testimony. "You know as well as I do that no court in the world ever pronounces justice; it merely passes judgments. Justice as such does not exist, it is made. And so accept the fact that I have to judge you. I have to judge you, understand, I have to!"

He had only to do his duty, like so many before and after him; I was sorry for him, especially since he pleaded with me somehow to provide him with a basis for the judgment he had to make anyway. We ransacked my military career.

"What's this about the commissar order?"

Unfortunately I had to assure him, with the best conscience, that I first heard about this after the war and that it had absolutely not been made known on the midsection of the Eastern front. But I knew of a particular case when the giving of such an order would have been justified. It was one of my first impressions of the Russian front. One of our antitank gun crews had defended itself down to the last cartridge, really down to the last cartridge. Over thirty dead Russians lay before their positions. They then had to surrender. While still alive they had their genitals cut off, their eyes poked out, and their bellies slit open. Russian prisoners to whom we showed this declared that such mutilations took place by order of the commissars. This was the first I had heard of such commissars.

The judge informed me that we did not have the right to justify our own crimes by those of the victor.

We looked further and came in my chronicles to the days at Staro Konstantinov. Should I tell him about it? I wanted to carry this charade to extremes and so I told him the story.

"You can be glad it's just the two of us here!" he shouted, and told me off because I apparently had still not clicked. Then he asked, "What do you know about the persecution of the Jews?"

Oh yes, I knew something about that, and it was so grotesque that I told him. One day in March some wagonloads of Jews had arrived in the internment camp in Recklinghausen. They came from England, having emigrated there at some time before the outbreak of war, and as they had not yet been naturalized they were interned there as German enemy aliens, and thus had spent the entire war sitting behind barbed wire. Now they were deported as burdensome Germans and brought to Recklinghausen, obviously in order to be denazified. He didn't want to believe this, but I assured him that these were the only Jews with whom I had associated up to then. They were fellow–sufferers and had really interesting things to tell, which the judge, in any case, did not wish to hear. On the other hand he noticed from my papers that after I was wounded in Russia I had had half a year's leave to study in Berlin, at a time when the Jews were already required to wear a yellow star. Surely I must have seen this.

Oh yes, I had seen this, and I had to laugh because nowadays everyone had their Jew to whom they'd been nice and helpful. Me too. I was standing in a line in front of a bakery at Bayrischer Platz. Lines like this were really disciplined. But one wrinkled old woman had to be an exception. She crept along the queue, stopped in front of me (I was the only one in uniform), cast me a brief glance, and pushed into the line in front of me. She could at least have asked politely or said "pardon," but since no one else objected, neither did I. It was only when she was paying that I noticed the yellow star on her blouse. It was actually my only encounter with a Jewish star, "and if you attach importance to it," I told the judge, "you can even interpret the story to show that I did everything to help the poor Jewish woman. But in the first place I saw the star too late, and in the second place, had she been younger I would have asked her to go to the end of the line, with or without a yellow star."

"Thank God," said the judge.

"What for?"

"Finally we have a basis on which to pass judgment!"

And now he dictated a legal text adorned with many subordinate clauses, according to which I must have been aware of the injustice done to the Jews and consequently I must also have known that I was serving a criminal regime. I wasn't at all in agreement with his making such a mountain out of a molehill, but he implored me to accept it, so much so that I once again felt sorry for him.

At the same time he added up how many days I had spent in the camp, multiplied them by a certain daily rate, and thus got the sentence of 1,830 marks which I had already paid through my internment. In other words I had been convicted before I was interned.

I would then receive a bill for the court costs, he disclosed to me, but I should simply tell the bailiff that I had no money—which was true.

Aware that my life was now at a new starting–point, I boarded the overcrowded train to Bremen. I had a three–hour wait there. Uncle Leo and Aunt Agnes lived not far from the station. As I was bursting with the need to tell of all I had been through—we had last seen one another four years before—I hurried through the city, trusting to luck, towards where I knew they had lived last. Looking around, I could scarcely hope that their house had been spared.

And yet at least half of the house was still standing. Were they still alive? While I poked among the ruins a window with a cardboard shutter opened. Uncle Leo!

"What are you doing here, boy? Come on in and see how it looks in here! Only the cellar is still all in one piece, thank God, since we had just been storing the most important things down there as if we suspected what was about to happen." He opened the door.

"The neighbor has given us two of her rooms, because her husband and both her sons have been killed. What luck for us! Heinz is in Bremerhaven and Luise is living in the country for a couple of days, at Elfriede's, you know her too. Come, sit down, I can make you a cup of coffee, real coffee from beans, since I now have to work in the harbor, punitive work, clearing up, unloading ships, like a coolie. Where have you come from? I've only just got home myself. I lost my job as slaughterhouse manager because I was a minor Party functionary. Plenty has happened here, that I must tell you."

And he told me.

I listened politely and gave up thinking about Chryseels and the boilerman, about the flight from Austria and the surprise at Uncle Theobald's. All this had occurred in the four years since I had last seen Uncle Leo.

But I listened. I had to look at every new, improvised piece of furniture and hear about where the individual parts had come from and what happy or unhappy event was associated with its creation. Then he described the nights during which the neighbors had lost their homes and their lives and the night they themselves had been hit: the first bomb over there, the second somewhat closer, and then the fateful third bomb: Ssssst–bang! He reconstructed everything he had thought, felt, and feared at the time and how lovely it was no longer to have to hide in the cellar and be afraid.

When he began with the comedy of his denazification my three hours were nearly up. He found it amusing, the way the commission had swallowed the story that he had joined the Party only in order to keep his professional standing and that he could not avoid being appointed cell–leader because he had, anyhow, been decent and helpful to people; and who knows how someone else would have behaved in his position? While I was already letting myself down the improvised steps I learned that thanks to his clever defense he had been classified only as a fellow–traveller, and then he told me how glad he was to see me again in one piece.

"Where are you coming from, actually?" he called after me. "Do you have something on your leg? Oh well, you must come back soon, there's still plenty to tell!"

21

While we were driving over the Tude bridge again on the way home Jeanette asked me, "Do you remember?"

I didn't know what she meant.

"That's where you all sat, the whole company. I was cycling to my aunt's in Chalais. I was all alone on the road, and you all sat there and waited for me."

"Waited for you?"

"No, not on purpose, but it seemed like that to me. Everyone looked at me, and I had to cycle past you all, past a whole line of soldiers. It was awful." She laughed.

"And then? What was so awful?"

"Nothing really, but I felt as if I were appearing on stage. And then you all clapped. Not you. I noticed that, I saw you. You didn't clap. We didn't know each other then; that is, we had said a few words to each other, but you didn't clap. Why not?"

I could recall this scene only dimly and, to tell the truth, I didn't remember that it was she who had cycled past our guard of honor. But I had watched with interest to see how the others would behave.

"Would you have preferred if no one had noticed you?"

"No, of course not. I thought the applause was nice."

"What actually did you think back then, when you heard that an entire company was going to be billetted on your village?"

"It was quite exciting for us girls, of course. We studied, observed, and judged each of you individually—only to the extent that you were interesting at all. We gave many of you nicknames. You were Lieutenant Werner and had no other nickname. Everyone agreed that you were really *gentil*. It made quite an impression that you knew French. But Toni was the handsomest; everyone was crazy about him. Naturally the boys in the village were very jealous, because now they had a lot of competition. They mimicked you, upright posture and walk, snappy greeting and so on. Before that, you know, they would stand in the street, careless, slouched, a cigarette hanging out of their mouths, and the remarks they made when a girl went by were often very, very suggestive. Later, after you'd gone, they tried to behave in a more disciplined fashion.

"My father was a patriot, a very patriotic soldier in the First World War. He once said that it would have done all young Frenchmen good to have been drilled once by you Germans; then France would not have lost the war."

"And what did he say when the war was lost for us?"

"He wasn't glad, no, not at all. He was angry, because France acted as if she had beaten the Germans."

"And your mother?"

"She was a good companion. She liked you a lot."

One more time I tried to ask how it had gone for her later, but I didn't know how to translate "experiences" into French in the correct sense, and so used the expression "adventure." But Jeanette evaded this by saying that Julien had been enough of an adventure for her and remembering that it was high time I booked into the hotel at the railway station.

Right! The present had suddenly escaped me. In the hotel they acted as though they had been expecting me. Everything was ready. They gave me a key and said I could come and go as I pleased. At Jeanette's all kinds of friends and acquaintances were already waiting who sized me up curiously and took Jeanette by the arm: *"Tu nages en bonheur?"* Julien was an eager host.

They chatted merrily, all at once, so that it was impossible for me to follow them; it gave me the opportunity to think about what my friends and acquaintances and the people in the factory would say when I brought Julien along and introduced him as my son. And Lore, Klaus, and Erika would shower me with questions which, I now realized, I wouldn't at all be able to answer because until now we had been completely wrapped up in the past—something they would not understand at all.

When I rejoined Lore, Klaus and Erika in Hendaye after two days, I did of course try to explain all that I felt then, and now. It was difficult but I guess I managed it. In any case, Lore still took it with more grace than I expected, and I loved her for it.

The day before I left I took Julien aside and asked him about all that he had learned and whether he had been a good pupil in school. A father naturally asks about how a child has done at school, and his judgment on this was quite different from that of his teachers'.

"And what do you want to do later on?"

First he wanted to do his military service in the Marines, and right after that go to Paris, to Aunt Monique, because here there were no decent schools and no industry. Preferably he would choose an occupation that allowed him to travel a good deal. He had once been to the Tyrol with his school class. "Do you know the Tyrol?" I asked whether he was good in foreign languages. Oh, yes! He recited some English sentences with a typical French accent. English would be quite useful in the Marines, and German, of course, was very similar to English, he would soon learn that too.

The next morning, right after a breakfast of fresh croissants and milky coffee, I drove with Julien to Monsieur Nicoline, the head of the secondary school. He lived just next to the school building and was not at all surprised to see us.

"Ton père, n'est-ce pas, Julien?"

He invited us into his bachelor pad and placed a carafe of red wine with two glasses on the table. His dentures clicked when he spoke an "s" sound.

"I've been told that you speak German and that you're a German teacher too; is that correct?"

"Yes, I speak German and I also have friends in Germany, in Saeckingen—do you know Saeckingen? My friends there are teachers too. Unfortunately not enough pupils here want to learn German, so at the moment there are no German classes. But hopefully that will change soon."

"I would very much like to bring you a pupil, Julien; could you teach him German?"

"Of course," he said. "As far as I'm concerned we can begin tomor-

row. It isn't a good idea for Julien to join the Marines right away. But
again, they haven't accepted him yet. Learning is better.''

"I think so too.''

"Will he be going to Germany later?''

"Yes.''

"What do you want to do with him in Germany?''

"I don't know yet, exactly. If he's a good student, he could continue
to study.''

"Then he has to learn properly and get his diploma in German. He
may manage that soon.''

"And maybe—depending on his talents—he could get into a technical
or commercial career.''

"What do you do, if I may ask; what line of work are you in?''

"I have a factory.''

"Oh, really? A factory? A real factory—I mean, do you have employees
there?''

"Of course, around a hundred factory workers and thirty other employees. We even export a lot to France.''

"What do you produce?''

"Synthetic materials, adhesive tape, and things like that.''

"Interesting, very interesting. We could use a factory like that here
in Chalais too. We only have one factory employing thirty people.''

"In any case I'm very grateful to you for wanting to teach Julien.
May I give you an advance payment right now? And then I'll send you
the payments on a monthly basis.''

"No, you may not do that.''

He glanced furtively at Julien and said, "He can stay here, since he
doesn't understand any German.''

What was he thinking of?

"This is the way it is. I was once with the Resistance—didn't anyone
tell you that?''

"No.'' I waited curiously for what was to follow.

"I was an average person in the Resistance, and you were in the
SS, the Waffen–SS, back then when you deployed the new Frundsberg
Division here in this area. You're wondering how I know all this, aren't
you? We observed you very closely and knew a lot about you.''

Oh no! Now what had I got myself into! It got even worse.

"Surely you also know about Oradour, Limoges and Tulle, right?''

What could I say? There are two sides to every coin. I knew the one side that was neither flattering nor heroic for the Resistance. Which side did he mean?

"A bad time for both sides," he continued, "with mistakes here and mistakes there. But that's not what I wanted to talk about. That's in the past. What I really mean is the time after that, when the German troops had withdrawn. Then all sorts of things happened that the amnesty simply cancelled out, as if they had never happened. It wasn't easy to win over good people for the Resistance. I was an idealist—or better, a patriot. I couldn't get over France's ignominious defeat in 1940 and wanted to save France's honor—to try to save at least a bit. There were all sorts of rabble in the Resistance, since we couldn't be choosy and took anyone who volunteered. As long as we were fighting the German troops we were relatively unified, but not after that. Then, when the danger was past, there were suddenly a lot of people who claimed to be Resistance fighters; and they made up in fighting against their own compatriots for what they missed in fighting against the Germans. They decided who were collaborators and took it out on them. A lot of injustices took place—including those against Julien's mother. Now I have the chance to make up for some of what my compatriots did in the name of the Resistance."

"That's . . . that's very generous of you."

"Please, don't mention it. Even the Germans are in the process of compensating for injustice. Injustice is injustice. But the war is over, we've all learned something from it, and if injustice isn't recognized and compensated for, it smolders again and stands in the way of reconciliation. Especially when all the blame is laid only on the losers."

I was moved.

"I have good friends in Germany. Not Resistance fighters, no, completely normal Germans, like you, decent, patriots like myself too. Most of them are teachers. I knew them even before the war. Some of them were officers, like you. I visited them some years ago. It is amazing, this Germany. So totally destroyed—nothing more to be seen of it. A miracle, and not just an economic miracle. Do you know what I learned from it?"

"No."

"It would have done France good, really, to lose this war. We did lose it, of course. But once again the Americans, who actually lost nothing at all here, forced Germany to its knees. We would have to have lost the war as totally as Germany did. It sounds brutal, I know, and of course one can't say out loud that it would have been better if we, too, had been laid waste.''

"I find this opinion amazing."

"Do you? We didn't win the First World War from our own strength, but we behaved like the victors, and every victor—you can see this all through history—behaves excessively in many respects. He wants to enslave his enemy in the sense that he wants to rest on his laurels at the enemy's expense. He wants to enjoy his victory. That didn't do France any good even after the First World War. We were threatened with becoming a dying nation—just as ancient Rome at the height of its powers looked only for pleasure and then collapsed. While we slept behind our Maginot Line, Germany had suddenly revived again under Hitler. Unlike France, which was split into so many parties, Germany had become strong simply through its unity, a unity of eighty million people. Our politicians kept Germany's true strength a secret from us in order not to discourage us from the next war before it even started.''

Suddenly, once again I had before my eyes that picture of the north of France from 1940. We were on a fast march with our antitank gun platoon to Aire, to help knock out a concentration of French tanks there. Our road was crossed by a rather large French convoy. In a few seconds our four cannon were in position and put on a small fireworks display. After a few minutes the French were waving white flags. Two heavy machine gun battalions, eight hundred men, surrendered. When the commander saw what a small gang he had surrendered to he was shocked and didn't speak a word to us. Some of the officers felt our camouflage jackets; they had heard they were made of paper. Others admired our machine guns, as they had believed that we would still be using the water–cooled Reiser–MGs from the First World War. They believed the motto ''Guns instead of butter'' and thought we were undernourished. They moaned about how much misinformation they had been given about the Germans.

"Two nations lost the last World War more totally than any nation had previously lost a war," Nicoline continued, "Germany and Japan, and both have risen like phoenixes out of their own ashes. Think of the blossoming of Baroque culture after the Thirty Years War. Do you know what I'm getting at?''

"No.''

"You can't destroy a nation by decimating it in war and robbing it of all its wealth, but you can do so by letting it rest on its laurels and degenerate in peace, freedom and welfare."

"That surprises me, but you could be right."

"I am right. And that's why it would have done France good to have lost this war as totally as possible. When I saw the ruins of Germany after the war and the exhaustion of the Germans, I thought Germany wouldn't recover in a hundred years. Naturally a war is a bitter thing which no one wants; it's still bitterer to lose it, but that's a healthy pain, and I'm convinced that we can grow only through the obstacles we meet. This is a law of nature: every development, whether in science, technology, society, or evolution, owes its decisive impetus to a necessity born of need or catastrophe."

"There's something in that."

"Just think of yourself! After all you've been through and what you had to endure after the war in persecution and injustice you could really have given in for the rest of your life. But did you? Had you won a war you would now perhaps be some big shot in the occupying force. Instead you had to work hard, to assert yourself, and you've achieved an economic miracle. Be glad you lost the war!"

That was truly a macabre suggestion, but it was worth discussing in more detail.

"When you come to Germany again," I said, "spend a few days with us, with me and my wife—and Julien."

"Gladly," he said, accompanying us to the door. "We had a French garrison in Germany, and there were also Franco–German children there—"

"No doubt," I said.

"But this is the first time I've ever met someone who is doing something about it."

Three years later he was our guest for two weeks. We talked about the war and the lessons one could learn from it. I had invited other friends, and we sat round the fireplace at the edge of the swimming pool and drank red wine from the Rhine and the Charante. Wilhelm pointed out the international character of our get–together: Polish pork, Dutch potatoes, French Resistance and a Waffen–SS in front of a fireplace in which German oak wood was burning. We sang about the Pont d'Avignon and ate sauerkraut with knuckle of pork.

Postscript

Notes on the characters:

The author retired in 1971, selling his business. Since then he has written and published many books on science and philosophy as well as a book on bridge. His most recent book, published in Germany in September 1990, is titled *The Deadly Fallacy of Materialism*. He lives with Lore in Remagen.

Julien finished his education and became an export sales manager for a German company. He is married to a German girl and has one daughter.

Klaus retired from his position as auditor to the British-American Tobacco Company a few years ago and lives with Erika in Hamburg.